Understanding
the Battle of Perryville

The Discovery of the Hafley Cabins
and its Impact on Historiography of the Battlefield

Jamie Gillum

"Understanding the Battle of Perryville: The Discovery of the Hafley Cabins and its Impact on Historiography of the Battlefield."

© 2022 ~ James F. Gillum
Spring Hill, Tennessee
Printed in the United States of America
LCCN: Pending
ISBN-13: 9798827637868
BISAC: Military History/United States/Civil War Period/Kentucky

Cover Image: Crosscupp and West engraving from Thomas Head's *Campaigns and Battles of the Sixteenth Regiment Tennessee Volunteers*, 1885.

CONSTRUCTED BATTLEFIELD MAPS:

Introduction and Acknowledgements

Much revisionist history of today is based on opinion or assumption—not cold, hard facts. There's no wonder why many revisionists get a bad reputation based on foolhardy attempts to alter ingrained historical understandings of people or events. However, occasionally long forgotten facts fester to the top after putrefying through many layers of historians' interpretations. In this case, revisionist history can be to the detriment of a very few—but the enlightenment of many. It is the very few who have unintentionally established a widespread and now entrenched misunderstanding of Perryville.

A historian's job is to analyze evidence and present the reader with a sound conclusion of events based on evidence. In the end, their conclusion is nothing more than an opinion that they have based on the evidence—that is, evidence they have used. Most people will take the historian at their word. Historians can't *cite* their own opinions; but, *their opinions* can—and will—be cited as fact. If written history repeats itself, this battle is a prime example. *Citing opinion that is asserted as fact is the foundation of misinformation that has altered history for the Battle of Perryville.* In this case, it didn't take someone traveling back in time to create a butterfly effect. After studying Perryville for more than a quarter of a century, I was never able to come to grips with some of the current interpretations of a *significant portion* of this strategically important battle.

The Battle of Perryville proved to end the Confederacy's hopes to unify Kentucky with the South and supplement their army's ranks with Kentuckians rushing to their standards. The success of the Rebel army at the battle—that most deem a Confederate *tactical* victory—was nonetheless strategically offset by the failure of the Confederates to consolidate and unify as one command. This failure was further complicated by the losses suffered on the bloody fields and hills north of Perryville along Chaplin's Hills and Doctor's Fork on October 8, 1862. Two separate Rebel commands had marched into Kentucky. One was under the command of Kirby Smith and the other under Braxton Bragg. The story of the movement into Kentucky and subsequent movement out by the Rebel army is not arguable. Historians have well founded conclusions as to the failures and successes—strategically speaking—of both the Federal and Confederate armies that confronted each other during the nearly month-long campaign.

At the tactical level, this research—that focuses more singularly on the northern flank of the battle of Perryville itself—did not reflect the same interpretations that other modern authors and historians have concluded. The primary source material that is picked through to condense the story of a battle is often overwhelming. The information age—with the ability to gain previously unattainable information due to time constraints, travel and expense—has enabled us to gather far more primary source material than has ever been available. This treasure trove continues to grow every day as more documents are scanned and added to massive data bases. It led me to conclude that much of what has been written in the last thirty years regarding the fight on the Confederate center and right has been misinterpreted through—by no fault of their own—historians' incomplete research.

So, you ask 'what has changed?' We know the end result of the battle; so, what could be so significant that it needs to be revisited? Although the out-come of the battle remains the same, if we revisit Cheatham's division and the right flank of the Army of the Mississippi, we can better understand how the battle unfolded and how the tactical success achieved by the Rebels came to fruition. It becomes clear how the fight actually evolved and how explanations of the battle to this point in time have missed the mark. Some of these historians' interpretations have literally altered the course of history for some units and brigades. Who engaged whom—and what units were engaged where—may be more easily explained and understood. This "new" interpretation does not alter the course of history, but rather *revisits the original history* that eventually became altered by modern scholarship lacking a depth of research that—in some cases—simply hasn't been available until now.

This is not to say that prior research was bad or lacked depth at the time. It is merely the recognition that condensing a fight in which hundreds of regiments participated can get confusing. It can be easy to misinterpret how a battle unfolded or evolved when given the entirety of the event and the huge numbers of sources that have been—and have become—available. That number of sources continues to grow daily. On the other hand, when only a portion of a battle is the focus, the depth of research can be confined to a much smaller number of units and leaders that participated in a particular part of the fight.

Simply put, this allows one to search much deeper within a centralized portion of a battlefield to uncover heretofore misrepresentations and identify previously unknown landmarks. This also enables the historian to use hundreds of accounts that focus on this small spectrum of the battlefield to get a much clearer picture of how and where specific actions took place.

Perryville—like all battlefields—was chaotic. The men who wrote of their experiences referenced the sights and scenes directly under their observation. These were always very localized and—if written too long after the fact—lacked in specific detail. One Federal participant made this clear in a letter he wrote only two weeks after the battle.

No one person can describe a battle. One's own view is very limited at best, and few see more than the movements of their own company, or possibly, their regiment. The sum total of every man's experience could only give a complete record. I saw the 105th in position, and there my view was limited to two or three companies on the left.[1]

Colonel John H. Savage
This photo is believed to have been taken in 1858 at Richmond, Virginia while Savage was still serving as a Congressman from Tennessee. The image was taken when he was forty-three years old. The day after the Battle of Perryville marked his forty-seventh birthday. (Public Domain)

This understanding of the complexities of the battlefield led me to write, *The Battle of Perryville and the Sixteenth Tennessee Infantry Regiment: A Reevaluation* in 2011. Independently published, the book saw a very limited audience, but at the same time raised eyebrows regarding the unfolding of the battle on the Confederate right—particularly Cheatham's division as a whole. The strength of the argument in the book hinged on the *belief* that a pair of cabins had occupied a position on the eastern slope of a hill now referred to as "Open Knob." The guts of the argument were strong, but lacking conclusive evidence of a structure at that specific location, some were understandably unwilling to accept any interpretation other than one concluded by the current histories of the battle.

First, the reader must understand that the intent of this work is to set the record straight—not defame nor diminish the work of previous historians. But this is not the first attempt to correctly relate the battle at Perryville. The Colonel of the Sixteenth Tennessee infantry regiment was a well-known man. John Houston Savage was born in McMinnville, Warren County, Tennessee on October 9, 1815. He had roots from Savage Station, Virginia and was the son of a well-to-do farmer. He studied military history at an early age and was full of ambition. Savage volunteered during the War for Texas Independence in 1836, but the war ended before his deployment. Shortly thereafter, he volunteered for service in the Second Seminole War and was discharged after six months of service in Florida. Returning home, he studied law, passed the bar and opened a practice in Smithville, Tennessee. Making connections and succeeding at his practice, he was appointed Attorney General of the 4th Congressional District from 1841 to 1847. He had just resigned to become a candidate for the U.S. Congress when he received a letter appointing him to Major of the 14th U.S. Infantry. He accepted the appointment and served with distinction in the Mexican War being wounded a Molino Del Rey. He was promoted to Lieutenant-colonel of the 11th U.S. Infantry shortly before the war ended. Returning home again, he was U.S. Congressman for his district from 1849 to 1853 and again from 1855 to 1859.

---

[1] "The 105th Regiment." *Cleveland Morning Leader* (Cleveland, OH) October 27, 1862, p. 2.

At the commencement of the Civil War, Savage was elected colonel of the Sixteenth Regiment Tennessee Volunteers on June 10, 1861. Savage loved the limelight and apparently had great aspirations. Additionally, Savage wanted credit where he felt it was due. This became especially evident in his autobiography that was published in 1903. *Life of Savage* was a tirade for all practical purposes. It appears that Savage was very opinionated, and clearly thought that his opinion was *the right opinion*. However, this historical record that Savage gave future generations was not *all* opinion or strictly the *Life of Savage*. A portion of the book is dedicated to the Civil War. As self-involved as Savage may have been, he truly had a love of the men he led. He was not an easy man. Savage proved to be a strict disciplinarian, and this worked to the regiment's benefit in their first major combat at Perryville. His regiment had seen early service under General Robert E. Lee in Western Virginia followed by coastal service in South Carolina when Lee personally saw to the unit's transfer there under his command. Even Robert E. Lee apparently saw something noteworthy in Savage. When the call came for reinforcements after the Battle of Shiloh, Donelson's Tennessee brigade (consisting of the Eighth and Sixteenth regiments) was immediately transferred to Corinth, Mississippi. As the Kentucky offensive began in September 1862, Savage's regiment was still in Brigadier General Daniel S. Donelson's brigade which had been supplemented by the addition of three more Tennessee regiments.[2]

Savage's autobiography was—at least partly—an attempt to set the record straight regarding the role his regiment played at Perryville. In the post-war years as books were published relating the history of the Army of the Mississippi and Army of Tennessee, Savage came to realize that written history was not relating the story of the battle accurately. He intended to right this wrong. Savage recognized that the accomplishments of his regiment were being claimed by other Confederate units at that battle. Additionally, after the publication of *The Official Records of the Union and Confederate Armies*, Savage noticed that no reports of the battle had been published by either his brigade commander or his division commander. Perhaps a conspiracy theorist to some degree, Savage believed the true story of his unit at the battle had been covered up. This was not the reality. In fact, both his brigade and division commanders wrote reports of the battle that eventually became part of a private collection of Civil War documents in the years following the war. Apparently when the search for official reports and correspondence was taken on for inclusion in the *Official Records*, either the purchase price was not right, or Marcus J. Wright (ironically, to whom one of the reports was written) was never made aware of the collection. With no report that even mentioned his regiment's sacrifice at Perryville, Savage clearly stewed over the lack of recognition his regiment received, while another brigade under General George Maney received all the credit in the written history of the battle.[3]

In his chapter regarding the Battle of Perryville, Colonel Savage clearly laid out the details of what happened that fateful afternoon and used convincing supporting evidence. No less than five members of the regiment—and General Maney himself—personally testified to the accuracy of Savage's account of the events. Surviving memoirs and diaries from other members of the regiment also tell the same story—a story very different than the one that current Perryville enthusiasts have come to know—and one that time has forgotten. But, the accounts by all these different men have one thing in common. They all tell the *same* story—a story that cannot be argued or explained away. Given the testimony, it will be shown that it is indisputable that Savage's Sixteenth regiment *did* participate in the destruction of Terrill's brigade and capture of Parsons' battery on Open Knob, and contrary to modern interpretations, their engagement at two cabins was not at the Widow Gibson's site but another home-site that had been lost to time.[4]

Now—with the discovery of the long-lost home-site and the name of the family that occupied it, a new and comprehensive attempt will be made to interpret the battle as the evidence clearly indicates. This interpretation of the evidence (*old and new*) will differ dramatically from current interpretations of the battlefield and will undeniably alter the over-all understanding of the progression of the battle. The new interpretation will

---

[2] Jamie Gillum, *The Battle of Perryville and the Sixteenth Tennessee Infantry Regiment: A Reevaluation* (Jamie Gillum, Spring Hill, TN, 2011) pp. 18-22.

[3] John Houston Savage, *Life of John Houston Savage*, (John Houston Savage, Nashville, TN, 1903) p. 128-31.

[4] John Houston Savage, *Life of John Houston Savage*, (John Houston Savage, Nashville, TN, 1903) p. 119, 124.

make the field far more comprehensive on the Confederate right. It will clarify how and where individual units attacked, whom they attacked, and the impact it had on the tactical outcome of the battle. This will also help us to understand how and why they achieved the level of success or failure on the field of battle.

Previous historians' interpretations will be challenged, and their citations will be put to the test. Arguments will be made as to why their interpretations or conclusions may—in some cases—be unreliable. A look at the primary sources themselves will be taken in an order to give them credibility or caution when considering their reliability. The concept of "cherry picking" will be addressed and how it is used to support some authors' and historians' conclusions. Also, the evidence will show how an inability to "think outside of the box" can limit one's ability to comprehend and interpret a battlefield. The battlefield itself will be framed, and an attempt to place units at various points of action will allow the confines of the battlefield to be more easily understood. Lastly, this **is not** a retelling of the Battle of Perryville. It is fresh look at old and new material that will help us to better understand portions of this bloody and **misunderstood** battlefield.

After numerous attempts to have reputable historians who have written on this subject comb through these ground breaking findings, only one offered any support. Christopher Kolakowski responded to communications and was willing to read through the manuscript. He offered encouragement and constructive criticism. The biggest criticisms were regarding what might be considered personal attacks. Although this is not a courtroom, I believe that the current written history of this battle has become so entrenched in the minds of many that a courtroom stance must be made to dispel these myths. In doing so, my passion to right the wrongs may seem abrasive, but are backed by hard evidence. I have no intention of hurting feelings, but I believe that when one finishes this manuscript, they will walk away with a very different view of this battle. My thanks also go out to my friends David Fraley and Dave Howells who offered so much encouragement along the way. If nothing else, let this contribution to the Perryville battlefield encourage conversation regarding this battle that Sam Watkins called *"a battle of giants… full of stifling smoke and fire, which seemed the very pit of hell, peopled by contending demons."* [5]

---

[5] Sam Watkins, *Co. Aytch*, Ruth Hill Fulton McAllister, Ed., (Providence House Publishers, Franklin, TN, 2007) p. 60.

Stumbling blocks that have caused the misunderstanding of the Battle of Perryville.

First, understand that *this* author struggled for years to make sense of this battle. Using the primary sources that were known until about ten years ago, I suffered with the same blinders that others still wear. The known sources related a *possible* chronology and execution of events as current histories most often relate. But after recognizing the existence of several previously unknown accounts and reports of the battle, I began to realize that Colonel Savage's puzzling chapter on Perryville made sense after all. The three stumbling blocks that stymied myself and others in a search for the truth at Perryville were closely related.

Over and again, an attempt was made to make the chronology of the battle and the existing reports of the battle coincide with one another. This was something that was truly impossible before the discovery of several heretofore picked over and unknown accounts of the battle. These included Frank Cheatham's and Daniel Donelson's reports of the battle, George Maney's, Marcus Toney's and several periphery accounts by men both blue and gray. Before these accounts were located and taken in their entirety, it was easy to believe the more recent conclusions made by historians in the last forty years. Three stumbling blocks have stood in the way of understanding the way the battle of Perryville unfolded. These stumbling blocks can prevent one from fully examining and understanding the accounts when taken in their entirety.

The first stumbling block was *caused* by a lack of deep research. More and more source material come to light on a regular basis in this information age. However, not having access to these sources years ago caused historians to make hasty conclusions based on the material they *had* uncovered. As none of the sources clearly explained what happened along General Cheatham's front, only short, abbreviated accounts explained tentatively what happened. This left a lot of guessing for the historians of the battle to explain in their own way how the battle unfolded. Since many of the known accounts and sources at the time were incomplete and shallow in clarification, it required historians to formulate an opinion that could *not* be corroborated by the known sources. This caused the historians to skillfully attempt to relate only portions of accounts and leave out other portions of those same accounts to relate the battle as *they* understood it. This—the first of the three stumbling blocks—is known as ***cherry picking***.

Cherry picking—at its core—is picking and choosing information that supports one's position and leaving available information out that may support some other position. It may also be known as suppressing evidence or the fallacy of incomplete evidence. Considering the limited number of source material available in the two largest works concerning this battle, one might understand why decisions were made to suppress (or at least leave out) parts of some of the documents that were available. It could also be recognized as a sort of selective attention—only noting the portions of an account that could be considered to support their theory. It made sense at the time—simply because the historians' conclusions could not be validated by the inclusion of the source accounts in their entirety.[6]

Closely associated with cherry picking is the second stumbling block—***confirmation bias***. Confirmation bias is "the tendency to search for, interpret, favor, and recall information in a way that confirms one's preexisting beliefs or hypotheses, while giving disproportionately less consideration to alternative possibilities." Historians can "display this bias when they gather or remember information selectively." It is suggested that the bias is even stronger when "deeply entrenched beliefs" are at stake. This is certainly the case at Perryville—where the same story has been told and retold for over thirty-five years. When new information comes to light, historians tend to interpret ambiguous evidence as supporting their existing position.[7] This leads us to the third stumbling block—***attitude polarization***.

Attitude polarization is "the tendency of people to search for and interpret evidence selectively, to reinforce their current beliefs or attitudes." It is very closely associated with confirmation bias. When new evidence comes to light it can result in the opposing sides "interpreting it as in support of their existing attitudes,

---

[6] https://en.wikipedia.org/wiki/Cherry_picking

[7] https://en.wikipedia.org/wiki/Confirmation_bias

widening rather than narrowing the disagreement between them." This has proven to be the case in several newly recognized sources on the battle.[8]

---

[8] https://en.wikipedia.org/wiki/Attitude_polarization
6

THE FIRST BOOK LENGTH WORKS ON PERRYVILLE

Although the Battle of Perryville was decisive in determining the fate of Kentucky, the brief but violent and bloody battle was overshadowed by events that took place right before and nearly right after it. The Battle of Perryville was fought October 8, 1862 and resulted in approximately 4,200 Federal casualties and 3,400 Confederate casualties for a combined total of about 7,600 killed, wounded and missing. In the eastern theater of war, the horrific Battle of Antietam had just been fought in Maryland only two weeks earlier on September 17, 1862. That was a one-day fight that resulted in as many as 23,000 casualties (that is: killed, wounded and missing) for both sides combined and was a decisive victory for the Union. Just over two months after the Battle of Perryville, the Battle of Fredericksburg, Virginia was fought in mid-December which resulted in a strategic loss for the Union and nearly 18,000 Yankee and Rebel casualties combined. Two weeks after Fredericksburg, Bragg's army—that had fought at Perryville—engaged Union forces at the Battle of Stones River or Murfreesboro, Tennessee from December 31, 1862 through January 2, 1863. That battle resulted in nearly 25,000 more combined casualties and was a strategic victory for the Union as well. Naturally, surrounded by battles that had much higher casualty rates and being fought on much greater scale, the Battle of Perryville quickly became an afterthought for newspapers and the populace in general, although its true importance was of the highest order. The fact is that the Confederacy would never have the ability to pull off another sizeable movement that could threaten Kentucky with Confederate dominance following Bragg's failed invasion of Kentucky in 1862.

In the post-war years, brief recollections of the battle were immortalized in publications such as *Confederate Veteran* and *The National Tribune*. Unfortunately, the battle failed to warrant a book length study until Dr. Kenneth Hafendorfer of Louisville, Kentucky finished the first in-depth history of the fight in 1981. This book—published 119 years after the battle—was titled, *Perryville: Battle for Kentucky*. Needless to say, there was little in the way of source material on the subject at hand. It certainly took years to dig up information in a period before the "information age" arrived. This book shed light on a battle that time and history had nearly forgotten. It became the staple on the Battle of Perryville until the publication of Auburn University's Professor Kenneth Noe's work was published twenty years later in 2001. *Perryville: This Grand Havoc of Battle* revisited the battlefield with some slightly differing interpretations of the field, but nothing that altered the over-all understanding. Noe had opportunities that Hafendorfer did not. The "information age" had kicked off by the time of Noe's publication. He cited Hafendorfer and added a fair number of new source materials in his bibliography. Portions of his book were neither what historians at the Battle of Perryville State Historic Site necessarily agreed with—nor his predecessor, Dr. Hafendorfer. However, these two works—combined—told the "definitive" story of Perryville from the opening of the battle until the close of action that night as the full moon shone over the battlefield.

It took nearly a decade before another attempt to interpret the campaign and battle was made. Following the release of the first two detailed works, a series of less detailed and broadly brushed general books came about. These include 2005's *The Battle of Perryville: Culmination of the Failed Kentucky Campaign* by Robert P. Broadwater, 2009's *The Civil War at Perryville: Battling for the Bluegrass* by Christopher Kolakowski, *Staff Ride Handbook for the Battle of Perryville, 8 October 1862* published in 2011 by Robert S. Cameron, and *Maney's Confederate Brigade at the Battle of Perryville*, 2014 by Stuart Sanders. All of these books perpetuate the stories as told by the first two major works on the battle. In some cases, there are subtle differences, but nothing particularly noteworthy. Sanders' more recent book on Maney's brigade goes even further entrenching some of the misunderstanding of the actions of Cheatham's division in the attack at Perryville. Apparently without *deeper* research, these very general summaries of the battle retell the same misconceptions that were unintentionally established by the combined efforts of both Hafendorfer and Noe. Now, an attempt to summarize the guts of these works as a collective whole will be laid before the reader to better understand how and when these misconceptions occurred.

Since there were no surviving witnesses to the battle or original battlefield one-hundred and twenty years after the conflict, only a conglomeration of letters, diaries, memoirs and hand-full of battle reports were available to give only the foggiest interpretations of what was where. The terrain—unquestionably—remained the same.

The topography of the field is dramatic to say the least. Deep draws and abrupt fingers and ridges range across the landscape north of Perryville dotted with commanding hilltops. However, war-time property lines, fences of stone and rail, home-sites, barns and other evidence of human habitation had long been destroyed, ruined or fallen into disrepair—eventually succumbing to the elements and by time itself. By the time the first book was written on the battle, only Squire Henry P. Bottom's home still rested on the gentle slope north of Doctor's Creek upon which the brigades of Anderson's Confederate division attacked Lytle's Federal brigade on the heights north of that home. One notable structure that was mentioned in both Confederate and Federal reports of the battle included the Russell House that stood a short distance south of the Mackville – Benton Crossroad. Unfortunately, that structure succumbed to fire in 1964—102 years after the battle.[9]

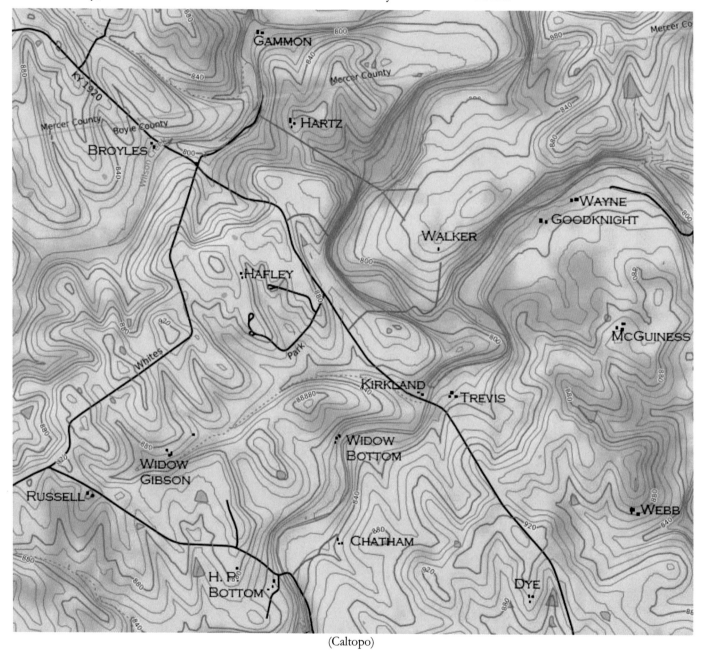

(Caltopo)

Other well-known landmarks and their locations were eventually identified through old battlefield maps, land records, soldiers' accounts and local lore, while others were forgotten and lost to time. The Widow Bottom

---

[9] *Owners of the Perryville Battlefield*, Document, (Perryville Battlefield State Historic Site: Perryville, KY, 2014) p. 6.

House, the Chatham House, the Yankey, Hart and Goodnight houses were all identified and mixed into the story of the battle. Additionally, another home that was *never actually identified by name* by any of the participants was included in that list. It was the home of Widow Gibson. The *exact* location of this structure is still uncertain, but it was believed to have been northeast of the Russell House. Although not mentioned by name, at least two Federal soldiers mentioned a structure on a finger of high ground that runs from Benton (White's) Road to the southeast. It is certain that the Widow Gibson—whose husband had died earlier in the year—occupied a cabin in this *vicinity*. An officer that reported the actions of Webster's brigade referred to a movement by the Fiftieth Ohio to the vicinity of a cabin situated on a hill. Additionally, a member of the Fiftieth Ohio—Erastus Winters—mentioned an "old log building" on a similar piece of terrain. However unlikely, this structure *may* have been the residence occupied by the Widow Gibson and her three children.[10] Although it was stated by battlefield park personnel that Widow Gibson's home was destroyed during the battle and no longer inhabited, a member of the Sixteenth Tennessee revisited the battlefield in May 1883. Whatever homesite the Sixteenth was engaged around was still standing when J. C. Biles visited the battlefield. He related that he "…was able to point out the ground over which the Sixteenth Regiment fought. The little log cabin is still standing, around which so many brave men of the regiment lost their lives."[11]

Given the reports of the battle and source materials that were available at the time, both historians Hafendorfer and Noe concluded that when the battle commenced the Confederate high command was unaware of the true location of the Federal left flank. The Confederate attack was supposed to commence from the Rebel right—first striking the enemy's left flank—and roll across the Federal front to the left. Both historians relate that when Cheatham's division commenced the forward infantry movement in this echelon attack, his lead unit mistakenly stepped off in the direction of the Federal center—instead of the enemy's flank as intended. As the lead brigade—under Brigadier General D. S. Donelson—neared the enemy lines, his force of three regiments was struck by heavy artillery fire. When Donelson realized that there was an error in direction, he sent for the lead regiment (the Sixteenth Tennessee) to correct its direction and await the two remaining regiments to close up for support. Both Noe and Hafendorfer assume that this initial advance was in the direction of Captain Samuel Harris' 19th Indiana battery. The correction would have caused the brigade to advance to the northwest against a battery commanded by Lieutenant Charles C. Parsons on the Open Knob. However, General Frank Cheatham had already sent a staff officer to rush the regiment forward in its original direction—that is— continuing toward Harris' battery. According to Hafendorfer and Noe's interpretations, this meant that Colonel Savage—who commanded the lead regiment—continued in his original direction in an all-out rush toward Harris' distant battery over a half mile away. The historians at the battlefield park today have a slightly different version of events. There, Kurt Holman—former director of the park—insists that the lead unit stepped off in the direction of Simonson's battery rather than Harris'. Simonson's battery was located fully five hundred yards southeast of Harris' battery. When the order to change direction was received, Holman concludes that the direction of march was corrected to advance against Harris' battery rather than Parsons' guns as suggested by both Hafendorfer and Noe.

By both interpretations, the Sixteenth Tennessee was followed by the Fifteenth and Thirty-eighth Tennessee regiments and continued their advance against the skirmishers of the Thirty-third Ohio and Second Ohio infantry regiments. At this juncture, the two interpretations take slightly different paths, but the guts of how the battle unfolded are nearly one in the same. By Noe's interpretation, at least the Sixteenth regiment under Colonel Savage fought its way through these two regiments and—between and beyond at least two other regiments—all the way to the grounds and structures of the Widow Gibson's cabin. This meant that the Sixteenth Tennessee regiment and its two supports had to smash their way through no less than two Yankee regiments (the Second and Thirty-third Ohio) under direct frontal fire of Harris' battery, enfilading fire from Simonson's 5th Indiana battery and the musketry fire of the Eightieth Indiana, Ninety-eighth and Fiftieth Ohio,

[10] Winters, Erastus. *Serving Uncle Sam in the 50th Ohio.* (East Walnut Hills, Ohio: 1905), 20.

[11] J. C. Biles, *Southern Standard*, McMinnville Tennessee, May 23, 1883, p. 3.

Tenth Wisconsin and the Twenty-fourth Illinois infantry regiments. That's the combined fire power of seven infantry regiments and two batteries of six cannon each.

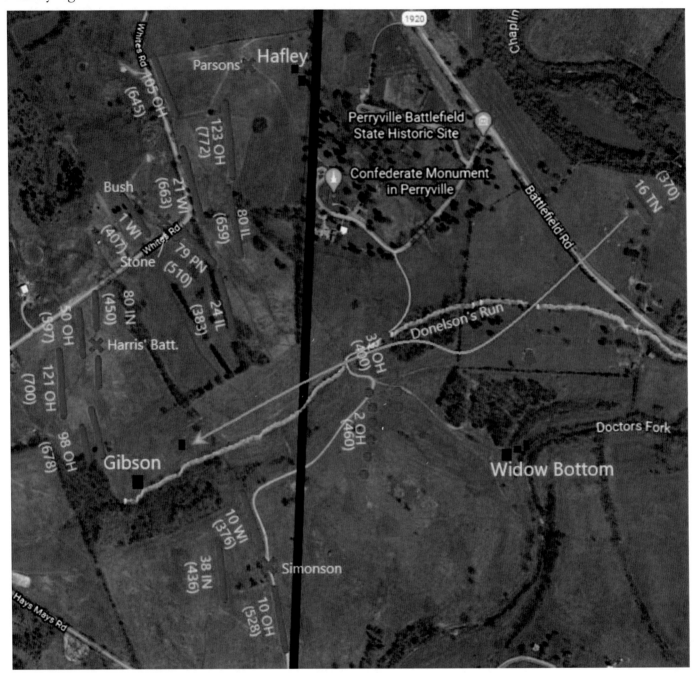

This graphic provides the current interpretation in which the Sixteenth Tennessee breaks through and between thousands of Federal troops—only to supposedly either retreat to their starting point (according to Noe) or are pinned down and await the support of sister units for **nearly three hours** according to the Park's interpretation. The numbers below unit designations are the approximate number of effective men that each unit reported. (Google earth)

Not to mention, the effective strength of Donelson's three Rebel regiments in this attack numbered not more than 1,000 men; while, just the Federal's Second and Thirty-third Ohio regiments combined—alone—numbered at least 848 effective men. The combined total of the Ninety-eighth Ohio and Eightieth Indiana regiments (that directly supported Harris' battery) came to a whopping 1,560 defenders. That's not even counting the Fiftieth Ohio (655 men), Tenth Wisconsin (376 men) nor the Twenty-fourth Illinois (383 men) who could have easily contributed to the repulse of Savage's Sixteenth Tennessee and its two supporting regiments.

If one counts only *half* of the infantry defending Harris' Federal battery, that number still comes to 1,723 infantrymen or more than 70 percent larger than the strength of the entire attacking force—the total strength of the Federal troops being over 3,775 men. Noe also declares that Parsons' battery—which would be more than 800 yards away—was still firing at them as they approached the Widow Gibson cabin. This is regardless of at least two wooded terrain features that would have deprived them of any line of sight to the regiment and the fact that their guns would have been firing in the direction of friendly forces at an angle of no less than 135° to the right of their original field of fire.

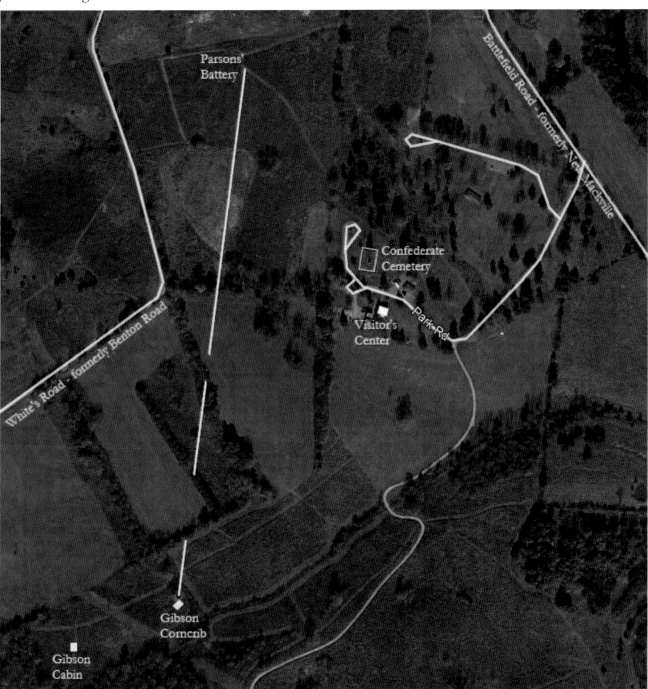

As noted in this map from Google Earth Pro using 3D line, the line of site from Parsons' battery is obstructed by at least two terrain features that would have made it impossible for Parsons' guns to have engaged the right of the Sixteenth Tennessee anywhere near the Gibson corncrib. This range was too far for canister to be effective at over 800 yards. This direction of fire would have the battery firing in rear of their own main line of defense.

Noe definitively states that it was the combined fire of these batteries and the infantry that led to such high casualties for the Sixteenth Tennessee whose losses approached sixty percent. That might sound like a reasonable assumption; however, making it that far against such imposing odds and incurring *only* sixty percent casualties would be nothing short of miraculous. Besides, the two supporting Rebel regiments—the Fifteenth and Thirty-eighth Tennessee regiments—sustained only seventy-six casualties *combined*—only about one-third of the casualties of the Sixteenth; while, the Sixteenth Tennessee suffered approximately 219 killed, wounded and missing. Still—somehow Noe concludes that after attaining its position *at the Widow Gibson cabin*, the Sixteenth Tennessee again attempted to "shift around to the right and attack Parsons' battery."[12] Noe apparently forgot that his narrative had already placed the attacking Rebel regiment at least 800 yards south of Parsons' guns—and no less than 250 yards behind the initial Federal main line. While his interpretation has Donelson's brigade achieve this deep penetration in the Yankee line, Noe then explained that the Rebel brigade had sustained such irreparable loss at the site of Widow Gibson's cabin that it must retreat. Continuing Noe's interpretation, Donelson's brigade then fell back in its entirety to (practically) its starting point nearly three-quarters of a mile to the east.[13] This—too—is regardless of the fact that Savage expressly stated in his autobiography, "We were ordered to fight. To order a retreat at the beginning of a great battle is not war. We must hold this position until supported, and it is the duty of our commanding officers to bring us support."[14] Clearly by Savage's account, as well as the accounts of his men in the ranks, there was no retreat conducted. It was only after the arrival of Maney's brigade—on their right—that the regiment received any form of relief. However, Noe's conclusion is challenged by the park's own interpretation.

Mr. Holman concurs with Noe's idea that the Sixteenth Tennessee fought against and through such overwhelming odds, but Holman's understanding changes when the regiment reached the cabins of the Widow Gibson. Holman relates that the regiment did not retreat, but instead, it held its ground behind enemy lines taking fire for over two and a-half hours until Maney arrived on the regiment's right flank. This is why—Holman insists—the Sixteenth regiment sustained more losses than any other Confederate regiment. But the hole in that interpretation is the fact that Maney never made an advance that took his brigade astride the site of the Widow Gibson cabin. Cheatham, Maney and his regimental commanders all explained that after several attempts to gain Starkweather's Heights—with limited success—Maney's force fell back to the foot of the hill at Benton Road and failed to participate in any more attacks. When they did advance—much later near dark—they met no resistance. The remaining assaults were conducted by Stewart's and Donelson's brigades.[15]

Critical to current interpretations is the idea that a massive gap had been left in the Federal center that day. If a massive inverted 'V' shaped gap was left in the center of the Federal lines—as Noe suggests—that contributed to the tactical defeat of Federal forces that day, the man responsible (Rousseau or McCook) would have stood next in line for a Court of Inquiry immediately following Buell's. There is no evidence of the commands of Lytle, Starkweather or Harris' brigades being mishandled that day. Not a single newspaper or letter home condemned anyone other than Buell and Gilbert for a failure to send reinforcements to the beleaguered Federal forces under McCook. Don't think—for a minute—that a commander that was negligent enough to leave a dangerous gap in the lines wouldn't have been reprimanded at the very least. A perfect example of this is Brigadier General Thomas J. Wood at Chickamauga nearly a year later.

For the next forty pages of text, Noe failed to mention Donelson's brigade. Only after the **unassisted** attack by Maney's brigade against Terrill's position and Parsons' battery on Open Knob does the reader get another hint of what faced Donelson's brigade according to Noe. Just before the advance of Stewart's brigade,

---

[12] Kenneth Noe, *Perryville: This Grand Havoc of Battle* (Lexington, KY: The University Press of Kentucky, 2001), 203.

[13] Kenneth Noe, *Perryville: This Grand Havoc of Battle* (Lexington, KY: The University Press of Kentucky, 2001), 204.

[14] John H. Savage, *Life of Savage* (Nashville, TN: John H. Savage, 1903), 122.

[15] Maj. Gen. B. F. Cheatham, *Report of Battle of Perryville* (William P. Palmer Collection: WRHS Collection: Box 1, Folder 6): Brig. Gen. George Maney, *Supplement to the Official Records of the Union and Confederate Armies*, Part 3, Vol. 2, Broadfoot Publishing Co., Wilmington, NC, 1994. p. 667.

he asserts that Donelson attempted another charge to seize Harris' battery. This is apparently after 3:30 p.m. which is around same time that he credits Maney's brigade with seizing Parsons' battery and Terrill's forces surrendering Open Knob. Contrary to **dozens** of Federal and Confederate accounts, Noe declares that Terrill held the hill (Open Knob) for up to an hour and a half. This declaration—if not outright stated—is at least implied. This early misconstruction of the development of the battlefield continues on the Federal left and left-center as Noe dissects, reorganizes, and splices accounts together to form any semblance of logic out of the quandary that his own misconception has birthed.

To add further to the confusion, Noe uses quotes from a member of the Sixteenth Tennessee to support this second attack on the Federal line which he insists was against Harris' battery—supported by Webster's Federal brigade.[16] The actual eyewitness accounts—taken literally—explain that all of these experiences took place in the **first thirty minutes** of the battle. Somehow, this is over-looked and apparently attributed to the idea that the *participant* was mistaken and the knowledge of the historian—writing 139 years after the fact—is right. While the majority of information regarding the Federal center is corroborated by Federal accounts and doesn't change what *they* experienced, it does affect the Confederate interpretation dramatically. If Donelson and Stewart's brigades didn't attack in the locations described by Noe and Hafendorfer—who did? That is what makes this forthcoming interpretation shed greater light on the Confederate center and right flank in an attempt to understand the development of Rebel success on the battlefield at Perryville.

Finally, it has become clear that all this confusion in the comprehension of the battlefield came from a lack of knowledge concerning the whereabouts of buildings or structures on the field. Three *key* Rebel commanders mentioned a structure or structures that faced the initial Rebel attack by Donelson's brigade in the *opening moments*. It's clear by their own words that these structures were *at the initial line* of defense established by the Federal troops. The structures were not located hundreds of yards behind the Federal front lines—but right at them. General Frank Cheatham called them "buildings," General Donelson called it "a small farm House," while Colonel Savage referred to them as "two cabins at the line of the enemy's forces." The mention of the cabins or buildings is made by at least three other members of the Sixteenth Tennessee. Private James R. Thompson calls them "two little log cabins." Private Carroll H. Clark referred to the site as "the little cabin on the hill," and Thomas Head: "an old log cabin." These seven accounts are unquestionably in reference to the same site. By each of these accounts, a battery of guns was within forty to one-hundred yards of the structures on an open hill. All the accounts of the soldiers of the Sixteenth Tennessee explain that this action occurred very early in the engagement—near the opening moments. They all state that this battery of enemy guns was *taken* by them with the assistance of Maney's brigade approximately *thirty minutes* after the commencement of the action. This implication is corroborated in the reports of both Generals Cheatham and Donelson.[17]

Finally, new research has yielded the discovery of a long-lost structure on the battlefield. This structure consisted of a cabin-dwelling with an additional barn or stable structure only a number of yards distant. The structures were located on the eastern slope of what has become recognized as Open Knob. On this same hilltop Parsons' Independent Federal battery was deployed. After exhaustive research, it was discovered that the location of the cabin and identity of its occupants sat in plain view for no less than 144 years. Long over-looked by historians, this family—by the name of Hafley—occupied this modest cabin that would become the scene of desperate fighting and bloody carnage. While Hafendorfer's and Noe's interpretations failed to get 100% approval from the management of the Perryville Battlefield site regarding their interpretations, this new interpretation of the battlefield has failed to get *any* approval. It's clear that Hafendorfer's and Noe's works have practically cemented history. From email correspondence with at least one of the authors and the Perryville Battlefield Park's former director, it became clear that this misconstruction of both the chronology of the battle and geographical placement of units on the battlefield came from the lack of knowledge regarding this newly

[16] Kenneth Noe, *Perryville: This Grand Havoc of Battle* (Lexington, KY: The University Press of Kentucky, 2001), 245.

[17] Maj. Gen. B. F. Cheatham, *Report of Battle of Perryville* (William P. Palmer Collection, WRHS Collection, Box 1, Folder 6): Brig. Gen. D. S. Donelson, Report of Battle of Perryville (William P. Palmer Collection, WRHS Collection, Box 28, Folder 9): John H. Savage, *Life of John H. Savage* (Nashville, TN: John H. Savage, 1903) 120: James R. Thompson, *Hear the Wax Fry* (Nellie P. Boyd, Ed., Cookeville, TN, 1966) 10.: Carroll H. Clark, *My Grandfather's Diary of the War* (C. W. Clark, Jr. Compiler, 1963, TN) Article #15.

found structure on the battlefield. Hopefully, with the discovery of this cabin location and a review of the evidence, the entrenched understanding of the battlefield based on insufficient research and mere *assumptions* will introduce a dramatic change in the understanding of the battlefield at Perryville.

Without the knowledge of another cabin structure *in the path of the initial advance* by Rebel forces, it would seem certain that any mention of manmade structures by participants could only be those belonging to the Widow Gibson. That belief is what has led historians to their current misrepresentations. If the only *known* structures were those of Widow Gibson, any references to cabins or buildings would *have* to pertain to Widow Gibson, or at least that was the *assumption* by historians. Unaware of any other structures on the battlefield, *opponents* to any *new* interpretation could argue it by declaring that *any mention of cabins* further bolstered the idea that Donelson's brigade fought at Widow Gibson's—which is the current bogus interpretation. Revisiting these sources—old and new—with knowledge of the long-lost cabin site *should* easily dispel these older interpretations of the fight on the Confederate right and center.

THE HAFLEY CABINS

CAPTAIN EDWARD RUGER

In July of 2014, while scanning documents and maps relative to the battle, a crucial map was rediscovered. Following the battle, both armies had their engineers draw maps to relate the positions that their forces occupied during the fight. The map that was drawn by order of Federal General Buell was created by Captain Edward Ruger and Lieutenant Anton Kilp. Ruger was Chief of the Topographical Engineers and had originally served in the 13th Wisconsin Infantry. Kilp served in the 1st Regiment Engineers, Missouri Volunteers. Ruger and Kilp took surveys of the surrounding countryside in the days following the battle and compiled their data. This original map was eventually used to create several different versions. To prevent crowding, many of the home-sites that were on their originally compiled map were left out of the version that was later submitted and published by the War Department. The version that appears in the *Atlas of the Official Records* lacks the details that an 1877 version of the same map included. The description of the 1877 Ruger and Kilp map in the Library of Congress indicates exactly what is *original* to the map.

"Authorities: surveys by Edward Ruger and Anton Kilp [and] official reports of officers of both armies." Map gives "position of General Gilbert's corps on the evening of October 7th" and the positions of both the Union and Confederate troops "on the 8th before being brought into action," "while engaged," and "after dark on the evening of the 8th." "Roads, the railroad from Lebanon to Stanford, drainage, vegetation, relief by hachures, houses, and the **names of residents** are also represented."[18]

This was the base map for all other maps that were made following the battle. It included all the above information: roads, relief, drainage, and *most importantly* "names of residents." This information was strictly from the 1862 survey taken by Ruger and Kilp. In 1860, Edward Ruger was living in Rock, Rock County, Wisconsin with his parents and was twenty-five years old working as a surveyor. He and his brother—William, an attorney—enlisted in the 13th Wisconsin at Janesville, Wisconsin in Rock County in October 1861. Edward was elected Captain of Company A and shortly thereafter detailed to the Engineers on the General's staff. He was mustered out of the army on November 18, 1864 at the expiration of his term. He is also found living in the same town (Rock, Wisconsin) with his wife in the 1870 census—no longer affiliated with the military, but working as a surveyor.

Interestingly on the 1877 Ruger/Kilp map, a word was located at nearly the exact point at which it was suspected the "mystery" cabins were located. After visiting the battlefield earlier that year and meeting with the park manager, it was noted that he had a poor copy of the same map on his wall. When it was suggested that the word may be a name, that hypothesis was quickly contested that the word was "hayfield" and represented such on the map. But seeing a much clearer image of the same map months later, it soon became certain that it was indeed a name. At first glance, it did appear that this word represented a *hayfield* on the battlefield, but zooming in on the word, it was clearly noted that it actually spelled "Hayflay." Upon closer investigation, a black square was seen adjacent to the word. These squares were regularly used to identify a structure or home-site. It was astounding that for all of these years, the *key* to this interpretation may have been over-looked or disregarded by so many.[19]

---

[18] https://www.loc.gov/resource/g3954p.cw0227000/?r=0.631,0.481,0.388,0.247,0

[19] Fold3: https://www.fold3.com/image/249/260559514

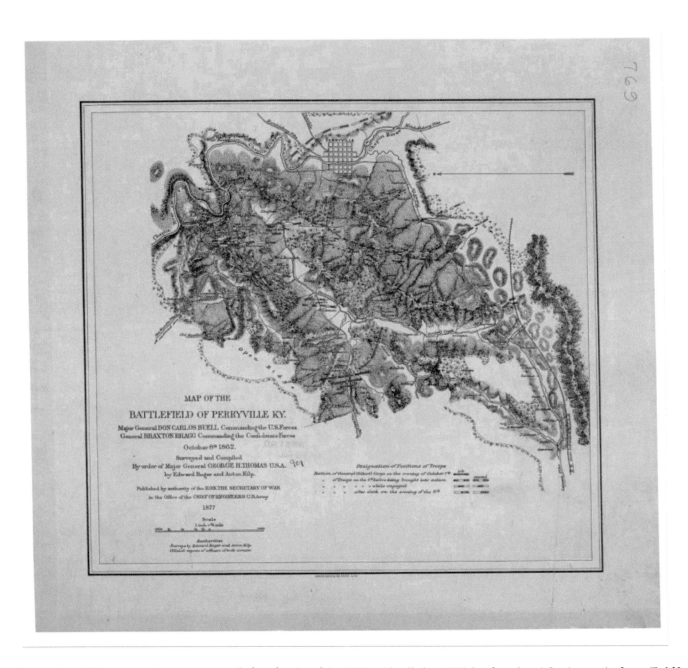

This is the 1877 version that was compiled and printed in 1877 with all the 1862 landmarks. The image is from Fold3 – Civil War maps – Kentucky – Battle of Perryville. A nearly illegible reproduction of this map has been sold at the Perryville Battlefield site for many years.

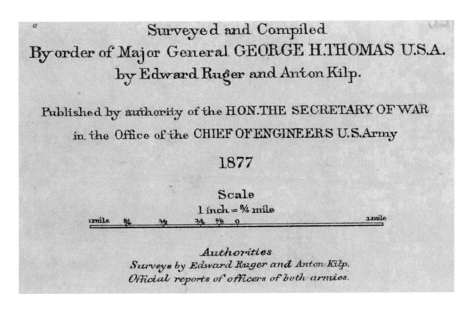

Note this portion of the 1877 map explains that the surveys were taken by Ruger and Kilp. They took the surveys in the days or weeks following the battle in 1862—not 1877. The site of the Confederate Cemetery had already been established after the battle when the vast majority of the Confederate dead were collected and buried in the vicinity of the deadliest fighting. Needless to say, this was on the finger of terrain only a short distance from the Hafley Cabins and Open Knob.

On a whim, Ancestry.com was accessed in hopes of finding evidence of a family by that name. Searching the 1860 census for Boyle County, Kentucky, the name "Hayflay" was searched. Luckily, Ancestry's site uses syllable recognition. In moments, at the very top of the list appeared the name, "Joseph C. Hafley." It was astounding when it was noted that the Hafley family (apparently pronounced Hayflay) had a Perryville post office. To confirm the find, a search of the 1850 census as well as the 1870 census was conducted. The family was not living with a Perryville post office in either of those censuses. The 1870 census confirmed that they lived several miles south of Perryville with a Mitchellsburg post office address—more than three and a half miles south of Perryville as the crow flies. In 1880, the family was living in Casey County a few miles further south. Joseph and his wife would die in Casey County after the turn of the century and were buried in the Lane Cemetery there. This further confirmed that the name was not added to an original map in the 1870s—but had only been at that location in the 1860 census. Deed records did not reflect property ownership by a "Hafley" family member; however, this was explained on further examination.

Joseph C. Hafley was the son of Henry Hafley of neighboring Washington County, Kentucky. Joseph was born in 1831 in Lincoln County. At some point, he moved to Boyle County as a young adult, and by late 1852 or early 1853, he had begun the courtship of a young lady ancestrally tied to the land that the battle would take place on. On March 27, 1853, twenty-three-year-old Joseph married twenty-one-year-old Francis A. Bottom. Francis was the daughter of Thomas Bottom and Sara Russell. Sara Russell's brother—John C. Russell—was the owner of what would become the famous "Russell House" landmark on the Perryville battlefield. Frances' father—Thomas Bottom—was the son of William S. Bottom and first cousin of Henry P. "Squire" Bottom. "Squire" Bottom's house and barn also became important landmarks on the battlefield. As well as being a subsistence farmer, Joseph Hafley worked as a hired hand for his uncle-in-law—"Squire" Bottom—from 1858 until the time of the battle primarily building fences for Bottom's property. Together, Joseph and Frances had three children by the time the census was taken in June of 1860. George, Thomas and Merit—all boys—were aged eight, six and three years old at the time of the battle.[20]

---

[20] http://perryvillebattlefield.org/html/battlefield_owners.html (Accessed August 14, 2021)

17

Note the name "Hayflay" near the center of the 1877 Ruger/Kilp map. North is oriented to the left of the map.

Joseph and Francis Hafley's net worth for their personal belongings was only $300 in 1860. With their feet not yet off the ground, the couple was offered the opportunity to live as tenants on property owned by Henry P. Bottom—this property may have actually belonged to his mother Mary Bottom who was now widowed and occupied the Widow Bottom House along Doctor's Fork. Both Thomas Bottom's family and his wife Sara's (Russell) side of the family probably owned nearly half of the ground that the hardest contested parts of the battle were fought on. The Hafley cabins were .86 miles or 1,508 yards (as the crow flies) from Henry "Squire" Bottom's front steps. It was also just less than 900 yards north-northwest of Widow Bottom's House—or about a half-mile. The Hafley home site consisted of two cabins located on the eastern slope of the Open Knob—land that would later be occupied by Parsons' Independent Federal battery and the brigade of Federal Brigadier General William Terrill. The structures were apparently rough-hewn log cabins. One structure acted as their home and the other was probably a stable or barn.

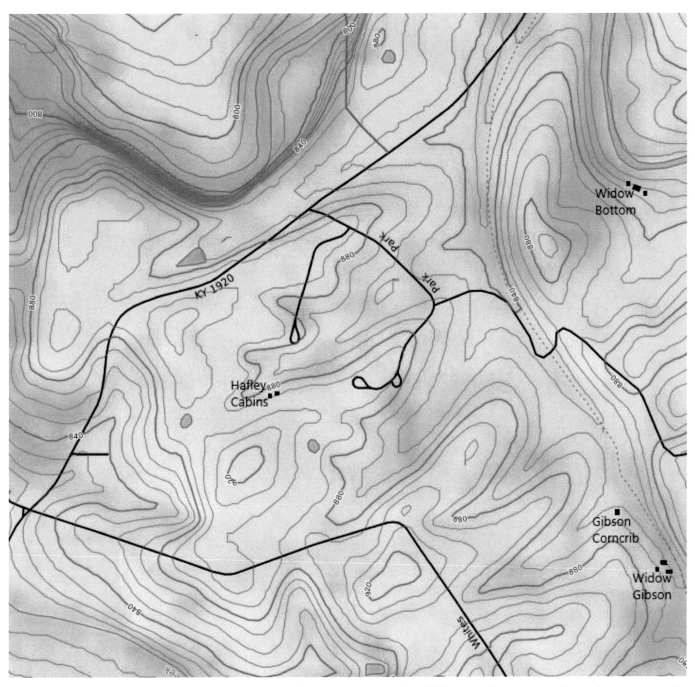

This map from CalTopo shows the same area and orientation as the 1877 map. Superimposed on the map are the homesites located there in October of 1862. North orientation is to the left on this map.

With the approach of Rebel cavalry around the 6th of October, local residents became uneasy of the possibility of a great battle. By the morning of the 7th, it became clear that a storm was brewing. When Federal forces approached—placing his home between the opposing lines—Joseph took his family and retreated out of harm's way just over a half mile north to the Gammon House that was located at the junction of Wilson's Creek and Chaplin River in Mercer County. A search of Joseph in the military turned up nothing definitive as to either side he may have served with, and it appears the war passed without his participation.

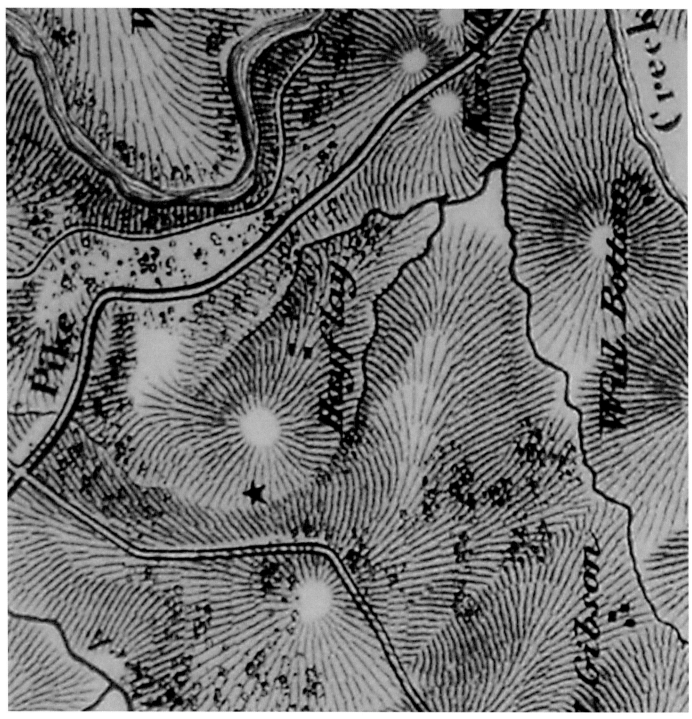

This map—from a French Atlas of the American Civil War—was also created from the Ruger/Kilp map and only located homesites just as the original survey did. North orientation is to the left on this map.

When this new information was submitted to the battlefield park, it was completely disregarded. In an attempt to get the park's leadership to recognize the existence of the cabins and Hafley family, a deeper search was conducted to find more proof of the dwelling structure. Finally, another piece of the puzzle was located on a historic map collection website. This map was from a French atlas about the American Civil War and was printed to be used in conjunction with *Histoire de la Guerre Civile en Amerique*. The interesting thing about this map is that it has no troop dispositions added to it. In fact, it merely shows the topography with hatch lines and locates all the home sites and names of families that occupied them at the time of the battle. These were all taken from the Ruger/Kilp survey of 1862. This is probably the closest to the actual Ruger/Kilp survey we will find unless the original surfaces someday. This additional find was also disregarded by the park. This author is of the belief that locating cabins at this particular site alters the story of the battlefield at Perryville so much that the park is unwilling to accept the probability that they may be wrong. With the most dependable authority, this second map further substantiates that a family named Hafley did indeed occupy a homesite on the southeastern slope of Open Knob. This missing link helps to solidify the hypothesis that the battle unfolded in a manner much different than how it has been interpreted for the last forty years. This discovery will hopefully be the glue needed to make the new interpretation comprehensive and valid. With the identification of the Hafley family and their cabin location, a vigorous argument will be made to show how current interpretations of the battle simply do not fit the complicated puzzle of the battlefield at Perryville.

UNBALANCED ODDS OF *CURRENT* INTERPRETATIONS

The story of Cheatham's division at the Battle of Perryville is a powerful one. This division—almost exclusively made up of Tennesseans—conducted an assault on Federal lines that crushed the Union army's left flank and nearly resulted in a Federal rout. It's clear that the success wreaked by Cheatham's division was inflicted as the result of the weight of the attack that was thrown on the "green" brigade of Federal Colonel William Terrill. Terrill's troops—nearly all newly formed within three weeks of the battle—were barely proficient in the manual of arms and lacked any depth of knowledge in transitioning formations. Terrill's Federal brigade numbered 2,270 effective infantrymen with a battery of eight guns in support—consisting of another 136 battery men—for a total of 2,406 bodies.[21]

Brigadier General George Maney's Confederate brigade opposed these Federal troops and was composed of five regiments totaling 1,885 effective infantrymen. This was a numerical advantage of 521 men for the Federal defenders of Open Knob. Still, only *four* Rebel regiments were committed in the attack against the Knob by Maney's brigade according to current interpretations. The Ninth and Sixth Tennessee with the assistance of the Forty-first Georgia and Twenty-seventh Tennessee single-handedly stormed the heights and over-powered the two Federal regiments that occupied its summit. The 123rd Illinois and the 105th Ohio were the only two Federal regiments that were formed in time to participate in the early defense of the Knob. Together, these two Federal regiments numbered 1,417 men. The combined total of the *four* Rebel regiments that made the attack numbered a mere 1,394 men. Thus, Maney was attacking a foe on dominant terrain supported by artillery with no numerical advantage at the outset and faced eight cannon that were in the act of being deployed in defense of the Knob. Before Open Knob fell to the Rebels, the Eightieth Illinois—consisting of another 659 men—and a small detachment under Colonel Theophilius Garrard with 194 men joined the fight. Both forces joined the fight to the right of Parsons' battery but were too late to prevent the capture of the guns. Still—according to current interpretations, nearly 1,400 men from four Rebel regiments were able to overcome the firepower of at least seven pieces of Federal artillery and over 1,400 Federal soldiers that were reinforced by another 853 men from the two aforementioned Federal regiments. That brought the total Federal force to more than 2,300 men defending the Knob against only 1,400 Rebel attackers. As the saying goes, if it sounds too good to be true—it *probably* is, and in turn, if it sounds improbable: it likely is.

If this act alone sounds nearly impossible, it would be even more astounding to believe that Maney's brigade went on to attack and force the retreat of Starkweather's brigade only four-hundred yards further in Terrill's rear. As currently related by Noe and Hafendorfer, Maney's brigade continued in pursuit of Terrill's men on to Starkweather's Hill with the assistance of only the extreme right regiments of Alexander P. Stewart's Rebel brigade. These were the Fourth, Fifth and Twenty-fourth Tennessee regiments per Hafendorfer. The Second Brigade under Brigadier General A. P. Stewart was the smallest in Cheatham's Rebel division. His brigade strength was listed at 1,490 effective troops on the day before the fight. The Fourth Tennessee mustered a mere 170 men that day, while the Twenty-fourth Tennessee mustered 375 men for the fight. Although the exact number is unknown, the Fifth Tennessee probably fared little better than the Fourth Tennessee after Shiloh with less than 200 effectives. This amounted to around 745 men of Stewart's brigade that came to the support of Maney. General Maney admitted in his report of the battle, that the lion's share of casualties in his brigade took place in the attack on Open Knob—excepting the First Tennessee whose mass casualties came in the assault on Starkweather's heights and the storming of Bush's Indiana battery.[22]

By reducing the known strength of Maney's three lead regiments by twenty-five percent to compensate for casualties, Maney's entire brigade strength probably amounted to around a mere 1,598 men after suffering at least 287 casualties in the attack on the Open Knob. This casualty figure may have been even higher, but it still

---

[21] All numbers given in reference to strength in this chapter are from Noe's *Perryville: This Grand Havoc of Battle* p. 369-80 and Hafendorfer's *Perryville: Battle for Kentucky* as well as contemporary newspaper articles.

[22] Report of Colonel John C. Starkweather, *The Louisville Daily Journal* (Louisville, Kentucky) Oct. 27, 1862, p. 3.

leaves almost 1,600 men in Maney's total force. This number—combined with Stewart's three regiments that Hafendorfer attributed to continuing the fight with Maney—brings the Rebel force attacking Starkweather's heights to approximately 2,345 effective Rebel troops.

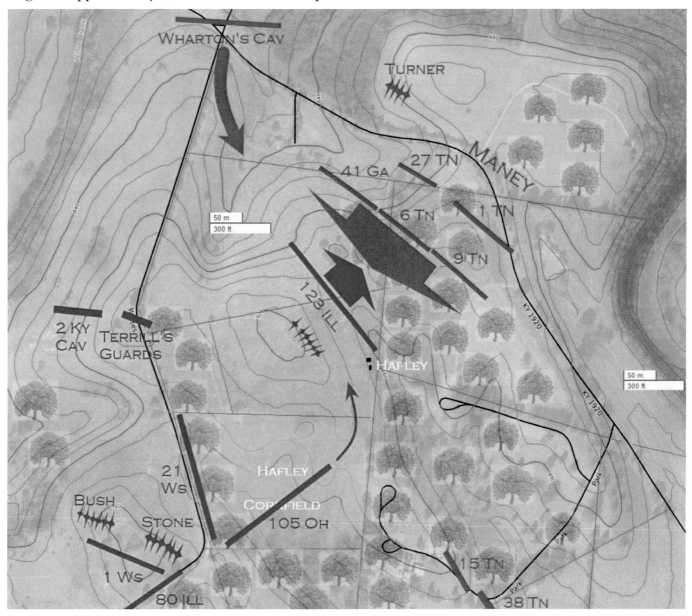

This map represents the current idea that Maney's brigade single-handedly over-ran Terrill's brigade capturing Parsons' battery. As is noted in the above image, Donelson's brigade is portrayed over a quarter of a mile south of Maney's brigade. Troop positions are from current histories that do not represent reported locations.

Terrill's Federal brigade was broken at this point, and his force of over 2,400 men was greatly diminished. Many—that had not been wounded—took to the woods and the safety of the rear. But still, Terrill managed to rally at least one-quarter of his force—and perhaps even more—in rear of Starkweather's troops that amounted to as many as 600 men. Colonel Starkweather's own brigade was supported by two batteries of artillery comprised of twelve cannons. His force of infantry and artillery consisted of no less than 2,189 men. Starkweather's force supplemented by Terrill's remnants made a defensive total of no less than 2,789 men. This force was later supplemented by the Ninety-fourth Ohio (500 men) and portions of other commands as the fight progressed.[23] This meant that according to Hafendorfer, Maney's and Stewart's forces (combined) totaling 2,345 troops at the outset of the attack on Starkweather's heights was able to practically defeat perhaps more than 3,300 Federal troops that defended commanding ground with massed artillery support.

While this is *somewhat* palatable, the fact remains that the Rebel forces conducting the attack were still outnumbered by nearly 1,000 defenders. Starkweather's forces were veteran troops, except for one regiment. The Twenty-first Wisconsin was fresh from home and numbered 663 effective troops that day. They had been placed at the foot of the hill in a cornfield in front of the remainder of his brigade that occupied the heights less than two-hundred yards west of Benton Road. This regiment was practically routed as Maney's men passed into the cornfield west of Open Knob, but Rousseau related that most of those men rallied and did good service after passing in rear of Starkweather's lines on the hill in their rear.

As the outnumbered Rebel's supposedly pummeled the Federal defenders of Starkweather's Hill, more improbable exploits were being conducted closer to the Federal center by Donelson's second attack with the support of two additional regiments. While the strengths of the Thirty-first and Thirty-third Tennessee regiments of A. P. Stewart's brigade are not conclusively known, these two regiments probably shared around the same number—each with approximately half of the remaining effectives in the brigade. Thus, these two regiments probably amounted to around 370 men each in line that day. The two regiments—according to Hafendorfer's account—advanced in rear of and to the support of Donelson's brigade as they crashed into the left of Harris' brigade and center of Webster's lines at Widow Gibson's home-site. By his interpretation, the reinforced line was able to penetrate even deeper into the Federal line which led to the capture of four guns from Captain Sam Harris' 19th Indiana battery. Hafendorfer states that the Rebels were able to seize the four guns around 4:45 p.m. This sounds feasible. These sequences of events appear possible, but all things possible are not necessarily *probable*.

A glance at the original records—diaries and accounts written in the days immediately following the battle—clearly indicate that the battery captured by the Sixteenth Tennessee regiment was not seized nearly three hours after the commencement of the action. In fact, the boys in the ranks indicated it was but a mere *thirty minutes* into the action when they captured the guns. There is no question that Harris' battery fell later in the fight—as late as 6 p.m. according to General McCook himself; the problem is the formula used to determine who captured the battery and when it was captured.[24] In fact, there is hard evidence that proves Donelson's brigade *did* participate in the capture of Harris' battery later in the evening. The later time frames nearly match up, and it is certain that they did play a role in the capture of those four guns—but not as described as either Hafendorfer's or Noe's chronology of events play out.

S. A. M. Wood's Rebel brigade was probably initially responsible for the capture of the four guns of Harris' battery. William Preston was a member of Company B, Thirty-third Alabama infantry in Wood's brigade. He explicitly stated that his regiment and the Thirty-second Mississippi regiments comprised a line that helped to capture a battery. In one of the final attacks of the day, Wood's brigade had advanced and crossed the dry bed of the intermittent stream that emptied into Doctor's Creek in the long valley running west to east. It was in this "valley" that the corn-crib, Widow Gibson's cabins and a small cemetery were located. Preston related that, "...we rushed their line which broke after our getting near the muzzle of their guns. Co. B on the left of the regiment passed between some of their four or more brass 12-pounder guns and pushed over the ridge, down the slope and into some timber where we met a line behind a fence."[25] There was only one battery in the Federal

---

[23] The Ninety-fourth Ohio of Harris's brigade was sent to the left as Terrill's brigade was being broken and after Parsons' guns had fallen on Open Knob. Its arrival to assist the preservation of the guns was too late, but just in time to assist in the defense of Starkweather's Heights. The Ninety-fourth remained on the left for the remainder of the fight. One wing of the Ninety-eighth Ohio was also sent to assist in the defense of Parsons' guns, but arriving too late, they were sent back to the center of the field to rejoin Webster's brigade. (Col. Frizell, OR, p. 114: Lieut. Kennon, OR, p. 154)

[24] Maj. Gen. Alexander M. McCook, "Report of the Battle of Perryville" OR. Vol. 16, Pt. 1, p. 1038 - 1044

[25] William E. Preston, *Diary of William E. Preston and History of the 33d Alabama*, Alabama Department of Archives and History, SPR393.

center that lost a gun that bloody evening. Captain Harris' Federal battery had been so hard pressed—that when their support began to give way—they only managed to limber up two of the six guns to make an escape. J. P. Cannon was a member of the Forty-fifth Mississippi also of Wood's brigade. His regiment was probably on the right of the Thirty-third and he mentioned confronting Indianians in his attack and subsequent retreat which were probably the Federal troops of the Eightieth Indiana. Wood's brigade may have initially captured the guns, but were forced back by a heavy counter-attack of Federal forces. Cannon stated that he "hardly time to catch my breath before a thrilling and welcome sight was presented – a line of gray almost a mile long, one of Polk's Divisions, coming to reinforce us."[26] The left of Wood's brigade was then reinforced by Cleburne's brigade arriving in their rear, while the right of the brigade received support from Donelson's brigade advancing to recapture the guns. General Donelson related that when he advanced to the attack, the Federals were conducting "a forward movement in the direction of the captured Battery evidently with a view to retake."[27] John S. Quarles was a member of the Eighth Tennessee infantry of Donelson's brigade. His recollection of the capture of Harris' battery was vivid.

> The Yankees ran from a point they had vigorously defended all day; we captured 4 cannon in this charge. The charge was made by the 8th and 51st Tenn. Inf. This was late in the evening. The battle had been very stubborn. When the enemy in our front gave way, the Gen. in command said, the 8th & 51st had won the day.[28]

These four guns fell into the hands of Donelson's brigade during their *final* assault. It's this in-depth investigation of the battle on the right that has revealed a whole new interpretation for the entire right and much of the center of the battlefield at Perryville. Revisiting the fight on the Confederate right provides ample evidence that it was the attack by Donelson's brigade that first engaged the Federal troops on the Open Knob— namely the Sixteenth Tennessee. This regiment assailed the right of Parsons' battery and the 123rd Illinois. The infantry and artillery of Terrill's brigade and the Sixteenth Tennessee of Donelson's brigade effectively pinned each other down creating high casualties until the arrival of Maney's brigade on the Rebel right flank. It was this fighting in the first thirty minutes of ferocious and bloody combat that had left the Sixteenth Tennessee "solitary and alone."[29]

[26] *The National Tribune* (Washington, D.C.) Dec. 8, 1898, p. 1-2. (newspapers.com)

[27] Brig. Gen. D. S. Donelson, *Report of Battle of Perryville* (William P. Palmer Collection, WRHS Collection, Box 28, Folder 9)

[28] John S. Quarles, *Memoir of John S. Quarles*, Copy on hand at Stones River National Battlefield.

[29] John H. Savage, *Life of Savage* (Nashville, TN: John H. Savage, 1903), 130.

RECONSTRUCTING THE BATTLEFIELD AND UNDERSTANDING TERRAIN

Understanding terrain and topography is crucial in understanding any battlefield. This particular USGS map from CalTopo was drawn using 10-foot interval contour lines. Contour lines are used to show ground elevation and contours in terrain. For this map it means the distance between each topographical contour line is 10 feet in **elevation**. The closer the lines are to one another represent steeper slopes, while those with greater distance between the contour lines represent more gently sloping terrain.

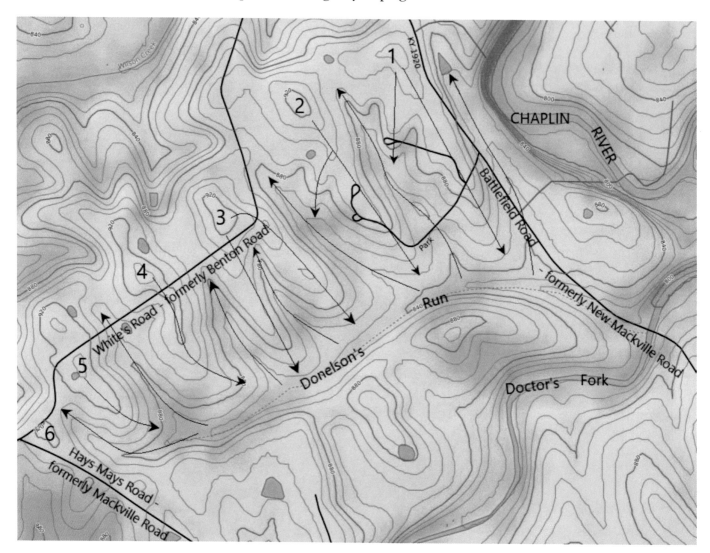

Topographical maps are easy to read if one knows what they are looking for. First, you must know what to look for. The Marine Corps has taught a simple example for many years now. If you ball your hand into a fist, you can identify the main terrain features that are most important to identify on a map. After making a fist, your 1ˢᵗ knuckles become **hilltops**. The row of four 1ˢᵗ knuckles is referred to as a **ridgeline**. The low points immediately between your knuckles are referred to as **saddles**. From each knuckle, follow your finger down to the second knuckle on the finger. These fingers are literally referred to as **fingers** of terrain in topography. That is, they are the higher ground that descends from hilltops to a larger draining area. They are sometimes referred to as spurs, but more-often they are recognized as fingers. Likewise, the low points between your fisted knuckles that we refer to as saddles become **draws or hollows**. These are the low points between the fingers that would naturally be drainage from higher elevations. On maps, fingers will direct themselves away from hilltops and appear more rounded at their ends more often than not. Draws—conversely—will appear more pointed more often than not and point towards higher ground. By making two fists and touching the second knuckles together, one has created two ridgelines that have fingers and draws that empty into a valley. This valley would likely have a stream with better than intermittent water flow. The valley itself is walled by numerous fingers and draws that flow toward the valley.

Running across the middle of the above map—diagonally from mid-top right to bottom left—are the numbers one thru six. These six numbers represent hilltops that ranged across the landscape from the northeast to the southwest in that order. This row of hill-tops is a ridgeline. From each number (hill-top) a thin line may be seen with an arrow pointing away from the hill-tops. These are fingers—higher terrain that slowly declines away from the hill-tops. Between each of these fingers are draws or "hollows" which are lower in elevation and separate the fingers of terrain. Thus, the arrows pointing toward the ridgeline represent the lower ground that may contain intermittent streams or creeks. The largest hollow in this image may be referred to as a valley. It is the low ground that contains the stream noted as "Donelson's Run" and runs a distance of nearly 9/10's of a mile. Fingers will often gently decrease in elevation for long distances from the hilltops. Note that the eastern most fingers extend south a distance of over 700 meters from the hilltops toward Donelson's Run. Likewise, other fingers descend in the direction of Doctor's Fork along the mid-bottom-right portion of the graphic. What we recognize as Open Knob—the position of Parsons' battery and Terrill's brigade—is listed as hill-top #2 in the image.

THE MAPS

Before modern topography was introduced with contour lines, hatch lines were drawn to show terrain relief. The following maps were based off of hatch line maps drawn by Ruger and Kilp in 1862.

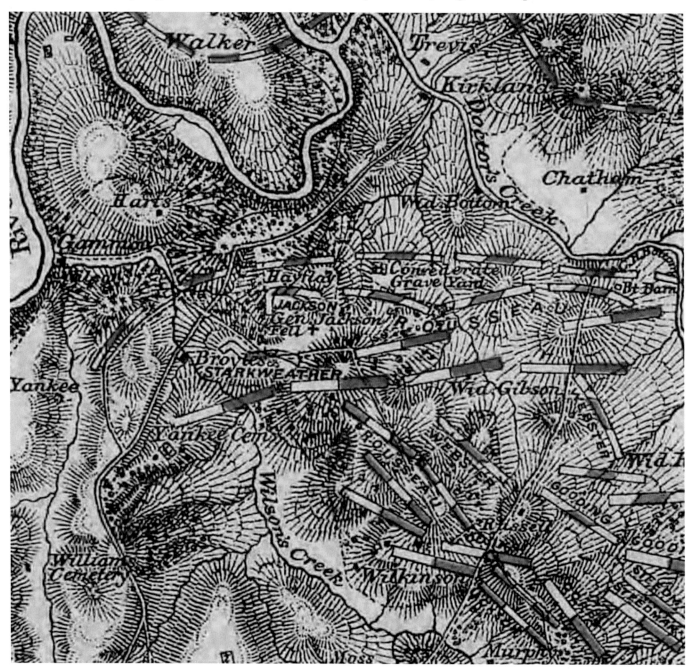

This is a portion of the original map that was published in 1877 by the authority of the Secretary of War from the office of the Chief Engineers of the U.S. Army. This map was intended for resale purposes. For orientation purposes, due north is to the left of the map. The authorities for the map, roads, home-sites and troop dispositions were compiled and located by Engineer officers Ruger and Kilp and the official reports of both armies in 1862. The Hafley homesite is legible just above Jackson's position near the middle of the map.

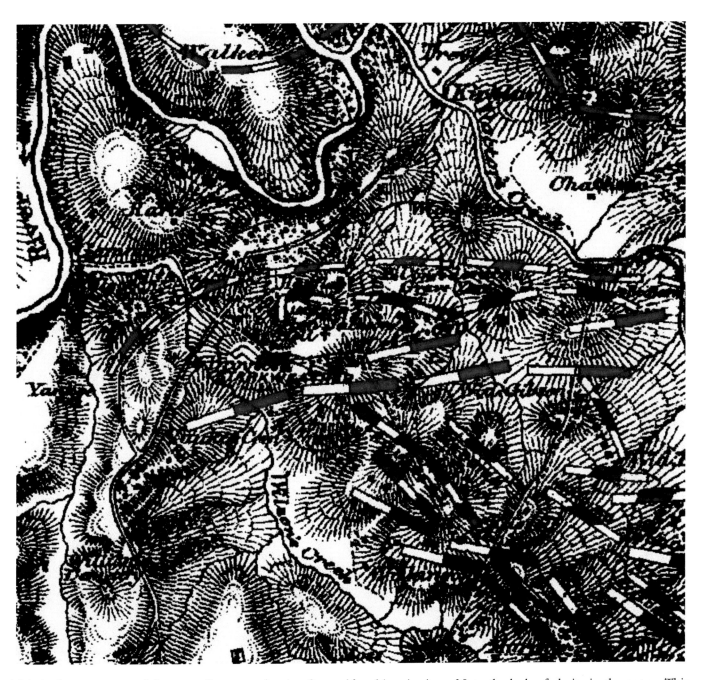

This is the same area of the preceding map that is often sold at historic sites. Note the lack of clarity in the copy. This poor version of the map is one of the main reasons why the Hafley home-site has never been identified. Only about half of the names on the map are legible.

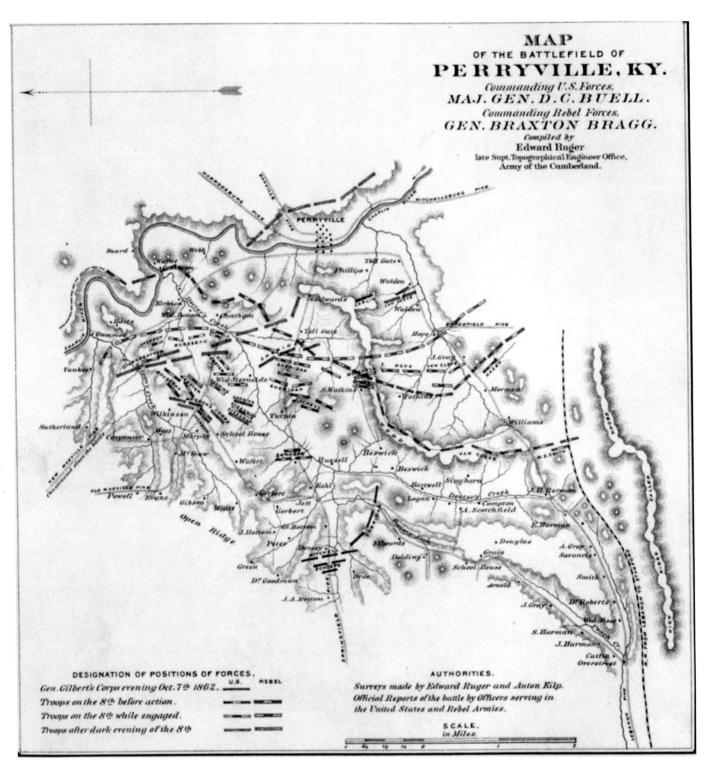

MAP
OF THE BATTLEFIELD OF
PERRYVILLE, KY.
Commanding U.S. Forces,
MAJ. GEN. D. C. BUELL.
Commanding Rebel Forces,
GEN. BRAXTON BRAGG.
Compiled by
Edward Ruger
late Supt. Topographical Engineer Office,
Army of the Cumberland.

DESIGNATION OF POSITIONS OF FORCES.
Gen. Gilbert's Corps evening Oct. 7th 1862.
Troops on the 8th before action.
Troops on the 8th while engaged.
Troops after dark evening of the 8th

AUTHORITIES.
Surveys made by Edward Ruger and Anton Kilp.
Official Reports of the battle by Officers serving in
the United States and Rebel Armies.

SCALE,
in Miles.

This version of the Ruger/Kilp map was compiled and used in the *History of the Army of the Cumberland* published in 1875.
North orientation is to the left of this map.

30

This close-up of the preceding map shows the main battlefield in the same orientation as the first. While it shows the Gammon, Chatham, Widow Bottom House and others, note the lack of the Russell, H. P. Bottom and Widow Gibson sites. The Hafley site is neglected as well. Why is this? Logic suggests it was to keep the troop positions more legible. The more that is crowded on the map, the harder it is to comprehend. North orientation is to the left on this map.

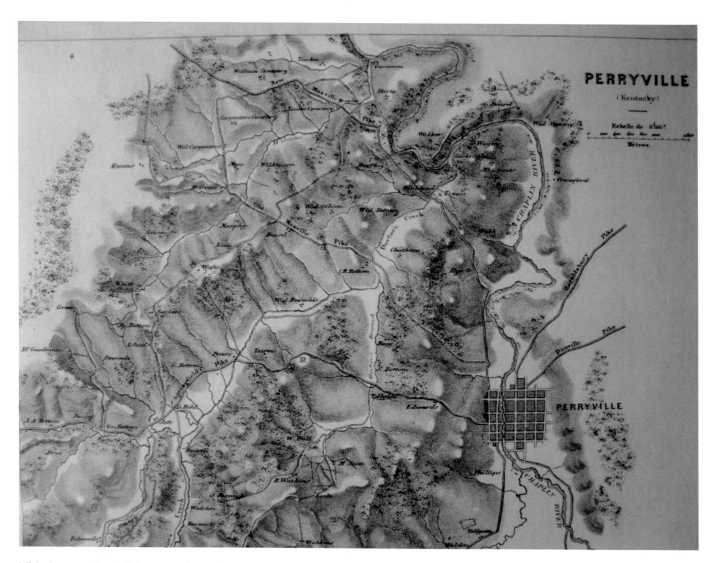

This is a portion of the map from the French atlas for: *Histoire de la Guerre Civile en Amerique*. The following close-ups of the map help us gain an even better comprehension of Ruger and Kilp's understanding of terrain and importance of community data. North is oriented to the top of this map.

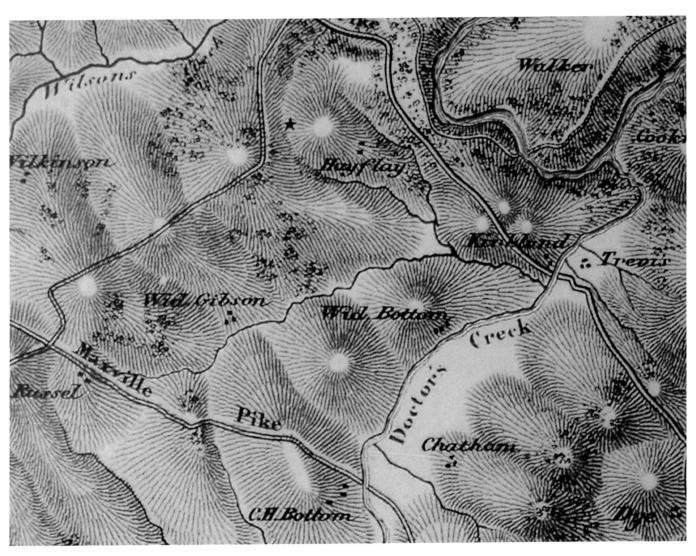

Here on the same map, the "Hayflay" (Hafley) name is clearly visible a short distance from Walker's Bend only about a quarter mile west of Chaplin River. South and slightly east is Widow Bottom nearly a half mile distant. Southwest of the Hafley family, Widow Gibson's site is a half mile distant. A quarter of a mile further, John C. Russell's home is visible just left of Maxville Pike. H.P. Bottom's home is incorrectly labeled C.H. Bottom. The Chatham, Walker, Wilkinson, Dye and Kirkland sites are also clearly listed. North orientation is the top of this map.

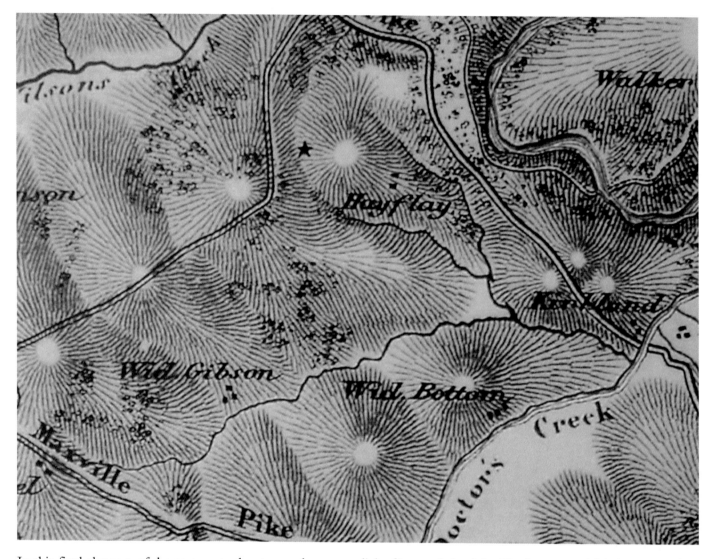

In this final close up of the map, note the star on the map a slight distance left of the Hayflay name. This is supposed to be the location at which General James S. Jackson expired after being hit by rifle-fire in the first few minutes of the action. To the southwest is the location of the Widow Gibson Cabin just over a half mile distant. North orientation is the top of this map.

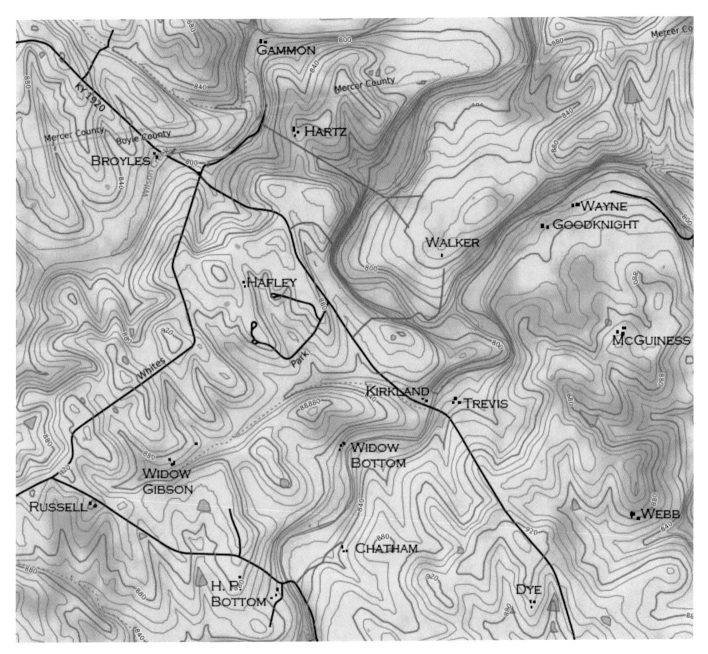

This CalTopo map includes most of the homesites and names from the 1862 Ruger and Kilp map. The names that have been transferred from the map include the Gammon family in Mercer County, Elizabeth Broyles, Hartz, Joseph C. Hafley, Widow Mary Bottom, Widow Mary Jane Gibson, R. F. Chatham, Henry P. Bottom and his barn that burned during the battle and John C. Russell. All the names had a Perryville post office address in the 1860 census—excepting Gammon which was in Mercer County and Hartz—whose records aren't located. North orientation is to the top of this map.

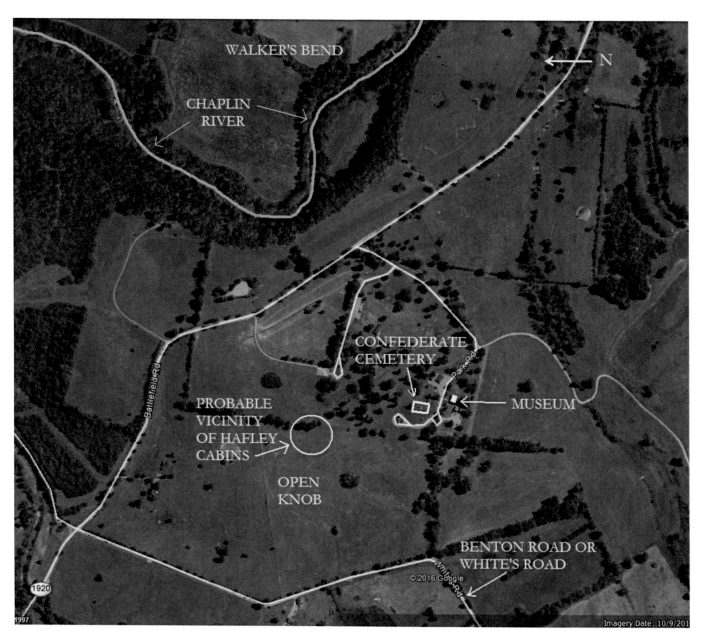

This view of the battlefield from Google Earth, shows Walker's Bend and Chaplin River at the top of the image. Note the north seeking arrow at the top right of the image indicates that the north orientation is also toward the left edge of the map. New Mackville Pike runs from the top-right to the bottom left. The road that runs from left to bottom-center was called Benton Road, but is now known as White's Road.

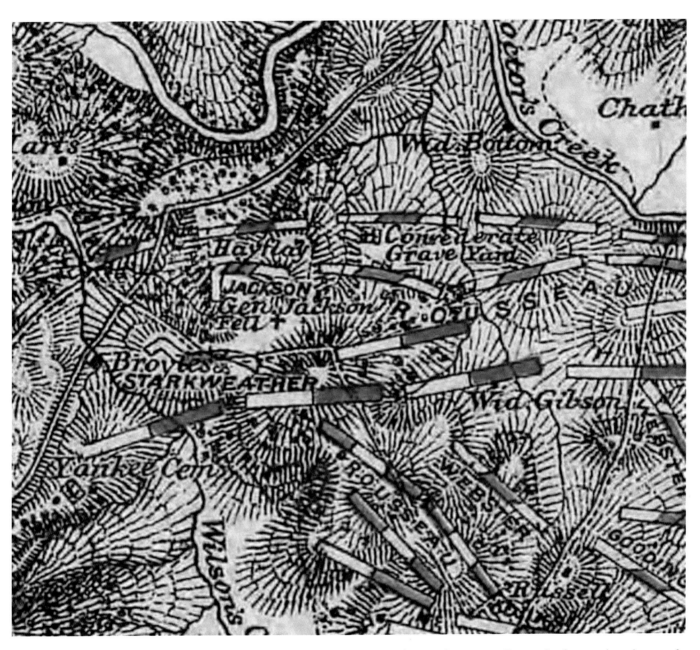

This close-up of the 1877 map is oriented to the same perspective as the previous map. Just as in the previous image, the left of the map is oriented north, the top of the map is east; right is south and the bottom is west. The following maps are aligned in the same manner and show the approximate same areas. They include a portion of Chaplin River at top, New Mackville Pike, Benton (White's) Road, Old Mackville Road, and Dixville Crossroads. Note the "Hayflay" name and the 'X' that denotes where General Jackson "fell" directly beneath it. To the right of the Hafley home-site, the Confederate Cemetery is noted.

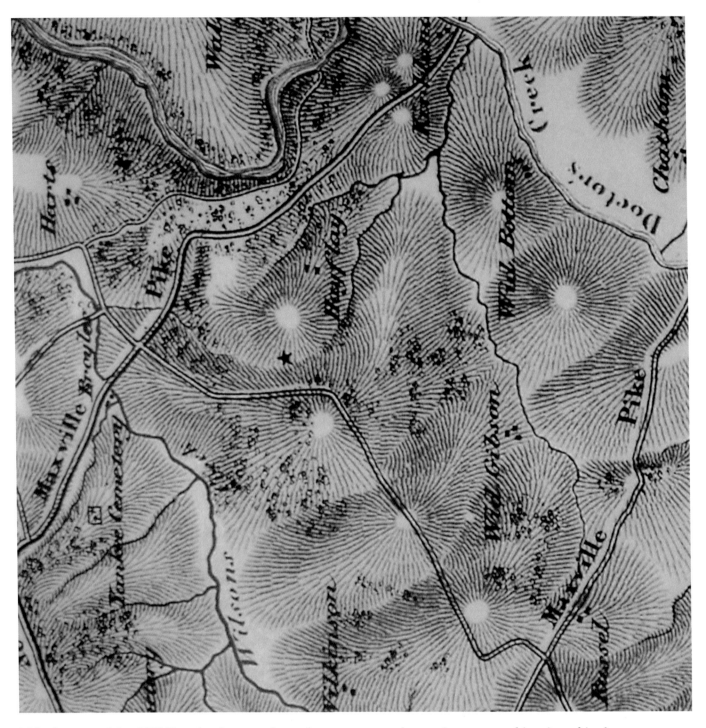

This close-up of the 1873 French atlas map shows the same area as the previous map and is oriented in the same manner. Note the two squares that represent the Hafley cabins just east and south of Open Knob. Also, note the star that probably represents the location at which General Jackson died.

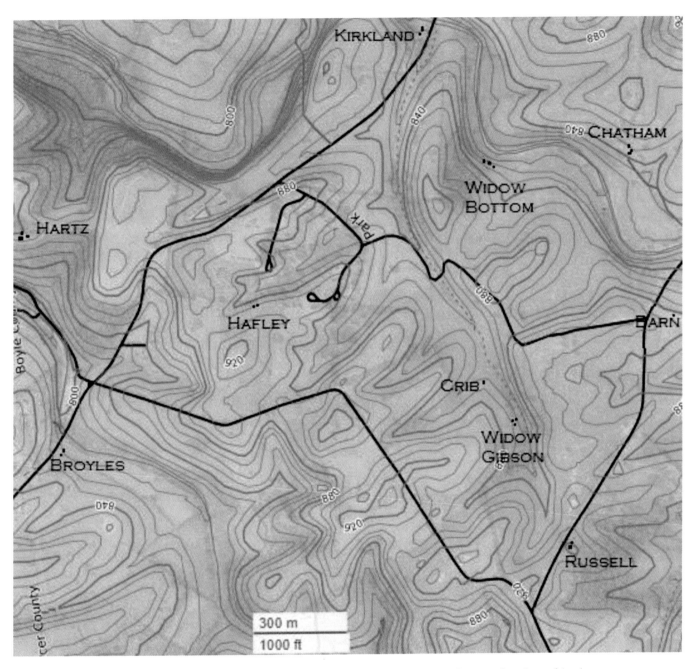

This is a portion of USGS Map Name: <u>Perryville, KY</u>   Map MRC: 37084F8. The map is oriented in the same manner as the previous map with homesites added. (CalTopo)

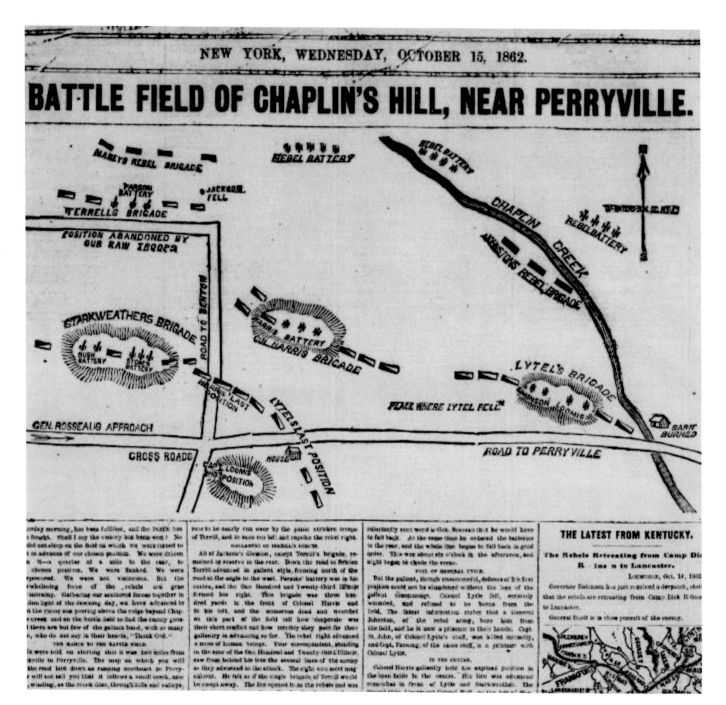

This map is from the *New York Herald*, October 15, 1862. It shows the deployment of Federal troops, where Jackson fell and where Lytle fell. The north orientation shown on map is incorrect. The left of the map would indicate north.

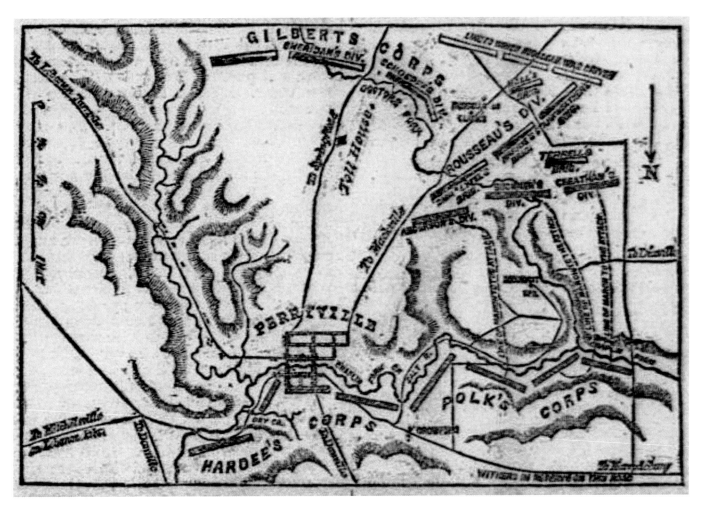

This map is from the June 19, 1884 edition of the *National Tribune*. It relates the advance of Anderson's, Buckner's and Cheatham's divisions. The north seeking arrow at top right is actually oriented east. The right edge of the map was actual north.

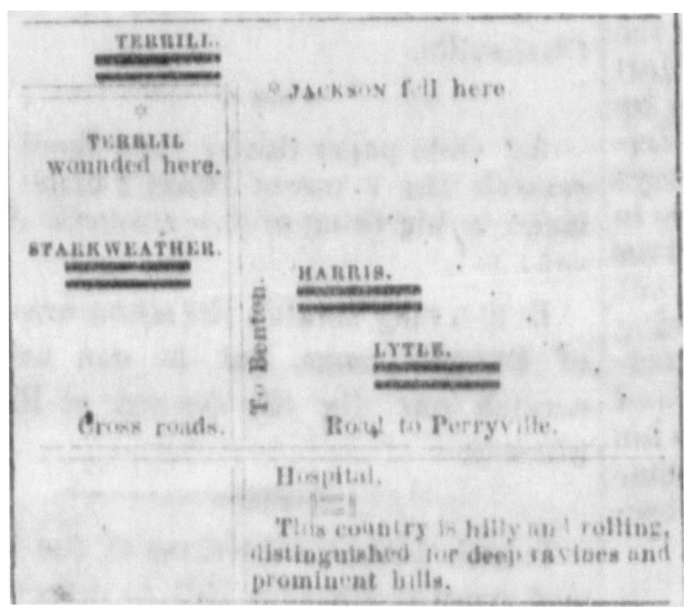

This is another period map that was included in the newspapers in the weeks following the battle. It also shows where Jackson and Terrill fell. The north orientation would be the left side of this map. *Nashville Daily Union, October 21, 1862, page 1.*

This photograph is from the *Mollus* collection. The photographs were taken in the first week of May, 1885 by E. H. Fox (photographer) out of Danville, Kentucky for *Century Magazine*. The photographs were used to make engravings which were printed in the magazine. The above photograph is identified as the corn-crib of the Widow Gibson. The same structure can be seen to the left of the tree-trunk in the next photograph. This photograph may show yet another mystery structure. A building can be seen on the hill in the distance just above the corn-crib possibly in the vicinity at which the Fiftieth Ohio moved to the front.

Pine Tree 100 years old
At left of Rosseau's position

This photograph was also taken by Fox. It is also in the *Mollus* Collection. This author believes that the cabin in the photograph belonged to Widow Gibson.

This is a close-up of the previous photograph. To the left of the tree trunk, the left of the corn-crib is barely discernible.

WHAT MAKES A SOURCE CREDIBLE?

Historians must often make decisions regarding a source's credibility based on a number of factors. These factors may include the witness' proximity to the event, how soon after the event the written record was made, and if the source is substantiated by other corroborating testimony. Any of these three questions can cause a liability for the historian if he chooses to use a source that was not in proximity of the event, writes the record many years after the fact, or lacks corroborating testimony.

Proximity to the event is the most important of the three questions. Regardless of when the record was written—if the source was at the epicenter of the described event, it is probable that the guts of the record are reliable. Descriptions of events that were recorded in the days and weeks following are the most reliable. These events fell under the direct eye of the contributor. Corroborating testimony is not positively necessary to sustain *personal* experiences, but it is certainly a welcome addition to any source that was at the epicenter of the event. An example of this might be the account of a soldier that participated in the actions his record refers to, or a soldier-correspondent for a newspaper who writes of events that fell under his direct observation. A poor example of this would be a paid correspondent for a newspaper that observed the event from a distance and relies heavily on rumor and innuendo in his reporting of the event. Naturally, diary entries and letters that were written in the days or weeks following the event are the most descriptive and accurate in names or units mentioned. This source equates to the best available.

Some sources were in the midst of the event they described, but the record was written dozens of years after the fact. It can be certain that personal experiences were likely the most memorable and can be given the most credibility. Often, these records will have errors in names and unit numbers, but the guts of the record can be taken as credible. Comparing names or unit numbers to contemporary sources may help to hash out inaccuracies. In this case, corroborating testimony is needed to support suggestions outside the accepted knowledge of events. Two or more of these type sources that corroborate one another can easily give more credibility to an event that is related by the record. Examples of this might include answers from post war Tennessee Civil War veteran questionnaires, late nineteenth century memoirs written from memory or letters written near the turn of the century to *Confederate Veteran* or *National Tribune*.

Corroborating testimony is always needed when dealing with a record that was written long after the event, but not so much when records were written within a reasonable time frame from the event they relate. Apparently, not all historians agree. Correspondence with one historian made it clear that his belief is apparently somewhere in between. In an email correspondence in the Spring of 2014, this scholar made it clear that—in his mind—some of the sources that I have used are not reliable. Oddly, these same sources were used in the publication of *Perryville: This Grand Havoc of Battle*. This may be a prime example of "cherry picking." For example, he used the account of the 1905 memoir *Privations of a Private* written by Marcus Toney of the First Tennessee Infantry regiment. Toney is mentioned on at least six pages of the narrative according to the index. However, when presented with another narrative that was published in 1912 by the same source (Toney), the Professor declared it unreliable. Apparently, this was primarily due to the assumption that Toney *should* remember the specific number and types of artillery pieces defending Open Knob—fifty years after the fact. Oddly, he was willing to use Toney as a credible source until the *same source* related something other than what his own comprehension of the battlefield was.

Informed common sense tells us that precise memories fade with time, but not the "guts"—*per se*—of the memory. It is easy to speak in generalities when explaining an event that took place long ago. Names and numbers may not always be correct, but the story at its core, has solid foundation. When two or more of these sources corroborate one another, they may certainly be classified as credible records. All records that corroborate one another give further credibility and support the statements of the record in question. The same may be said for maps.

EXAMPLES OF *"CHERRY PICKING"*

Private Marcus Toney was a member of the First Tennessee Infantry regiment that served in George Maney's brigade at the Battle of Perryville. He wrote a fairly well-known memoir following the war that was copyrighted in 1905 and published in 1907. *Privations of a Private* was a post-war memoir that gave his personal recollections of the war based off a very detailed diary that he had kept. His wartime experiences were summed up in 120 pages of his memoir. Thirty additional pages covered his post-war privations. Simply put, nearly four years of war were summarized in this brief memoir that was meant to inform and entertain future generations.

When the year 1912 came around and Toney found he was still full of life, he wrote an article that was published in the *Nashville Banner* on October 5, 1912. The article was entitled, *Fifty Years Ago Tuesday Perryville was Fought*. Interestingly, this record of the battle included many details that his memoirs had failed to include, but of course, the memoirs were merely a sketch of his personal experiences during and after the war. This article, however, included incredible details of the fight that his memoirs had failed to reveal. Certainly, using his personal wartime diary as his most direct source, Toney detailed the battle to a degree that future historians *could* gain a much deeper understanding of the events on the Confederate right. While his *memoirs* brushed the surface concerning the fight at Perryville, this more detailed description of the battle—revealed in his article to the *Nashville Banner*—shed even greater light on what his regiment saw and experienced in that battle. The following abstract comes from *his memoir*. It—alone—clearly detailed a scenario different from what current histories relate. It included valuable information that historians *purposefully* left out of their studies of the battlefield. It's also clear that for time and space Toney left out many details of the fight itself.

> There had been some skirmishing before our arrival, and about three o'clock the musketry and cannonading became quite brisk, the shells falling around us as we climbed the fence in battle line. We crossed Chaplin River, ascended a high bluff, and when we reached the height *Colonel Savage's Sixteenth Regiment was hotly engaged with the enemy. To uncover from Colonel Savage we had to move by the right flank,* and while executing this move some of our men were wounded. When we uncovered, we again moved by the left flank. General Leonidas Polk rode up and asked: "What regiment is this?" The answer was: "The First Tennessee." He then said: "Capture that battery."
>
> It was Parsons's *[sic]* eight-gun battery, supported by an Ohio brigade (Germans) in command of General Jackson, of Hopkinsville, Ky. They would not stand the charge, but ran in great disorder, leaving the battery in our possession. In attempting to rally them General Jackson was killed, and his body fell in our line of march.[30]

In the foregoing account, Toney revealed that his regiment approached the battlefield in *rear* of the Sixteenth Tennessee while they were "hotly engaged." Toney's regiment was instructed to "move by the right flank" in order to get out from behind the Sixteenth regiment. This statement—alone—not only suggests, but clearly indicates, that the proximity of the two regiments was very close. He added that Polk ordered his regiment to capture "Parsons' eight-gun battery." For whatever reason, this mention of the Sixteenth Tennessee was disregarded by historians—probably due to the lack of understanding Napoleonic tactics and the concept of support on a battlefield. This excerpt from Toney's memoir is informative, but it lacks specific details as to *exactly* what was unfolding in the First Tennessee's immediate front. However, the following excerpt is from Toney's *newspaper article* that—published only five years later—revealed even more startling evidence from the same diary entries that cannot be dismissed by historians.

> The firing of the pickets and the booming of the enemy's cannon told the battle would soon begin. From our position in the valley we could not effectively use artillery. Near the bluff General Buell had seven pieces of a Parrott battery. Our regiment, after crossing the stream, nearly dry, climbed the steep bluff and *came up in rear of the Sixteenth Tennessee commanded by Colonel John H. Savage,* which he called "the Panthers."

---

[30] Marcus B. Toney, *Privations of a Private* (Publishing House of M. E. Church, Nashville, TN, 1907) 42-3. *Emphasis added.*

The Sixteenth was engaged in a hot contest to capture the Parrott guns which were supported by a brigade of Illinois soldiers and Ohio soldiers commanded by General Jackson, from Hopkinsville, Kentucky. As we were moving by the right flank *in the rear of Colonel Savage* and endeavoring to uncover from his right, several of our men were shot before we got into action.

While laying down awaiting orders, General Leonidas Polk rode up and asked: "What Regiment?" The reply: "First Tennessee." He ordered Colonel Fields as soon as he uncovered from Colonel Savage to move by the left flank and *assist Colonel Savage to capture that battery*.

When we got into line of battle, the firing was furious, but as soon as we fired the Ohio troops fled and we captured the Parrott guns. In the meantime, Bush's Indiana Battery, supported by the First and Twenty-first Wisconsin, were reinforced by an entire brigade. The First Tennessee rushed forward under a storm of shot and shell which seemed to mow down our boys as grain by the sickle, but our thin ranks would close up and charge again only to meet with death. We had advanced so far in front of our line that we were without support, and the enemy, having no foes in their immediate front, turned their fire upon us and many of our boys were killed and wounded by this enfilade fire. Nowhere on the firing line was it so furious as where the First Tennessee was engaged, and some of our men fell in ten feet of Bush's Battery but we could not take it. Every man and horse of the battery was either killed or wounded. *When we charged the Ohio brigade with Colonel Savage of the Sixteenth Tennessee* and Colonel George C. Porter of the 6th Tennessee, General Jackson, with sword drawn, attempted to rally his men but he was killed and his body fell in the line of company F, Captain Jack Butler (which was known as the Nashville and Chattanooga Railway boys). Tip Greenhalge of the company captured General Jackson's watch.[31]

As revealed in this unabbreviated account of the action, Toney left out details in his memoirs merely to save space, but when he wrote the article specifically about the battle, he included far more information that also certainly came from his wartime diary. Twice, he clearly stated that his regiment was ordered to *charge the battery with the Sixteenth Tennessee*. It would seem that Toney's account would be clear enough to comprehend what truly happened on the Rebel right; but this was *not* the case. When this 1912 article was shared with the Perryville Battlefield and Professor Noe—neither of which had been aware of its existence—there was no interest in what Toney's very own words revealed. Since Toney's later account referred to the captured guns as "seven pieces of a Parrot battery," Noe argued that Toney couldn't have been referencing Parsons' guns. He asserted that since it is well known that Parsons' battery consisted of six brass twelve-pounder Napoleons, one Parrott gun and one brass howitzer that the guns Toney was referring to could be a reference to any battery *other than* those of Parsons' battery. This is where historical methodology becomes clouded by *assumptions*. There were certainly many things that Toney recorded in his diary regarding the fight that day. The majority of events were probably included in the article, but as previously noted by the member of the 105th Ohio, "One's own view is very limited at best, and few see more than the movements of their own company, or possibly, their regiment."

Is it reasonable to assume that Toney visually inspected and identified each and every gun of the battery, or is it more reasonable to deduce that Toney was aware that there was a battery of seven or eight guns in his front? Perhaps later, he was simply told they were Parrott guns. The Rebels on the field, including the commanders, mistakenly referred to Bush's and Stone's guns as "Loomis's" battery. Additionally—only *forty days* after the battle, Frank Cheatham—personally—referred to Parsons' guns as "a Battery of Eight Guns (12 lb. Napoleons) of the Enemy…"[32] In the end, it is clear that exactly *what types* of guns are confronting an attacker is not important—thus not remembered. What *is* important is that seven or eight enemy artillery pieces manned by Federal soldiers were confronting the Rebels—all hell bent on destroying anyone that tried to take their guns.

---

[31] "Fifty Year Ago Tuesday The Battle Of Perryville Was Fought." Marcus B. Toney. *Nashville Banner* (Nashville TN) October 12, 1912. *Emphasis added.*

[32] Maj. Gen. B. F. Cheatham, *Report of Battle of Perryville* (William P. Palmer Collection, WRHS Collection, Box 1, Folder 6)

This is what the attacking Rebels were well aware of. Some historians were willing to "cherry pick" Toney's memoir as a primary source in their books, but disregard Toney's article that was published only five years later based on entries from the same diary in much more detail apparently *assuming* that it is not credible. The same account was practically swept under the rug by the leadership at the Perryville battlefield. I was never given a reason for this lack of interest in the Toney article.

Two more previously unknown accounts by Marcus Toney were recently discovered. Both of these include the above information, but relate it in slightly different versions—adding even more detail to these pivotal accounts. They were both written for the anniversary of the battle—one in 1893 and the other in 1904—prior to the publication *Privations of a Private*. The 1893 account made it clear that the First Tennessee's initial attack was made in conjunction with the Sixteenth Tennessee.

I was a member of Company B, Rock City Guards, and we went into that fight thirty-three strong, and when it closed fourteen were killed and thirteen wounded. **Our regiment, with Savage's, was ordered to take the enemies' artillery**, and in the effort were almost destroyed. In that fight the gallant First began a record which became more glorious as the war progressed. **We took Parsons' splendid battery…**[33]

The second account was from much longer article that Toney wrote regarding the invasion of Kentucky in 1904. In it, he added even more detail. In this article he expresses the sorrow that both Colonel Savage and Maney felt at the massive losses in their commands.

About 3 o'clock the artillery from the enemy began to boom, followed by musketry. The First Tennessee moved in line of battle across Chaplin River and up the bluff. When we reached the summit **we came upon Gen. [sic] Savage's regiment and he was hotly engaged with the enemy**. Gen. Polk rode up and asked what regiment. The answer from Col. Fields, the First Tennessee.

The next command was, "Move your regiment by the right flank." As soon **as we uncovered from Col. Savage's right** we moved against the enemy, which in our immediate front was Gen. Jackson's brigade of Ohio troops, although they were all Germans.

When we charged they fled precipitately, and in attempting to rally them Gen. Jackson was killed. **We captured Parsons' eight-gun battery in Col. Savage's onslaught**. He had lost heavily, and when we made another charge to capture Bush's Indiana battery, which appeared to be supported by a double line of troops, we exposed our left flank to an enfilade fire, which mowed our men like grass before the sickle. Ten men were shot down with the colors, all of whom were killed or died.

Subsequently, all of Company B except six men were place hors de combat. The regimental loss was about 250. Col. Savage lost about 199, and in the space of two hours the battle was over. …

I did not wonder that **Col. Jno. H. Savage of the Sixteenth Tennessee, and Col. George Maney of the First Tennessee, wept bitterly**, for the flower of their regiments were dead or bleeding.[34]

Another example of this "cherry picking" is dissecting the "guts" of a historical record and forcing it to mold to one's understanding—yet failing to use the whole of the record—or use it in context. This method is frequent time and again in Hafendorfer's work on Perryville and repeated in Noe's work. The best example of this is the dissection of numerous diary entries and memoirs that relate the capture of Harris' Federal battery in their interpretations. As related in source after source, the men in the Sixteenth Tennessee *definitively state* that the battery that they captured in conjunction with Maney's brigade was seized in the first *thirty or forty minutes* of action. Hafendorfer's use of the same sources span over 120 pages of narrative and a period of no less than *three*

[33] "Anniversary of Perryville." *The Tennessean* (Nashville, Tennessee) October 9, 1893, p.3. **Emphasis added**.

[34] "Invasion of Kentucky by Gen. Braxton Bragg." Marcus B. Toney. *Nashville Banner* (Nashville, Tennessee) June 14, 1904, p. 40. **Emphasis added**.

hours of action before he describes the capture of Harris' battery. Records do show that Harris' battery fell late in the action, but historians' accounts of the action—and the manner in which it developed—do not share the eyewitness description of events nor coincide with the given time frames.

Another example of this cherry-picking is in the latest work that relates the experiences of *Maney's Confederate Brigade at the Battle of Perryville*. The author uses the report of Federal Colonel Albert Hall to describe the fighting on Starkweather's Heights in defense of Bush's battery from the attacks of the First Tennessee. The passage the author uses is quoted precisely as it is recorded in the book.

> *The fire at this moment was terrific beyond description, and the running through my line of a six-horse team drawing a caisson created some disorder in my center. At almost the same moment of this repulse of the enemy* [Stewart's brigade] *a determined assault was made by them* [the 1st Tennessee] *on our left. A battery opened on us from the enemy's right* [Carnes' battery], *and from the form of the ground nearly enfiladed my line.*[35]

At a glance, that description gives an intimate view of the conflict for Bush's guns and the fight for Starkweather's Heights. The author even helped aid the reader by inserting brackets to better understand what units were involved and action as it unfolded. However, upon simple examination, the source actually reveals a completely different story. The *very next lines* from Hall's report explain that this action was—in fact—not taking place on Starkweather's line or near Bush's guns at all.

> Parsons' battery was stationed on a sharp crest of open ground about 80 yards from a wood occupied by the enemy. From this crest the ground descended to the woods and then ascended, so that the enemy delivered us the fire of consecutive battalions in rear of each other. The battery was also on a crest which abruptly terminated on the left a few yards from the guns, exposing the support to a cross-fire from the enemy's extreme right, of which the enemy, as before described, promptly availed themselves.

> Thus at the distance of 80 yards, in an open field, did Parsons' battery and the One hundred and fifth Regiment Ohio Volunteer Infantry deliver to the enemy a most terrible and destructive fire, receiving in return the fire of an enfilading battery and of a rebel brigade concealed in the woods.[36]

Clearly revealed, the scene that Colonel Hall was describing was the defense of Open Knob—an action that took place fully twenty minutes prior to the assault on the batteries atop Starkweather's Heights. Is this simply an oversight or was it a conscious effort to mislead the reader? Under the circumstances, it seems hard to believe that one could mistake the quote to be in reference to an attack on Starkweather's position, but mistakes can happen, and there would be no reason to purposefully mislead the reader.

Far from condemning anyone's historical methodology, it is clear that some have apparently made a conscious decision to *not* include some records that relate a chronology or summation different from what *they* have concluded occurred on the battlefield. Others have taken the liberty of using "picked" lines to support their theories or conclusions. And still, others manipulate the chronology of the records to better fit their beliefs and understandings of the field. This sort of picking and choosing or altering of sources can completely change the *actual* chronology of events. If one chose to leave out the *"guts"* of most of the accounts from members of the Sixteenth Tennessee and its sister regiments, one could easily conclude that the battle played out in the manner these historians have heretofore narrated. The evidence will show that the men in the ranks that day told a *far different* story than what historians have revealed to their audience thus far.

---

[35] Stuart W. Sanders, *Maney's Confederate Brigade at the Battle of Perryville*, History Press, Charleston, 2014, p. 107.

[36] Albert S. Hall, *Report of the Battle of Perryville*, OR, Series I, Vol. 16, Pt. I, p. 1065.

DECIPHERING PRIMARY SOURCE MATERIALS

John H. Savage's *Life of Savage* is a primary source that has been used time and again to explain the events that took place at Perryville. Like with most primary records, one must look very closely to decipher what is said versus what is not said. Sometimes the key to interpreting primary records is realizing the things that *are not said*. The sole purpose for Savage's chapter on the Battle of Perryville was to place blame where it was due (in his eyes) for the loss of so many men in his regiment. Secondly, he was trying to right the wrongs that had been misstated in the annals of *Confederate Military History* and had failed to relate the accomplishments of his regiment. Savage was prideful to say the least. When he realized that his regiment failed to get the recognition it deserved, he wanted to set the record straight. Part of his argument was that neither Donelson nor Cheatham had prepared or submitted reports of the battle. That was not actually the case.

As stated earlier, the two reports of these officers had been placed in a personal collection of war-time documents. They were never included in the Official Records of the war. Based on this, Savage assumed that no reports were ever prepared. Had Savage seen these reports, he would have been pleased to see that he and his regiment received praise from both Donelson and Cheatham. Although the coolness between Donelson and Savage prevented the brigade commander from specifically commending Savage, he described the advance of his three regiments "amid yells and cheers at every step."[37] He also made note of Savage's wounding. Cheatham went further in his description of the opening attack of the Sixteenth Tennessee and her two sister regiments. "…with a cheer which rang through all the surrounding woods, these brave men rushed forward with a determination and impetuosity which not even superior numbers or advantage of position could resist, the Enemy was driven back into the woods, leaving his former lines thickly strewed with dead and wounded." Cheatham did not stop at that. He also noted the losses sustained by the Sixteenth Tennessee.

> This daring and desperate charge however was not accomplished without most serious loss. Over one third of the men engaged were killed or wounded, among whom were some of the most valuable officers in the command. Col. Jno. H. Savage, commanding the 16th Tenn. Regiment, received a serious wound from a minnie ball in his left leg, and was painfully bruised by the fragment of a shell, and had his horse shot while gallantly leading his men against the enemy's lines.[38]

While Savage would have felt vindicated to some degree—had he known of these reports, he may have still been convinced that both of his commanders wouldn't have minded learning of his death. Savage attributed the sacrifice of his regiment to one of three possibilities. First: "From undue excitement by the presence of the batteries and main line of the Yankee army, dethroning their reason and banishing their common sense." The evidence suggests that Cheatham was aware of the location of the enemy's flank, but through some misunderstanding—perhaps Donelson's poor eyesight or an optical illusion—Donelson ordered Savage to initially advance on the wrong enemy battery. Donelson attempted to correct this misdirection, but the angle of the corrected axis of advance on the enemy brought the brigade diagonally across the adversary's front toward the battery. The Sixteenth Tennessee was then punished by a very heavy infantry and artillery fire at extremely close range. Second: "From drinking liquor to stimulate their courage to meet the dangers in the impending battle." Savage admits that he had no proof of such, but he speculated that alcohol may have been a cause. Third: "To cause the death of the disrespectful, disobedient and insubordinate Colonel Savage, who was constantly declaring that the army should be reorganized, Davis removed and a dictator appointed, or the conquest of the South by the abolitionists was a certainty."[39] This was likely sheer paranoia. True, Savage did not get along with Donelson on many matters, but to represent that Cheatham felt discontent with Savage would

---

[37] Brig. Gen. D. S. Donelson, *Report of Battle of Perryville* (William P. Palmer Collection, WRHS Collection, Box 28, Folder 9)

[38] Maj. Gen. B. F. Cheatham, *Report of Battle of Perryville* (William P. Palmer Collection, WRHS Collection, Box 1, Folder 6)

[39] John H. Savage, *Life of John H. Savage* (Nashville, TN: John H. Savage, 1903) 136.

be stretching the truth. If Cheatham had any displeasure with Savage, it would probably have been over Savage's constant harping about how someone better suited should lead the army—or the Confederacy. There is little doubt that Savage would have thought *himself* better suited to fill *either* position.

In addition to blaming both Donelson and Cheatham for his regiment's losses, he intended to prove—conclusively—that his regiment was responsible for the capture of Parsons' battery and the death of Major General James S. Jackson. Unfortunately, Savage failed to name the battery that his regiment captured—or even the regiments that supported it. Perhaps, Savage thought that information to be common knowledge. But in the end, his failure to include some details left holes for the historians of the battle to fill in. The testimony that he used came from no less than five members of the Sixteenth regiment and a personal letter from General George Maney. The following is a summary of Savage's account.

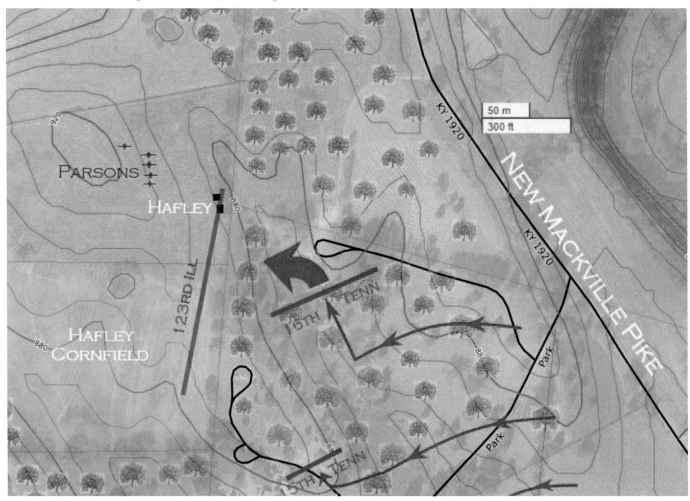

According to Savage, his regiment advanced in the direction of an enemy battery that he estimated to be about two hundred yards away. As his regiment reached the lowest point of a hollow, a staff officer from General Cheatham came with a message for him to redirect the advance. The messenger stated that "the enemy was in the woods at the *head of the hollow at the right.*" Savage halted the regiment and "ordered my color bearers to the front and ordered the regiment to dress on them so as to march in the new direction indicated by Cheatham's order." By his account, they continued in the new direction of march until they reached "an open beech forest on the top of the hill." Suddenly a battery opened fire on them from about one hundred and fifty yards which enfiladed at least a portion of the regiment and mowed down a swath of men. To get out of the range of the battery, he ordered his regiment forward toward the enemy. Although this sounds odd, staying in position would have been more foolish. By advancing, he could enter a position of defilade caused by the sloping of the ground. But this too brought about another deadly threat. "Descending the hill some forty or fifty yards, we were fired on by the main line of the Yankee army, not more than fifty or sixty yards distant, concealed behind a rail fence which was a prolongation of the fence enclosing the field in which the battery was situated."[40]

Another dozen or more men were felled by this blast of rifle fire from the infantry force in their front. Savage took note of "a fence and a field on my right running up to *two cabins* at the line of the enemy's forces." A skirmish line occupied the fence and fired on his flank and rear as the regiment advanced, while the boys hugged the ground and sought what protection was afforded from "a few trees in the forest."[41] Savage knew that to remain under fire without action that his men would suffer even more. "I ordered a charge." They rose up with a yell, and with wild eyes charged and drove the enemy "from behind the fences, killing many of them as they fled." The right of his regiment had reached the two cabins which then provided cover for more of the boys. Some of the guns of the enemy battery that had opened fire were then within "thirty or forty yards" of these cabins. Savage watched the as the battery men loaded the guns and would shout out, "Lie low, boys; he is going to fire!"[42]

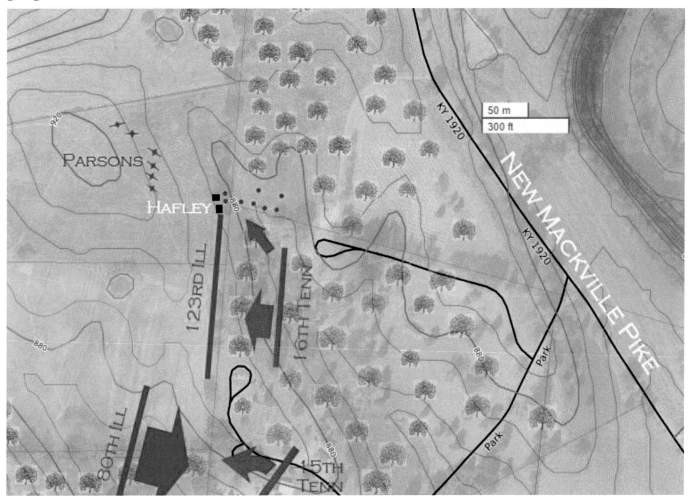

The regiment loaded and fired as rapidly as possible, and at least twice, they charged the fence on the left only to fall back for the protection of the trees at the edge of the woods. During the hottest part of the fight, his lieutenant colonel came to Savage and requested that he order a retreat. Lt. Colonel Donnell exclaimed, "We are losing all our men and are not supported." Colonel Savage replied that Lt. Colonel Donnell should protect his

---

[40] Ibid, p. 121. (*Emphasis added.*)

[41] Ibid, p. 121. (*Emphasis added*)

[42] Ibid, p. 122.

wing by the trees and fence on the left of the regiment while he protected the right wing by the cabins. Certainly, with a determined look, Savage reportedly turned to Donnell with balls flying thick and furious.

> We were ordered to fight. To order a retreat at the beginning of a great battle is not war. We must hold this position until supported, and it is the duty of our commanding officers to bring us support.[43]

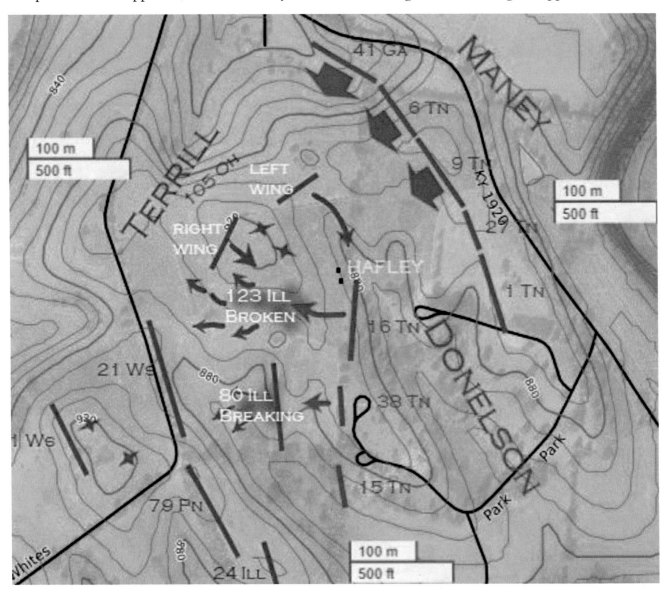

Colonel Savage and the right wing of the regiment found itself pinned down around the Hafley cabins and scattered trees that surrounded it while "a fire of small arms from the line of battle was directed upon these cabins." On their own initiative, some of the regiment started to make a dash for the guns, but just then an enemy force was detected moving to his right and right-rear. Another Yankee regiment—believed to be a wing of the 105th Ohio—had arrived and was sending a column to envelope the Sixteenth's right flank. Just at this crucial moment, Maney's brigade arrived at the fence about a hundred yards to Savage's right. The sudden presence of Maney's brigade forced the enemy that was approaching Savage's flank to break for cover themselves. In the midst of this action, Savage was struck by a wooden sabot from a canister charge that ricocheted off the adjacent cabin and was struck in the left calf by a minnie ball at nearly the same instant. After losing so many men in the fight for the battery, and although his regiment had not advanced in perfect line of

---

[43] Ibid, p. 123.

battle and seized the guns themselves, Savage stated to his lieutenant colonel to "Take charge. Go to the battery. It belongs to the Sixteenth."[44]

Unfortunately for Colonel Savage and the Sixteenth Tennessee—because neither his report nor the reports of the brigade and division commanders were located and placed in the Official Records, Maney's brigade would be the only unit officially credited with the capture of Parsons' battery on Open Knob. According to Savage, his entire account of the fighting transpired in the *first thirty minutes* of action and was supported by five members of the regiment. "To corroborate and sustain my report, I have taken the statements of five soldiers of the Sixteenth Regiment, now residing in Warren County—James C. Biles, Jesse Walling, E. S. Rowan, Huel Moffit and William H. White—who all remember the facts as I report them…"[45] To corroborate his account even further, Savage wrote Brigadier General George Maney for additional confirmation that "…the regiment was engaged for half an hour before Maney's brigade appeared on the right." Maney's response was just as Savage had hoped.

> I very well remember in conversation having stated to you that it had been engaged for not less than thirty minutes before my command came to your assistance by attacking at your right, and having so stated it verbally, of course am willing at your pleasure to place it in writing as I here do. On this point I am persuaded that though wounded, you were still with your command when I went into action, and you had not been borne off the field, so your memory will thoroughly concur with mine, and here again intervening events involving time in occurrence may be relied on as conclusive support.[46]

Savage's account is very informative, and taken literally, it can hardly be comprehended in more than one way. Savage was clearly relating the attack on Open Knob, the Hafley cabins and the push against Parsons' battery and the 123rd Illinois. These accounts state—that according to both Savage and Maney—Maney's brigade was directly assisting Savage's right flank only *thirty minutes* into the fight. This could not have happened *unless* the action was on Open Knob. This is not what other historians would conclude however. Misunderstanding Savage's account and without knowledge of the Hafley home-site, a story was concocted that explained that Savage, the Sixteenth Tennessee and the other two regiments of Donelson's brigade attacked Harris' battery in the center of the Federal line over a half mile south-southwest of Parsons' position. That equates to a distance over eight football fields away from the location that Savage and Maney *both* relate their experiences. Without knowledge of any other structures on the battlefield, historians had no other way to interpret the statements of Savage's record. Historians had to manipulate the accounts to conclude that the regiment fought at the Widow Gibson's home-site. Historians *had to force* the first-person accounts to *support their assumptions*. But yet another problem was presented by historians' interpretations that forced even more manipulation of the primary sources.

General Donelson's report of the battle described the advance of his brigade. After crossing his command over Chaplin River and ascending the nearly vertical bluff, Donelson's lines were immediately formed. Two of his regiments had been detached to support Captain Carnes' battery of his brigade. He had already sent Major James G. Martin to get permission to have the Eighth and Fifty-first Tennessee regiments rejoin his command, but the order to advance was received before Martin returned with the remainder of the brigade. With only three regiments, Donelson's brigade commenced the advance against an enemy battery that was apparently in clear view in the distance. After traversing the terrain for a short distance and "proceeding in the direction of the Enemy battery, I soon ascertained from the fire of another Battery of the Enemy's further on our right that I did not have the proper direction."[47] That statement by General Donelson may have explained

---

[44] John H. Savage, *Life of John H. Savage* (Nashville, TN: John H. Savage, 1903) 122.

[45] Ibid, p. 124.

[46] Ibid, p. 119.

[47] Brig. Gen. D. S. Donelson, *Report of Battle of Perryville* (William P. Palmer Collection, WRHS Collection, Box 28, Folder 9)

why many historians suggest that the Rebel command was unaware of where the Federal flank truly rested. The assumption by historians was that a poor reconnaissance did not reveal the actual extremity of the Federal line. Although that quote by Donelson aided in blurring the historians' understanding of the battlefield, Donelson's next statement confused historians even more-so. Whatever the cause of the misdirection, Donelson continued:

> I accordingly gave orders for a change of direction further to the right, in making this move I sent forward a staff officer to order Col Savage Comdg Regt on the right to halt when in the proper direction, until I could bring up the other two Regts in line of battle.

The foregoing sentence was the statement that *really* caused problems for the historian. What may have been over-looked is the fact that *two orders* were given in the preceding quote. The *first order* was to "*change direction.*" The *second order* was to "*halt when in the proper direction*" in order to await the formation of the two supporting regiments—the Fifteenth and Thirty-eighth Tennessee. Understanding that *two orders* were explicitly given in this sentence from his report, Donelson's very next sentence can create even more confusion if taken *out of context.*

> *This order was not obeyed* because as I have since learned one of Genl Cheatham's Staff ordered said Regts to move forward rapidly.[48]

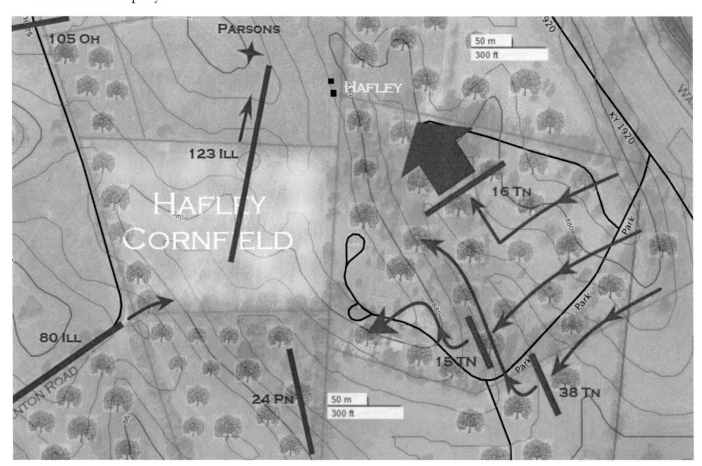

Apparently, some historians have only noted the first order—to *change direction*. With that understanding, they concluded that it was the order *to change direction* that was countermanded by the staff officer from General Cheatham. According to one historian, one of Cheatham's staff officers instructed Colonel Savage to "continue

---

[48] Brig. Gen. D. S. Donelson, *Report of Battle of Perryville* (William P. Palmer Collection, WRHS Collection, Box 28, Folder 9) *Emphasis added.*

pushing straight ahead" with the other two regiments on their original axis of advance.[49] This may have been an oversight. However, given the fact that the only known cabins that existed on the field were those of Widow Gibson, once again historians had to *mold the facts* to fit their understanding of the field. Thus, Donelson's sentence was often dissected, used out of context, or left out in its entirety—yet still cited. Whether this was an oversight, or the only way to make sense of the recorded resources is hardly questionable. Without *altering* the context of Donelson's comment, historians could not make sense of Savage's regiment advancing toward cabins on the Open Knob that—according to modern scholarship and their own comprehension of the field—didn't exist.

Reviewing the same sentence *in context* of the subject matter *with* knowledge of the Hafley cabins, it is irrefutable that it was not the order to *change direction* that was over-ridden by General Cheatham, but rather it was Donelson's order to *halt* to wait for the supporting regiments that was overridden by Colonel Savage. Obviously after committing to the attack, Cheatham didn't want *any hesitation* pressing forward in the assault. Thus—after making the change in direction and having committed to the attack, the order to *halt and await the formation of the two supporting regiments (Fifteenth and Thirty-eighth) was not obeyed* by Colonel Savage. This was the order that Cheatham's staff officer had conveyed to Savage: that is, to "*move forward rapidly.*"[50] Savage did as he was instructed. He quickly changed direction of his regiment and rapidly charged headlong in the *new direction* toward the supposed enemy line that his regiment now confronted. Following far in his rear were the two supporting regiments that had fallen far behind the Sixteenth Tennessee regiment while reorienting their lines. In this attack, Savage's regiment was also acting as the guide unit for the brigade. A guide is an individual or unit upon whose movements a larger force traces or conducts its movement. While the Fifteenth and Thirty-eighth regiments reformed and aligned for the new direction, the Sixteenth Tennessee raced ahead—at an angle of nearly ninety degrees *to the right* of their original direction of march.[51]

It's certain that without knowledge of the Hafley cabin site—and the *belief* that Cheatham instructed Savage to continue in the *original* direction of march—historians *had* to conclude that Donelson's advance took them up the long valley south and west of their attack position. This valley contains an intermittent stream that is referred to as "Donelson's Run" at the battlefield today—a name that may be more appropriately referred to as "Wood's" or "Jones' Run." By historians' interpretations, the Sixteenth Tennessee's attack ended at the only *known* structures on the battlefield—Widow Gibson's cabins. In that now *dated and erroneous* interpretation, the Sixteenth Tennessee fought its way through and past the Thirty-third Ohio and forced them back wounding its commander in the process.

Lieutenant Colonel Oscar F. Moore commanded the Thirty-third Ohio that day. He never filed a report of his actions, and it is unclear *exactly* where his unit was engaged. However, it is known that his unit was partly deployed as skirmishers before the full-fledged Confederate assault took place, and that they became engaged with Rebel skirmishers early on. Moore's subordinate—Major Frederick Lock—reported that Moore was wounded "at an early period of the action."[52] Another account by a member of the Thirty-third Ohio indicates that the majority of their losses came in the first "ten minutes" of action.

> It entered the fight with four hundred muskets, and lost one hundred and twenty-nine men killed, and wounded *in less than ten minutes*. The first onset of the rebels was by a regiment of cavalry, and these the Thirty-third put to the right-about and emptied half their saddles. Then the main line came up and the work was short and sharp, and ended by the Thirty-third being compelled to fall back upon the main body,

---

[49] Kenneth Noe, *Perryville: This Grand Havoc of Battle* (Lexington, KY: The University Press of Kentucky, 2001), 199-200.

[50] Brig. Gen. D. S. Donelson, *Report of Battle of Perryville* (William P. Palmer Collection, WRHS Collection, Box 28, Folder 9) *Emphasis added*.

[51] John H. Savage, *Life of John H. Savage* (Nashville, TN: John H. Savage, 1903) 126.

[52] Major Frederick J. Lock, *OR*, p. 1053.

leaving their dead and wounded upon the field. It was here that Colonel Moore was wounded while gallantly holding the regiment up to the unequal contest.[53]

Hints that point to where the Thirty-third Ohio was deployed as skirmishers can be found in some of Moore's superiors' reports. General Alexander McCook commanded the Federal First corps that was approaching Perryville on Mackville Pike. He related that he had ordered General Rousseau to "throw forward a line of skirmishers to examine the woods on our left and front."[54] The two lead brigades of Rousseau's division were led by Colonel William Lytle and Colonel Leonard Harris. Apparently, Lytle sent forward the Forty-second Indiana straight down Mackville Pike while Harris pushed the Thirty-third Ohio into the tree line to the left of Mackville Pike. Colonel George Webster's brigade took up position to the left and rear of Harris's brigade along dominant terrain. Only minutes before the Rebels began their advance with Cheatham's division, McCook had ordered the occupation of Open Knob that commanded approaches to the Federal left flank. This position was assumed by Colonel William Terrill's brigade of green troops that were hardly drilled and had only a few weeks of military service under their belts. Finally—to Harris' left, Colonel John C. Starkweather's last brigade of Rousseau's division took position on the heights along the road to Benton connecting with Harris' left. Both Terrill's and Webster's brigades fell under the command of Brigadier General James S. Jackson who commanded the Tenth division. Terrill's brigade—that was to assume position on the knob—was "ordered to advance a body of skirmishers cautiously down the slope of the hill to the water *as soon as the line was formed.*"[55]

Since the Federal line was extending to the left, it would appear that the initial advance of the skirmishers of the Thirty-third Ohio would have been in the woods overlooking Doctor's Creek. That position would have placed them in the vicinity of Widow Bottom's house and in front of the forces commanded by both Buckner's and Anderson's Rebel divisions of infantry. More specifically, they were probably initially in front of Wood's brigade and portions of Brown's brigade at the outset of the action. On the Federal left, since Terrill was ordered to advance skirmishers "as soon as the line was formed," it appears that no major Federal skirmisher screen had been advanced east of Open Knob prior to Terrill's advance to that point. Additionally, any Federal skirmishers that were advanced from the knob would have been from Jackson's own division. We know that some had been sent forward, as a "wooded eminence" had to be cleared by Wharton's cavalry before the advance of Rebel infantry could cross Chaplin River and ascend the steep bluffs. Although we don't know which regiment of Jackson's Federal division advanced skirmishers, we do know that Wharton's "gallant" charge had caused them to retrograde and at least halt their advance.[56]

Looking at the Confederate point of view from the sources that are available, it appears that Donelson's advance was not hindered in any way by the fire of enemy skirmishers as they had been cleared away already. The first mention that members of the Sixteenth Tennessee give in regard to the enemy is that of striking the enemy's "line of battle." General Donelson specifically related that in the advance to that point, "for more than ½ mile the Brigade was subjected to the cross firing of two of the Enemy's Batteries killing and wounding several although shot and shell fell in profusion there was no faltering on the part of men or officers."[57] At least Savage's regiment didn't suffer *much or any* from artillery fire during the initial advance. He and others in the regiment related that until they were fired on by the battery on their right, they had not yet been engaged with infantry. In fact, this battery fire that took effect on the regiment occurred only *after* the change of direction was made and their movement toward Open Knob on their *new* axis of advance.

---

[53] "War Times." *Portsmouth Daily Times* (Portsmouth, OH) Sept. 4, 1886, p. 3. *Emphasis added.*

[54] Major General Alexander McCook, *OR*, p. 1039.

[55] Maj. Gen. Alexander McCook, *OR*, p. 1039. (Emphasis added.)

[56] Maj. Gen. B. F. Cheatham, *Report of Battle of Perryville* (William P. Palmer Collection, WRHS Collection, Box 1, Folder 6)

[57] Brig. Gen. D. S. Donelson, *Report of Battle of Perryville* (William P. Palmer Collection, WRHS Collection, Box 28, Folder 9)

So where did historians get the idea that Colonel Savage engaged Lieutenant Colonel Moore's Thirty-third Ohio when the Sixteenth Tennessee's advance most likely took them far north of Moore's position? Colonel Savage mentioned Colonel Moore on two pages of his autobiography. Apparently, part of this confusion came when Captain J. J. Womack of Company E informed Savage *after the fight* that he had found Lt. Col. Oscar F. Moore wounded on the field "about dusk."[58] Specifically, Savage stated that Womack "directed a Rebel and a Yankee soldier to carry Colonel Moore to the Rebel hospital, about dusk." Later in the narrative, Savage stated that "the Sixteenth charged and drove from its line of battle formed behind a fence the Thirty-third Ohio Regiment, and wounded and captured its colonel, Oscar F. Moore, with whom Savage served in Congress, and that Savage directed his doctor to take the same care of Colonel Moore as he would take of himself if wounded."[59]

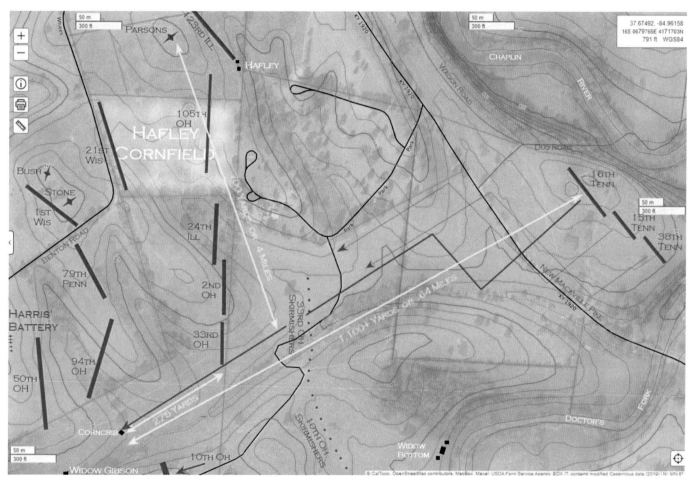

This image shows—generally—the *traditional* understanding of the Sixteenth Tennessee's attack against Harris' battery that wouldn't have even taken them to Harris' battery, but instead took them 300 yards south-east of the battery. Their starting position is from the hilltop just south of the Dug Road. The range from Parsons' battery was beyond canister shot and would have them firing along the length of their friendly lines. The yellow arrow from Parsons' position represents the only line of sight that the battery may have had, but likely didn't owing to trees and vegetation at the time. The Federal troop dispositions—applied to this map and taken from current histories of the battle—do not represent their actual locations according to official reports. (CalTopo)

[58] John H. Savage, *Life of John H. Savage* (Nashville, TN: John H. Savage, 1903) 125.

[59] John H. Savage, *Life of John H. Savage* (Nashville, TN: John H. Savage, 1903) 128.

Just as with Marcus Toney's incorrect identification of the type of guns utilized by the enemy battery that were seized, it is probable that Savage merely *assumed* his regiment had engaged the Thirty-third Ohio. In the heat of combat, it's highly unlikely that Savage was aware of exactly which regiment *his* regiment confronted. Besides, Savage was only made aware of Moore's wounding and capture "about dusk." Savage's regiment had—by then—been reformed and recommitted to the attack at least one more time in a different location as will be seen in Donelson's report. It is only with the combination of accounts that we can gain an understanding of *whom* they engaged and *where* they were engaged. Just as the soldier-correspondent of the *Cleveland Morning Leader* stated, "One's own view is very limited at best, and few see more than the movements of their own company, or possibly, their regiment." This understanding cannot be reiterated enough.

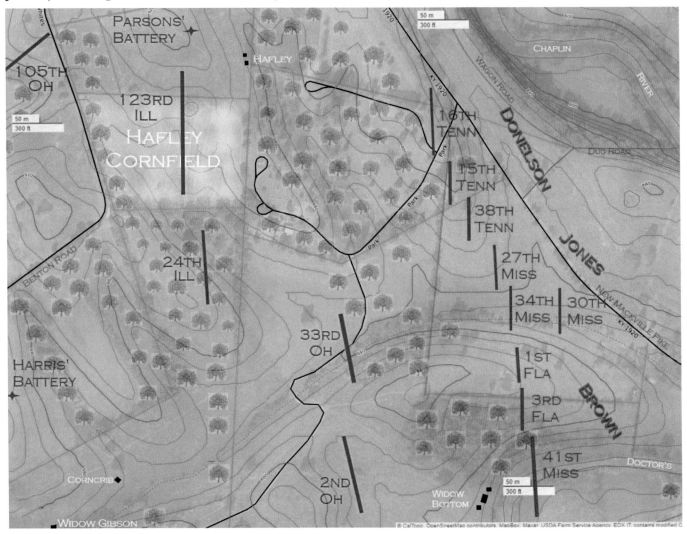

This map shows the more probable disposition of troops just before the attack commenced. Donelson's brigade begins its advance from the vicinity of the park's entrance in a westerly direction. Jones' brigade traces Donelson's movement to the west followed by Brown's brigade on the left of Jones.

Following the chronology of Federal reports, Generals McCook, Rousseau and Colonel Harris explained that the Thirty-third Ohio was supported by the Second Ohio that came into skirmish order near its right flank as skirmishing grew hotter. However, the Second Ohio became engaged "before it arrived on the ground where the Thirty-third was fighting."[60] It appears that this support came into action at nearly the onset of Cheatham's advance. Brown's brigade had already been in attack position waiting for Cheatham's division to move into

---

[60] McCook, *OR*, 1040: Rousseau, *OR*, 1045: Harris, *OR*, 1049.

position. The skirmishers of Wood's brigade had already been advanced, and it is more probable that it was *his* force or Brown's brigade to his left that was engaging the Federal troops of the Thirty-third Ohio. When Buckner was moving his forces into position to prepare for the attack, he placed Wood's brigade on the right in his front line. In this position, they were already on the north side of Doctor's Creek and in the vicinity of Widow Bottom's. General Buckner even stated that, "Wood's skirmishers became engaged with the enemy and drove them to the wood to the right of my line, which covers the heights in the rear of the valley of Doctor's Fork of Chaplin's Fork."[61] Buckner continued that when General Wood advanced to the woods in his right-front, that it created a gap in his front line "which was afterwards filled by the brigade of Brigadier-General John Brown, of Anderson's Division."[62]

General Buckner noted that during all this time, Cheatham's division was "taking position on my right."[63] Later when Wood's brigade advanced, it advanced with a slight left-oblique in rear of Colonel Jones' brigade of Anderson's division that had also been ordered to help plug the gap.[64] This may have been due to Donelson's initial misdirection. While Donelson's direction was corrected, it may be that Jones' direction continued on its slight oblique to the left. This sent Jones' brigade directly up the long valley that contains Donelson's Run and empties into Doctor's Fork not far from its terminus with Chaplin River. Shortly after the Second Ohio was sent to support the Thirty-third Ohio's *right* flank, General Rousseau personally led the Twenty-fourth Illinois— of Starkweather's brigade—into action initially deploying them as skirmishers to the *left* of Thirty-third Ohio. Thus, the Second Ohio—of Harris' brigade—was most likely engaged with either the extreme right of Johnson's brigade or more likely confronted Brown's brigade as it advanced. In turn, Jones' brigade would have assailed the Thirty-third Ohio.

Even Federal Colonel John C. Starkweather stated in his official report that "Gen. Donelson's brigade at this moment engaged the 24th Illinois and 79th Pennsylvania on the right…"[65] If the Sixteenth Tennessee was the right most (northern most) unit in Donelson's brigade—as it is clearly known to be, it would only make sense that the Sixteenth Tennessee was engaging the 123rd Illinois while the Fifteenth and Thirty-eighth Tennessee regiments engaged those Federal units further south—(i.e. the Twenty-fourth Illinois and Seventy-ninth Pennsylvania). However, if the Sixteenth Tennessee had in fact been engaged with the Thirty-third Ohio as current interpretations suggest—who was engaging the Twenty-fourth Illinois that would have been further to the Tennessee regiment's right? Donelson is clearly recognized as the first brigade to advance to the attack and the only regiments *initially* supporting the Sixteenth Tennessee were to its left flank (or south). Maney's brigade didn't join the fight for at least thirty minutes according to the participants. Thus, it is literally impossible that Donelson's brigade (or at least the Sixteenth Tennessee) was engaged with the Thirty-third Ohio. It may not be unreasonable for a brigade commander to assume what brigade he was opposing. Certainly, from captured enemy soldiers the commanders might form an opinion – which is certainly what Savage had done after Moore's capture, but pinpointing a brigade may be easier than a specific regiment.

[61] Maj. Gen. Simon Bolivar Buckner, *Report of the battle of Perryville*, Simon Bolivar Buckner Collection, The Huntington Library, San Marino, California.

[62] Maj. Gen. Simon Bolivar Buckner, *Report of the battle of Perryville*, Simon Bolivar Buckner Collection, The Huntington Library, San Marino, California.

[63] Maj. Gen. Simon Bolivar Buckner, *Report of the battle of Perryville*, Simon Bolivar Buckner Collection, The Huntington Library, San Marino, California.

[64] Maj. Gen. Simon Bolivar Buckner, *Report of the battle of Perryville*, Simon Bolivar Buckner Collection, The Huntington Library, San Marino, California. 'From General Bragg's Army." *Memphis Daily Appeal* (Memphis, Tennessee) November 4, 1862, Page 2.

[65] "Colonel Starkweather's report of the Twenty-Eighth Brigade." Col. John C. Starkweather, *Louisville Daily Journal* (Louisville, KY) October 27, 1862, p. 3.

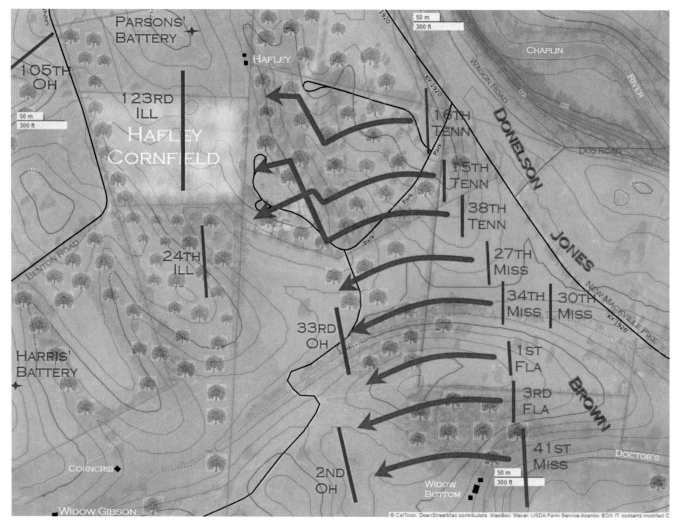

Knowing that the Twenty-fourth Illinois was the extreme right regiment of Starkweather's brigade—and Starkweather's direct front and left was practically covered by the mass of Terrill's brigade, only Starkweather's infantry on the extreme right could become engaged in the opening moments of the fight. His brigade was still in the act of deploying as the combat evolved. The combined number of effective troops with the Seventy-ninth Pennsylvania and Twenty-fourth Illinois amounted to 913 men. This force was nearly the strength of the combined forces of the Fifteenth, Sixteenth and Thirty-eighth Tennessee regiments which numbered less than 1,000 Rebel troops altogether. Naturally, those two Federal regiments could nearly fill the entire frontage of Donelson's brigade. After the Rebel change of direction, the Sixteenth Tennessee continued as the guiding unit on the *right* of the brigade. They quickly advanced up the draw and slope of the finger of terrain in the direction of Parsons' battery and the Hafley cabins on Open Knob. The two remaining Rebel regiments—the Fifteenth and Thirty-eighth—realigned their axis of advance and moved to position themselves on the Sixteenth's left flank. As they did so, they apparently came under the fire of the Twenty-fourth Illinois that had just been led forward by Rousseau himself. Coming under fire before reaching the Sixteenth's position, the Fifteenth Tennessee fronted toward the primarily German immigrant force that suddenly confronted their left-front. The Thirty-eighth Tennessee also came under fire, and to close the gap between the Fifteenth and Sixteenth regiments, they may have eventually moved to their right between these two regiments.

While the Fifteenth and Thirty-eighth Tennessee regiments directed their attention to the Twenty-fourth Illinois and Seventy-ninth Pennsylvania, the Sixteenth continued their advance in a northwesterly direction confronting the right of Parsons' battery and came under the fire of the fresh recruits of the 123rd Illinois. Colonel Starkweather was able to stymie the attack by the Fifteenth and Thirty-eighth Tennessee while the Sixteenth Tennessee's attack veered into Terrill's right-front. Starkweather stated that the force from Donelson's brigade that confronted him was "driven from the field after desperate fighting."[66] While Starkweather momentarily repulsed the left of Donelson's command, Savage's Sixteenth Tennessee—on the right flank of Donelson's brigade—pressed the right-front and right flank of Terrill's brigade and was fortunately shielded by terrain from some of Starkweather's fire. There, the Sixteenth conducted at least two desperate charges gaining a little more ground each time. They then kept up a steady fire on the growing force of infantry, artillerymen and horses until the arrival of Maney's brigade nearly a hundred yards to their right. Together, the combined forces of the Sixteenth Tennessee and Maney's brigade then mounted the all-out charge that carried Parsons' battery and shattered the brigade of General Terrill. Immediately following the collapse of Terrill's brigade, Starkweather admitted that the remainder of his infantry forces had barely taken position when "Gen. Maning's [sic – Maney's] brigade attacked me in front; assisted by a battery and General Donelson's brigade again attacked me on the extreme right…"[67]

Therefore—with Donelson's brigade's change of direction toward Open Knob and the Sixteenth Tennessee maintaining their position on the right of the brigade, it is highly *improbable* that the Sixteenth engaged the forces of the Thirty-third Ohio. When the brigade was withdrawn to resupply their ammunition around 5 P.M., it's most probable that when it was recommitted in the attack against Harris' battery—at about 5:30 P.M.—or its withdrawal near dusk that Lt. Col. Moore was identified on the field and carried to the rear. The original historian of the Sixteenth Tennessee also mentioned Colonel Moore and the fight against the Thirty-third Ohio and *Seventh Ohio*. The Seventh Ohio was not even engaged at Perryville and yet another indication that time can erode specifics of the memory. However, Thomas Head went on to briefly summarize the guts of their experiences and stated that "the enemy bending his line around the right flank of the Sixteenth Tennessee Regiment near an *old log cabin*, an enfilading fire of musketry and artillery was poured into its ranks; yet the regiment held its ground for *half an hour*, when Maney's brigade came up and formed on its right."[68] This is another indication that the Sixteenth Tennessee held its ground around the Hafley cabins and did not retreat. With the arrival of Maney's brigade, every member of the Sixteenth could corroborate the fact that they "with our assistance [sic] now taken the battery on our right."[69] Contrary to one historian's explanation of the battle, neither Donelson's brigade nor the Sixteenth Tennessee were withdrawn from action until about 5 P.M. as related by one of the Captains in the Sixteenth Tennessee.[70]

To further corroborate Savage's testimony, General Cheatham's record is of even greater assistance. In the explanation of the attack on Parsons' battery and Terrill's Federal brigade, Cheatham described the "daring and desperate charge" of Donelson's brigade against the enemy on Open Knob. We can now recognize that he was referencing Open Knob and Parsons' guns, as his first mention of the enemy was regarding an enemy line of battle—a fence, buildings, artillery and advantage of position (i.e. – a hilltop).

> Gen. Donelson's Brigade moving steadily and rapidly forward was soon engaged under a heavy fire from the *Artillery* and *infantry lines* of the Enemy, who were discovered posted under protection of a skirt of woods and also protected by a *fence* and *some buildings*, without hesitating for a moment, although under a most terrible fire of grape, canister and musketry, and having a command of three Regiments only in hand—this gallant leader gave the order to charge, the order was repeated rapidly along the line, and with a cheer which rang through all the surrounding woods, these brave men rushed forward with a

---

[66] "Colonel Starkweather's report of the Twenty-Eighth Brigade." Col. John C. Starkweather, *Louisville Daily Journal* (Louisville, KY) October 27, 1862, p. 3.

[67] "Colonel Starkweather's report of the Twenty-Eighth Brigade." Col. John C. Starkweather, *Louisville Daily Journal* (Louisville, KY) October 27, 1862, p. 3.

[68] Thomas A. Head, *Campaigns and Battles of the Sixteenth Regiment Tennessee Volunteers* (Cumberland Presbyterian Printing House: Nashville, TN, 1885) p. 96.

[69] Thomas R. Hooper, 1862 Diary (Photo copy in Regimental Files at Stones River National Battlefield: Murfreesboro, TN) p. 75-6.

[70] J. J. Womack, *The Civil War Diary of Captain J. J. Womack* (Womack Printing Co.: McMinnville, TN, 1961) p. 63.

determination and impetuosity which not even superior numbers or *advantage of position* could resist, the Enemy was driven back into the woods, leaving his former lines thickly strewed with dead and wounded.[71]

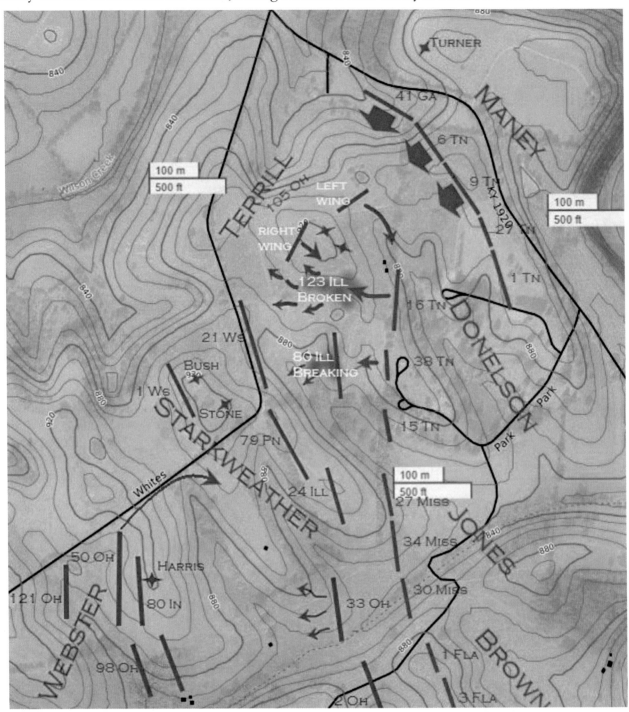

The references Cheatham made clearly indicated where—and upon what force—the attack was directed. Cheatham's reference to the enemy's "advantage of position" is easily recognized as the commanding position on Open Knob. The "infantry *lines* of the enemy" represent Terrill's brigade arriving in line of battle. His mention of "artillery" and protection "by a fence and some buildings" should be clearly recognizable as Parsons' battery and the fences and buildings of the Hafley home-site. This will become even more evident in the

[71] Maj. Gen. B. F. Cheatham, *Report of Battle of Perryville* (William P. Palmer Collection, WRHS Collection, Box 1, Folder 6) *Emphasis added.*

forthcoming remarks by Cheatham. To suggest that the preceding description is in reference to Donelson's brigade coming under fire against Harris' battery around Widow Gibson's would be a stretch to say the least. Widow Gibson's corn crib was *behind* the enemy line of battle by as much as 250 yards and in rear of—or beyond the flanks of—no less than *six* Federal regiments. The actual Widow Gibson homesite was another two hundred yards or so further west. Cheatham then related that as soon as he sent Donelson forward from his attack position, he immediately gave orders to General Maney "to move his command to the right, and attack and press the left flank of the Enemy."[72]

Cheatham or his staff apparently observed the advance of Donelson's brigade and sent an officer to correct Colonel Savage's direction when they realized the brigade was moving on the wrong axis of advance. When Cheatham's staff officer relayed this information to Savage, the colonel quickly reformed his line of battle on the correct axis and commenced his movement—not obeying Donelson's order to await the supporting units. Cheatham then observed the Tennesseans in their steady tread up the hill and the sudden storm of rifle and artillery fire that greeted the right of Donelson's brigade. Watching the resulting blood-bath, he dispatched an order to General Maney—who was still moving through the timber and aligning his brigade—"to move rapidly through the woods and attack and carry a Battery of Eight Guns (12 lb Napoleons) of the Enemy, planted on an eminence in an open field." Parsons' battery was comprised of eight guns and was in fact on an "eminence" in an "open field." Cheatham's own words related that this battery "was fiercely opposing my advance, and had *almost destroyed Genl. Donelson's Command on my left*."[73]

If Donelson was not attacking Parsons' battery as some suggest, how could Parsons' battery "fiercely" oppose Cheatham's (Donelson's) advance. How could that battery have "almost destroyed" the Sixteenth Tennessee in its trek to Widow Gibson's? By Noe's account, Donelson did come under fire from Parsons' battery, but the brigade had by-passed it by more than seven-hundred yards in its advance against Harris' battery. Cheatham makes it clear that his first brigade (Donelson's) was advancing *against* the eight-gun battery (Parsons') and it was devastating his troops. When Maney commenced his attack, Cheatham continued that the battery's attention "was immediately turned to meet this new attack" by Maney. Only yards from the action, Cheatham watched from the extreme Rebel right flank as Maney brought his brigade into battle. Cheatham later related that "I had placed myself about one hundred yards to the right of Maney's brigade and on a line with them, where I could look down the lines between the contending forces (the first and last time that I had found the enemy's flank sticking out in the air)."[74]

Leaving a Staff Officer to form and bring up his reserve, Maney led forward his three Regts already in line, and here commenced one of the most desperate conflicts I have ever witnessed. The Battery's attention was immediately turned to meet this new attack, but notwithstanding, its heavy fire of shot and shell, our line pressed onward rapidly and in fine order, until it reached the fence which separated the woods and open field, in which the Battery was situated, here the entire Eight guns together with their strong support poured their fire with deadly and crushing effect full upon it. For a moment the line is staggered and halts. Maney's horse was knocked from under him, but passing along this line on foot, he urged and cheered his men forward, this was all that was needed, the gallant line responded with a cheer, and with desperate courage again rushed rapidly forward, silencing the Battery and driving the gunners from the pieces…[75]

As if this doesn't corroborate Savage's account enough, General George Maney's record and accounts by members of Stewart's brigade fit the remaining pieces of the puzzle perfectly. General Maney's report was

---

[72] Maj. Gen. B. F. Cheatham, *Report of Battle of Perryville* (William P. Palmer Collection, WRHS Collection, Box 1, Folder 6)

[73] Maj. Gen. B. F. Cheatham, *Report of Battle of Perryville* (William P. Palmer Collection, WRHS Collection, Box 1, Folder 6) *Emphasis added*

[74] B. F. Cheatham "The Battle of Perryville." *Southern Bivouac*, Louisville, KY, April 1886, pp. 704-5.

[75] Maj. Gen. B. F. Cheatham, *Report of Battle of Perryville* (William P. Palmer Collection, WRHS Collection, Box 1, Folder 6)

eventually included in the *Supplements to the Official Records of the Union and Confederate Armies*. The Battle of Perryville State Historic Site was unaware of the existence of this report until it was shared with them in 2012. Professor Noe must not have been aware of it either, as it was not included it in his bibliography nor did he quote any of its content. Oddly, the historic site *did* have a 'transcribed' copy of a report that was allegedly written by General Maney; however, that report is *clearly* falsified when compared with the true report published in the supplements written by the general at the end of October 1862. Although the source of the 'fake' report is attributed to "unknown," it's troubling that the report was even considered possibly reliable and is still available at the site. General Maney's actual report from the "supplements" mirrors that of Cheatham and notes the proximity of his brigade to that of General Donelson.

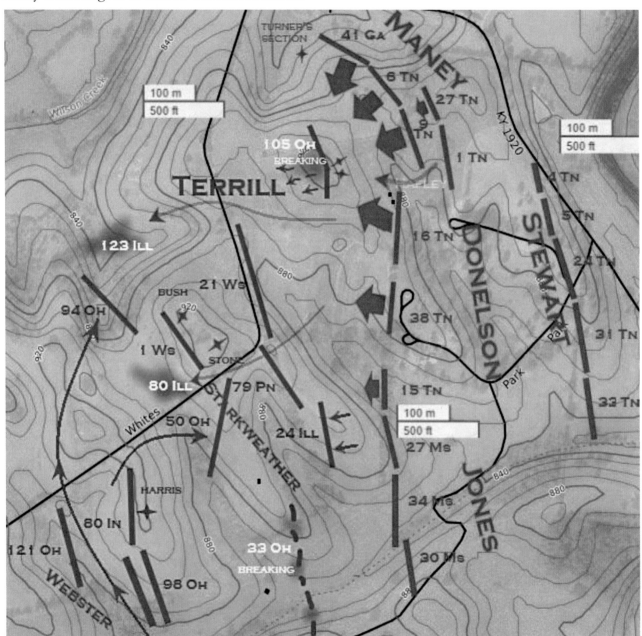

Maney's published report explains that his brigade moved by the right flank and crossed Chaplin River on the north side of Walker's Bend. Colonel Wharton's cavalry had just rushed through the woods and hills west of the bend in order to clear away enemy skirmishers. Maney then received orders to "advance as rapidly as practicable through the woods toward the enemy; attack, drive, and press him." Maney deployed his force into one long line. His brigade advanced "several hundred yards" when he was informed that "General Donelson had become hotly engaged and was in great need of reinforcements. The action seemed but *a short distance to my front* and appeared to be fiercely waged, both with infantry and artillery." Moving forward, Maney realized that his left flank was overlapping Donelson's brigade, and owing to the direction from which he was approaching, only three regiments could be "brought to bear advantageously against the battery." While the First and Twenty-seventh Tennessee regiments moved from *in rear of* the Sixteenth Tennessee to form a supporting line, Maney rode forward to survey the field by "personal reconnaissance."[76]

> Facing my approach and slightly to the right of General Donelson's command was a strong battery placed on a hilltop in an open field and less than 120 yards from the nearest edge of the woods, in which I was. The battery was actively engaged, partly on *Donelson's command at short range* and partly in firing into the woods through which I was approaching.[77]

Maney clearly stated that the battery was "actively engaged" on Donelson's command at "short range." First, this makes it clear that the instant Maney went into action he was immediately in support of the right flank of Donelson's brigade. He personally witnessed the battery engaging Donelson's men. If the Sixteenth Tennessee was a half mile from Open Knob—as Noe describes—Maney would not have been able to witness what he described as the battery engaging Donelson's men—especially at *"short"* range. Interestingly, he noted that his force was about one-hundred and twenty yards from the guns of Parsons' battery, but referred to the guns firing at *"short range"* on Donelson's command. This certainly implies that the guns that were engaging Donelson and the Sixteenth Tennessee were even nearer each other *than his own force to the enemy battery*. Maney's remaining description then encompassed the attack of his brigade against Parsons' guns. But—the evidence doesn't stop there.

After relating "the battery having fallen," Cheatham's report states that he sent forward "Gen. Stewart which had come up and relieved Gen. Donelson's Brigade, which latter I ordered to reform in a ravine *about one hundred yards to the rear*." If Donelson's men had fallen back after a failed attempt to seize Harris' guns as historians assert, the entire brigade would have had to withdraw over a quarter of a mile—over 400 yards. In Cheatham's report, he made it clear that the guns Donelson assailed had "fallen" to Maney's assault.[78] Thus, a quick glance at the topographical map shows that there is in fact a "ravine" around 100 yards east of Open Knob that Donelson's men reformed in—the balance of the brigade that is. This was the "hollow" that Savage had referred to in which he knew he could realign his forces in without threat of contact prior to his initial assault. He stated in his autobiography that prior to the attack that there was "a long hollow about half way between the battery and where the regiment was in line."[79] The order given by Cheatham to reform was directed to take place there. This was not an order to retreat; it was simply an order to *reform*. As soon as that was done, it appears that Donelson continued in the attack with his three regiments supporting both Maney's and Stewart's brigades. Many members of the Fifteenth, Thirty-eighth and Sixteenth Tennessee regiments failed to stop and reform; instead, they advanced with the relief of Stewart and Maney and continued in the fight intermingled with their comrades.[80]

In support of Marcus Toney's account of the First Tennessee that was related earlier, two more records from adjacent units that shed light on the attack against Parsons' battery also incorrectly relate both Federal and

---

[76] Brigadier General George Maney, Report of the Battle of Perryville, *Supplement to the Official Records of the Union and Confederate Armies*. (Broadfoot Publishing Co., 1999) Part 2, Volume 3, p. 667.

[77] Brigadier General George Maney, Report of the Battle of Perryville, *Supplement to the Official Records of the Union and Confederate Armies*. (Broadfoot Publishing Co., 1999) Part 2, Volume 3, p. 667. *Emphasis added.*

[78] Maj. Gen. B. F. Cheatham, *Report of Battle of Perryville* (William P. Palmer Collection, WRHS Collection, Box 1, Folder 6)

[79] John H. Savage, *Life of John H. Savage*, Nashville, TN, 1903, p. 120.

[80] Thomas R. Hooper, *Hooper Diary*, October 8, 1862, Photocopy on hand at Stones River National Battlefield.

Confederate unit designations. However, the general knowledge of who was fighting whom was related in sufficient detail to determine which units were actually engaging one another. These records were likely compiled from diary entries as well. This guess is based off the amount of detail that was included in the description of the battle. While both of the records come from members of Stewart's brigade, the first account was related by a member of the Fifth Tennessee. First Sergeant Edwin H. Rennolds of Company D, Fifth Tennessee witnessed that "after climbing the steep declivity, we were deployed into line and ordered to lie down in the timber of small growth, in support of Donelson's Brigade."[81] He continued that a few minutes later, Donelson was "ordered to charge Chaplin's Hill, on top of which was posted the Fifth Missouri Battery of eight guns supported by the One Hundred and Seventeenth Ohio and One Hundred and Fifth Illinois Regiments." It seems certain that the mention of "Chaplin's Hill" is in fact Open Knob. If this is the case, then the battery of eight guns he mentioned were in reference to Parsons' battery. He was correct in his mention of Ohio and Illinois units, but incorrect in the numerical identification. It was actually the One-hundred and Twenty-third Illinois and One-hundred and Fifth Ohio regiments defending the battery.

Rennolds watched with the rest of his command while "with a yell, Donelson's brave Tennesseans rushed over the intervening space of 100 yards, firing as they ran," and the Federal troops broke to the rear leaving their battery to be captured. As General Maney stated in his report, Stewart's brigade was not yet formed when his brigade began the advance to the attack. Thus, by the time Maney had closed up on Donelson's right, Stewart's brigade had made it into line to observe the last charges on Parsons' battery. Rennolds added that the "sound of firing receded very rapidly as the Confederates pursued the fleeing enemy." Next, Rennold's regiment of General Stewart's brigade was ordered to advance—just as Cheatham stated in his report. "When we reached the crest of the hill we passed between the guns of the captured battery, and saw the dead body of the Federal Brigadier-General Armstrong lying near." This was in fact the body of General James S. Jackson. Passing the battery, "we then came into full view of the conflict our comrades were engaged in at a lane about 150 yards down the slope, where they encountered the enemy's second line." It appears certain that Rennolds and his regiment were then in view of the Twenty-first Wisconsin in the Hafley cornfield with the Eightieth Illinois and remnants of the 105th Ohio and 123rd Illinois that were attempting a stand near Benton Road. "But few of the first line could be halted there to help in resisting Donelson's terrible onslaught."[82] That is what Rennolds wrote verbatim; however, he was watching the onslaught of both Donelson's remnants and Maney's brigade. Maney's brigade had apparently approached the battery and advanced from a position hidden from Stewart's brigades' view due to trees, terrain and vegetation to their right-front. This corroborating testimony is strong, but this record combined with Marcus Toney's and yet another member of Stewart's brigade helps in understanding the unfolding of events.

Joseph E. Riley was a private in the Thirty-third Tennessee also in Stewart's brigade. Much like other accounts, his record incorrectly identifies specific regiments, but Riley was aware of what brigade was in his front. He was also *unaware* of what units were in what positions in the brigade that he was supporting. This account is nonetheless informative in the chronology of the fight. Riley's reference to Donelson's brigade is brief but reliable when coupled with the other two enlisted men's accounts.

Donaldson's [sic] brigade made a charge upon a battery of seven guns. These guns poured a storm of grape and canister upon this brave unflinching brigade. We were lying down watching their irresistible onslaught. My attention was directed mainly to the 5th Tenn., the Irish regiment. On, on they went as the volleys from the guns would mow a swath of brave fellows from their ranks; they would close up their ranks and keep on that dead run. They captured the battery and halted. At this moment we were ordered to their relief. Orders were passed down the line "Reserve your fire." We got up running, not a double

[81] Lieut. Edwin H. Rennolds, *A History of the Henry County Commands*. (Sun Publishing Company, Jacksonville, FL, 1904) p. 45.

[82] Lieut. Edwin H. Rennolds, *A History of the Henry County Commands*. (Sun Publishing Company, Jacksonville, FL, 1904) p. 46.

quick but on a dead run. We halted at the battery for the Federal General, Jackson, had rallied and was making a desperate onslaught with three lines of battle.[83]

Riley's account identified Donelson's brigade, but his mention of the Fifth Tennessee (that was actually in his own brigade) is possibly a reference to the Fifteenth Tennessee that had many Irishmen in its ranks and hailed primarily from Memphis. It may be even more likely that this is a reference to the Sixteenth Tennessee that was on the extreme right of Donelson's brigade and directly confronted the guns of Parsons' battery. Regardless of which regiment his reference was made, his representation of the battlefield mirrors the indication that Donelson's brigade attacked Parsons' guns. Just as Cheatham represented, when the guns fell to his forces, he ordered Stewart's brigade forward which passed through the ranks of Donelson's command and past the guns that had just fallen. Riley's description of the scenes around the battery left an impression he could never forget. "Around that battery Mars had held high carnival, for dead were piled upon the dead, with here and there, a writhing mass of wounded flesh, twisting, groaning, and sometimes cursing, under the overwhelming weight of dead piled upon him."[84] Riley's account coupled with Rennolds', Cheatham's, Maney's, Donelson's, Marcus Toney's and other members of the Sixteenth Tennessee clearly relate a *far different story* than the one that modern historians have told.

---

[83] Gustavus W. Dyer & John Trotwood Moore, *The Tennessee Civil War Veterans Questionnaires*. (Rev. Silad Emmett Lucas, Jr., Southern Historical Press, Inc., Easley, SC) Joseph E. Riley, Volume 5, p. 1847.

[84] Gustavus W. Dyer & John Trotwood Moore, *The Tennessee Civil War Veterans Questionnaires*. (Rev. Silad Emmett Lucas, Jr., Southern Historical Press, Inc., Easley, SC) Joseph E. Riley, Volume 5, p. 1847.

COLONEL THOMAS M. JONES

Thomas Marshall Jones was born in Virginia. He was eighteen years old in the 1850 census and listed as a fourth-class cadet at West Point alongside James B. McPherson, John M. Schofield and William Terrill. He graduated from the United States Military Academy at West Point, New York in the same 1853 class with John Bell Hood.[85] While Hood graduated forty-fourth out of a class of fifty-two, Jones' position was that of forty-seventh. Jones was commissioned a Brevet Second Lieutenant in the U.S. Army on July 1, 1853. He served on garrison duty at Fort Columbus, New York thru 1854 and then transferred to frontier duty serving first at Ringgold Barracks, Texas and then Fort Davis, Texas until 1859. From 1857 through 1859, he served as Second Lieutenant and Quartermaster for the Eighth U.S. Infantry. Jones was promoted to First Lieutenant in July, 1858 and served as Adjutant of the Eighth Infantry until December, 1860 when he was appointed Aide-de-Camp to Bvt. Major General Twiggs until February 28, 1861. On that date, he resigned to find his fortunes with the Confederacy.[86]

On March 16, 1861, Jones was appointed Captain in the Confederate States Army and was in charge of the corps artillery at Pensacola, Florida by April 4, 1861. In October of that year, he was appointed Major and assigned Chief Commissary of Subsistence on Braxton Bragg's staff at Montgomery, Alabama. In mid-January of 1862, Jones was appointed colonel of the Twenty-seventh Mississippi infantry regiment stationed at Pensacola.[87] Sources from the regiment suggest that they hardly knew him. He was a Virginian and his regiment's companies were from Mississippi. In fact, Jones had hardly any contact with the regiment before he was placed in command of a brigade. Left in command of the forces there while Bragg moved to northern Mississippi, he was responsible for the evacuation of supplies and stores from Pensacola when capture of that city by Federal forces seemed imminent. Some of the naval authorities complained that more stores might have been saved when Pensacola did fall to Federal forces, but Jones argued that given the situation, nothing else could be done. By late May, Jones moved with his brigade to join Bragg and the Army of the Mississippi at Corinth.

Jones participated in the Kentucky Campaign as a brigade commander in Patton Anderson's division. His command was comprised of three Mississippi regiments—the Twenty-seventh (his own), Thirtieth and Thirty-seventh (later known as the Thirty-fourth) Mississippi infantry regiments. At Perryville, his brigade appears to have attacked on the immediate left of Cheatham's wing and may have been under the direct command of Cheatham (as right-wing commander) during the battle. Before the battle, as Wood's skirmishers forced back a federal skirmisher screen north of Doctor's Fork, Brown's brigade and—shortly thereafter—Jones' brigade were sent to fill a gap that had been caused by Wood's advance. Later, Cheatham would relate in his reminiscences of the battle that Mississippians from two different regiments were mixed up with his wounded Tennesseans after the battle.[88] He couldn't account for this, but it is likely that Jones' brigade fought over ground that Cheatham's left later passed over. Jones' men had been poorly armed and attacked up the long valley that empties into Doctor's Fork just before its junction with Chaplin River. His men had been uncovered by the woods in the location that historians have—in fact—placed Donelson's brigade. Passing through the woods and appearing in the low ground, Jones' Mississippians were crushed by Federal rifle fire from the brigades of Colonel Leonard Harris' left and Colonel John C. Starkweather's right—as well as the artillery of

[85] Retrieved from:
https://www.ancestry.com/interactive/8054/4202541_00349?pid=7929046&backurl=http://search.ancestry.com/cgi-bin/sse.dll?indiv%3Dtry%26dbid%3D8054%26h%3D7929046&treeid=&personid=&hintid=&usePUB=true&usePUBJs=true#?imageId=4202541_00352

[86] Retrieved from:
http://penelope.uchicago.edu/Thayer/E/Gazetteer/Places/America/United_States/Army/USMA/Cullums_Register/1625*.html

[87] *Fold3*, Civil War, Service Records, Confederate, Officers, Thomas M. Jones.

[88] B. F. Cheatham "The Battle of Perryville." *Southern Bivouac*, Louisville, KY, April 1886, pp. 704-5.

Captain Sam Harris' battery of Webster's brigade directly in their front. They held their ground and even tried to push forward several times, but eventually, they were overwhelmed by sheer concentrated firepower and forced to retire. Later, his brigade was recommitted and faced heavy losses near darkness. Jones' *brigade* suffered approximately *fifty percent* casualties in the slaughter. That is the highest loss of *any brigade* in the Army of Mississippi—*by more than twelve percent*—at the Battle of Perryville. The Twenty-seventh Mississippi lost 140 men killed and wounded of the 260 that were effective in the fight amounting to a staggering fifty-four percent casualties.[89] The losses sustained by the Thirty-fourth Mississippi came to fifty-six percent. Their losses were only surpassed by the casualties of the Sixteenth Tennessee regiment of Donelson's brigade with an astonishing 58.8%.

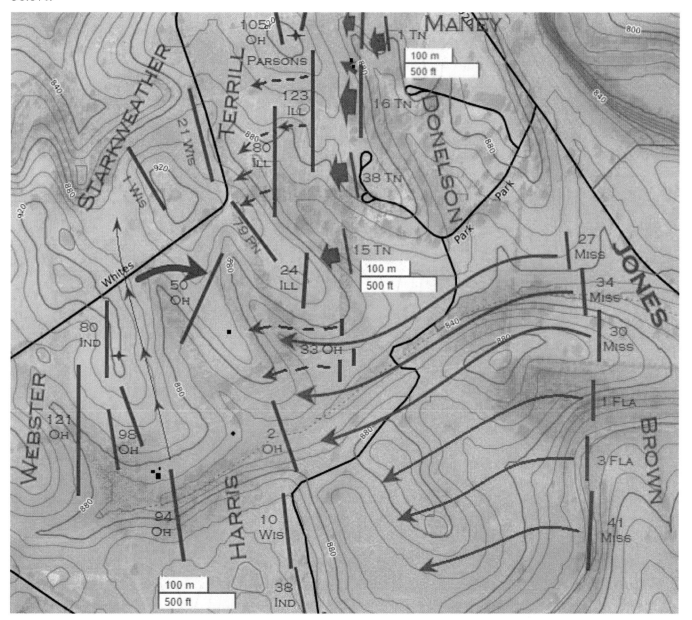

In February 1863, no less than two politicians wrote the president or secretary of war to provide written commendations and recommendations for Jones' promotion to brigadier general. The first was an Attorney General and later Governor of Alabama named Thomas H. Watts. He described Jones as "energetic, *[of]* sober habit and skill, and his gravity of manner won praise from all." The present Governor John G. Shorter of

---

[89] *Memphis Daily Appeal*, November 8, 1862, p. 2.

Alabama also wrote Secretary Seddon with his recommendations in February 1863. He stated that Jones exhibited "great skill and good judgment." Interestingly, none of the recommendations came from military men. Only four days later, Brigadier General W. H. C. Whiting wrote the War Department requesting that Colonel Jones report to his department at Wilmington, North Carolina.[90]

Jones felt slighted. He had been passed over in promotion by many others that had not engaged in the same responsibilities that he had to endure. He complained that he had been in command of a brigade since early in 1862. This was a position that was normally filled by a brigadier general. All that time he was "still doing the duty of Brig. Gen'l in command of a brigade which was in the thickest of the desperately fought battle of Perryville." Unfortunately, no reports of his brigade are known to have survived, and he received no special mention or praise in reports by his commanders. He continued that he "retained command of a brigade till a few weeks before the battle of Murfreesboro when on the reorganization and breaking up of the division to which I belonged I fell in command of my Regt." Jones was dumbfounded at the lack of recognition he received. You can imagine how the members of the Twenty-seventh Mississippi felt when their brigade commander and former regimental commander came back to them—with hardly any association. As far as Jones knew, he had done nothing wrong. "During this service to which I have referred I was not aware that my conduct as a soldier met with anything but the approbation of my superiors, yet I find officers my juniors who had not discharged half so responsible duties as myself have been promoted to the rank of Brig. & some to Major Gen'ls." Jones ended his resignation letter as colonel of the Twenty-seventh Mississippi with the simple question, "why have I been neglected?"[91]

Kenneth Noe devoted two pages to Jones' attack that day. His scenario suggested that Jones moved forward on his own without orders, and since he is not found in command of his brigade later on, that he must have failed in some manner that day. Jones was not mentioned in any of the reports of the commanding officers that day. This was probably due to the likelihood that no particular commander was aware of who was directly responsible for Jones' brigade. Whether Jones failed in some way that day is debatable—as his brigade sustained the highest casualty percentage of any brigade in the army; however, Patton Anderson's division had been splintered into four separate (practically) independent commands.

Anderson's four brigades were commanded by Colonel Samuel Powell, Brigadier General D. W. Adams, Brigadier General John C. Brown and Colonel Thomas Jones. Powell's brigade covered the Springfield Pike nearly three-fourths of a mile southwest of Brigadier General D. W. Adams' brigade that supported the left flank of Buckner's division. The other two brigades under command of Brown and Jones had at first maintained some level of cohesion with their division, but by about one p.m., these two brigades had been sent northeast to fill a gap. The gap was created by General Sam Wood's brigade forcing back the skirmishers of Harris' brigade composed of the Thirty-third Ohio. General Buckner had allowed Wood to push the enemy skirmishers to the north side of Doctor's Creek and into a wood north of that stream. This gap had to have been at least three to four hundred yards wide and created an open void between Buckner's brigades commanded by Wood and Johnson. Buckner wrote in his official report that "Wood's skirmishers became engaged with the enemy and drove them to the wood to the right of my line, which covers the heights in the rear of the valley of Doctor's Fork of Chaplin's Fork. By direction of General Bragg this brigade remained in occupancy of that wood, making a gap in my line which was afterwards filled by the brigade of Brigadier-General John Brown, of Anderson's Division."[92]

Interestingly, Buckner nor Anderson made any mention of Jones' brigade, and it's probable that Anderson spent the majority of his time conducting the movements and actions of Powell's and Adams' brigades. The only mention of Jones' brigade is made by the left-wing commander—Major General William J.

[90] *Fold3*, Civil War, Service Records, Confederate Records, Officers, Thomas M. Jones.

[91] *Fold3*, Civil War, Service Records, Confederate Records, Officers, Thomas M. Jones.

[92] Report of Major-General Simon Bolivar Buckner, C.S. Army, on the Battle of Perryville, Kentucky, October 8, 1862. *Simon Bolivar Buckner Collection*, The Huntington Library, San Marino, California.

Hardee. He stated that Jones and Brown were both sent to plug the gap between Buckner's and Cheatham's divisions.[93] Accordingly, Brigadier General Brown was possibly placed in command of this demi-division of his own and Jones' brigades, but he was wounded very early in the action and failed to submit a report of the battle. Acting as right-wing commander during the battle, Major General Frank Cheatham also failed to mention Jones' brigade, but the fact that he mentioned casualties from two Mississippi regiments at his field hospital point to the probability that Jones initially advanced to Donelson's immediate left. Those troops would have been put in the hellish scenario that historians maintain Donelson's brigade to have experienced—without of course—making it all the way to Widow Gibson's cabin. That is—that they advanced up the 'run' that separates Doctor's Fork from Chaplin Hills and Open Knob. The 'run' is currently referred to as "Donelson's Run," but would more appropriately be called "Jones' Run" or even "Wood's Run." This 'run' was called "Crazy Creek" at the time M. Quad wrote his story of the battle in the autumn of 1882.[94] This—too—could explain why Jones' brigade sustained the highest casualty rate of any Confederate brigade on the field that day.

No report of Colonel Jones is known to exist, and it appears that details of his brigade's actions are not reported by any commanding officers. Being aware of the scheme of maneuver, Jones was apparently placed on the right of Brown's brigade and to the left of Donelson. Wood's brigade was—more than likely—initially placed in reserve as they had conducted the skirmishing in the hours preceding the fight. Jones' direction took him up the length of "Crazy Creek" or "Donelson's Run"—just north of Doctor's Creek—where he engaged the Thirty-third Ohio and portions of the Second Ohio. His men also faced the direct frontal fire of Captain Harris' Nineteenth Indiana battery of Webster's brigade. In this initial action, he was probably engaged up to an hour. Taking high casualties and running low on ammunition, he was probably withdrawn and likely taken charge of by his division commander—Patton Anderson. This may explain why his last charge was apparently made on the west side of Old Mackville Pike against a section of howitzers belonging to the Second Minnesota battery near the Russell House.

Two things are certain in regards to Jones' brigade at the Battle of Perryville. They conducted no less than two separate attacks at the battle. The first was in the opening minutes of the fight upon the movement of Donelson's brigade to their immediate right. Stanford's battery had been separated from Stewart's brigade to which it belonged. Jones' brigade had moved to the right to fill the gap between Donelson' brigade and Buckner's division. Jones' brigade was placed on the left of Cheatham's division and Stewart's brigade. This is confirmed in an article written by a member of Stanford's battery. "The 30th Mississippi regiment, Colonel Neill, lay immediately behind our battery, while the 33d, belonging to Buckner's division, followed it as a reserve, when the charge was made."[95] The Thirtieth Mississippi was in Jones' brigade, while the Thirty-third Mississippi was a regiment of Wood's brigade. The second attack took place shortly before nightfall and aided in the rout of Federal troops from the grounds of the Russell House. There is no doubt that between the two attacks, the brigade had fallen back some distance to replenish cartridges and reform. At least an hour—or perhaps two—had passed between the time they first moved into action and the time that they charged a section of the 2nd Minnesota Light Artillery near sunset.[96]

---

[93] Report of Major General William J. Hardee, C.S. Army, commanding Left Wing. *OR*, Vol. 16, Pt. 1, p. 1119 – 1122.

[94] *The Spirit of Democracy* (Woodsfield, OH) June 13, 1882, Page 1.

[95] 'From General Bragg's Army." *Memphis Daily Appeal* (Memphis, Tennessee) November 4, 1862, Page 2. The mention of the "33d" must be in regard to the 33rd Mississippi of Wood's brigade of Buckner's division.

[96] "Letter from the Second Battery." *St. Cloud Democrat* (Saint Cloud, Minnesota) November 27, 1862, Page 2.

WHARTON'S FAILED CAVALRY RECONNAISSANCE?

Controversy and speculation must make for great reading—at least that would be the assumption. In Noe's book, the author takes the stance that his understanding of the situation on October 8, 1862 is much clearer than those on the field that day. While discussing Wharton's reconnaissance that—according to him— "failed miserably," he states with limited source material that the Thirty-third Ohio had pushed forward to the point at which Frank Cheatham's division was to launch their attack.[97]

According to Noe, Wharton's cavalry had just been brushed away from Benton Road north of Open Knob by artillery fire from Captain Stone's Indiana battery. From there, Noe explains that the cavalry swept east and then south down the New Mackville Pike and near the current park entrance. There, the cavalry chased two companies of the Thirty-third Ohio back up the ridge. He further adds that in the meantime McCook had sent the rest of the Thirty-third to support the two companies. He then used an account by Angus Waddle to support the idea that the Thirty-third Ohio fired a volley that emptied many saddles and "caused them *[the rebel cavalry]* to quickly disappear." The narrative is well written, and sounds reliable. However, in the same paragraph he described that Waddle was riding forward to give an order to the Thirty-third when a volley of musketry was fired that frightened his horse and he returned to the rear without delivering the order. But only a sentence or two later, he quotes Waddle stating that "A volley from our regiment emptied many of their saddles and caused them to quickly disappear."[98] How did Waddle witness the volley and its results if he turned back to the rear? Waddle's own accounts (taken from two different sources) are contrary to one another. The account in which Waddle mentioned that he turned back before delivering the order came from a letter written to his sister only three days after the battle. The other account which declares that the volley emptied saddles and forced the Rebel cavalry to retire is from his book *Three Years in the Army of the Cumberland*. It's likely that Waddle witnessed nothing other than his horse turning to the rear that day.[99] Lastly, it's noted that Waddle's accounts are the only ones used to support the theory that Wharton's reconnaissance failed in a two-page explanation by Noe as to why the whole Rebel attack was doomed from—nearly—the beginning. No other primary source accounts state or suggest such a theory.

From there, Noe goes on to describe how Wharton returned to General Polk and reported "the cavalryman's obviously exaggerated account." Noe then relates the portion of Polk's report that praised Wharton's accomplishment of driving back the Federal infantry several hundred yards. He then adds, "Wharton, of course, had not driven back the 33rd Ohio at all, they instead had forced him to the rear with a single volley."[100] The irony here is that there are no less than four accounts by Confederate commanders and/or soldiers that witnessed Wharton's foray that *did in fact* clear "an eminence of great importance" for Confederate success on the right. Being cavalry, it's clear that Wharton's mission would not have been to attack and drive the enemy in his front, but rather to disperse the enemy skirmishers and create a safe passage for the forthcoming infantry's assault position.

The first account was a member of Wharton's command. G. L. MacMurphy was a member of Terry's Texas Rangers that helped clear the hill of Federal forces that afternoon. MacMurphy related that his brigade, "made a charge at the enemy on a thick wooded hill so as to cover the advance of our Infantry, and it was successful that far but we could not sustain ourselves against the numbers brought to bear on us."[101] Wharton's

---

[97] Noe, *Perryville: This Grand Havoc of Battle*, p. 192.

[98] Ibid.

[99] Noe, *Perryville: This Grand Havoc of Battle*, p. 192, (Endnotes, p. 418).

[100] Noe, *Perryville: This Grand Havoc of Battle*, p. 193.

[101] MacMurphy, G. L., *Online Archive of Terry's Texas Rangers*. Retrieved from http://www.terrystexasrangers.org/diaries/macmurphy_gl/index.html

force did successfully clear the hill, but they faced superior numbers and retired as friendly infantry advanced. He continued his account describing the advance of Rebel infantry.

…meantime our Infantry advanced across an open field unperceived when the enemy finding out the movement fell back behind a battery on a *bald hill* overlooking the wooded hill they had just left, our Infantry advanced steadily to the foot of the hill, the enemy laying upon the top of it at that place I saw the most desperate fight at close quarters it has ever been my lot to witness The distance could not have exceeded 30 yards when the firing first began and after *the first fire* our troops commenced advancing, the enemy falling back, I became separated from the regiment on the wooded hill spoken of above, and got with the Infantry cheering them and doing all I could to add success to our cause.[102]

This account—clearly—does not coincide with the description that one volley from the Thirty-third Ohio dispersed the Rebel cavalry. First, neither Noe nor Holman believe that the Thirty-third Ohio was in such close proximity to Open Knob—referred to above as a "bald hill" with a battery on it. This description clearly indicates that MacMurphy was referring to Open Knob and Parsons' battery. He also mentioned that the infantry began advancing after "*the first fire.*" The first fire did not take place upon Maney's arrival. All accounts by Noe, Hafendorfer and Holman recognize that Donelson's brigade was the first to become engaged and participate in the initial infantry attacks. The contradiction comes when they fail to recognize that by all accounts—Federal and Confederate—the first attacks made by the Confederates fell on the Federal left—not the center as they describe.

A. B. Briscoe was also a member of the Rangers. His account is found in L. G. Biles book on the 8th Texas Cavalry regiment. After describing the movement through the infantry lines and crossing a wooden bridge that probably spanned Wilson's Creek, he states they charged in column of fours at "2 p.m."

After crossing, each squadron formed left front into line, which made us present five lines, one behind the other, and in this order we charged up the hill, into the woods and among the Yankees. This whole movement was made in a sweeping gallop and as if on parade. How different from the way we were handled at Shiloh! The Yankees were brushed back from the hill and woods and when the bugle sounded the recall and we returned, our own infantry and artillery had crossed the creek and were taking position on the hills from which we had driven the enemy.[103]

Briscoe's description aids us in understanding that Wharton *did* actually clear the wooded hill west of the bed of Chaplin River enabling Rebel infantry to cross over and form only a few hundred yards from Open Knob. The evidence doesn't stop there however. In addition to General Polk's description of Wharton's advance, this never before published portion of General Cheatham's long-overlooked report aids us even further. After describing the initial attack by Donelson's brigade, Cheatham described what had happened just before Donelson stepped off in the attack.

… Maney with his Brigade, which had been moved across the creek to my right, came forward in the woods from which the Enemy's skirmishers had been driven a few moments previously by a furious and gallant charge of Col. Wharton's Cavalry…[104]

---

[102] MacMurphy, G. L., *Online Archive of Terry's Texas Rangers*. Retrieved from http://www.terrystexasrangers.org/diaries/macmurphy_gl/index.html *(Emphasis added.)*

[103] J.K.P. Blackburn, L. B. Giles, E.S. Dodd, *Terry Texas Rangers Trilogy* (State House Press, Austin, TX) p. 35.

[104] Maj. Gen. B. F. Cheatham, *Report of Battle of Perryville* (William P. Palmer Collection, WRHS Collection, Box 1, Folder 6)

General Maney seconded Cheatham's mention of Wharton's accomplishment. Maney described moving by the flank to the north in order to cross the river on the north side of Walker's bend of Chaplin River about the same time that Wharton made his "gallant dash."[105]

There had been considerable firing, but the movement of our cavalry appeared a success in clearing the woods, and deeming it important to appropriate the advantage of any confusion which might exist with the enemy, in consequence, I pressed on with all rapidity practicable, turning to the left after crossing the creek bed and following the sound of the action. In passing through the wood, I encountered much of our cavalry, which had been engaged in the dash just made, and knowing that when deployed my command was to constitute the extreme right of our infantry line, and being unable at the moment to find the commanding officer, I instructed the cavalry whether in squads or companies to pass rapidly to the right, so as not to enfilade my infantry movement, and to take position for the protection of my right flank. Meeting COL. Wharton a few moments afterwards, I mentioned my action and wishes with respect to his cavalry and requested his personal efforts in carrying them out, which was promptly given.[106]

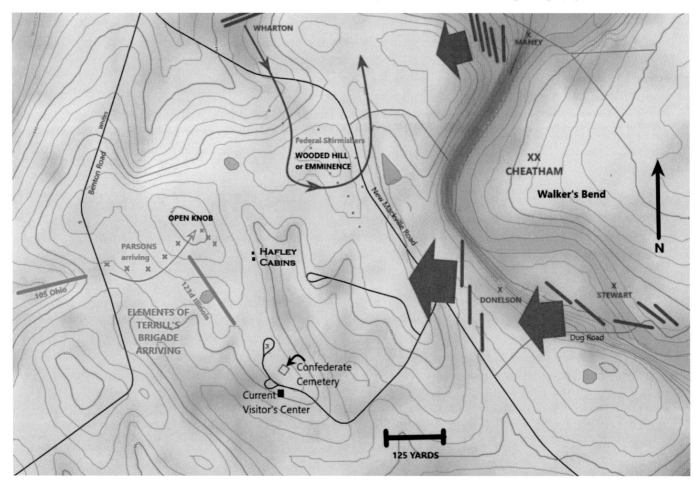

Now that it's clear that Wharton did in fact clear the way for Rebel infantry, we must delve more deeply into the concept of the Confederate attack. Noe rightly states that it was to conduct a "surprise flanking

---

[105] Brig. Gen. George Maney, *Supplement to the Official Records of the Union and Confederate Armies*, Part 3, Vol. 2, Broadfoot Publishing Co., Wilmington, NC, p. 667.

[106] Brig. Gen. George Maney, *Supplement to the Official Records of the Union and Confederate Armies*, Part 3, Vol. 2, Broadfoot Publishing Co., Wilmington, NC, p. 667.

movement against an unanchored Federal left."[107] He then goes on to suggest however, that Wharton failed through "a function of timing, topography, and perhaps fate." He declares that Wharton had only seen "a few mounted men—conceivably cavalry, but in fact were several generals with their staffs—on top of the Open Knob." He attributes optical illusion—which is prevalent among the terrain of Chaplin Hills—to Wharton's supposed failure to recognize the true location of the Federal's northern flank.[108] This argument seems logical until we address the guts of Polk's report that substantiate the fact that the Rebels knew that more Federal forces were still in route to the northern Federal flank.

Regarding the plan of attack and known positions of the Federal army at Perryville, General Polk's report seems clear when he stated that he was informed that a force was moving on Old Mackville Pike toward the enemy's left. Although he had received an order from Bragg to "assume the offensive" around one p.m., he recorded that "our chances of success were greater against the line in my front even when re-enforced than it would be by attacking it as it stood and exposing my flank to the approaching force…"[109] There were two brigades of Federal infantry that were approaching the battlefield at that time. The two brigades were under the command of Union Brigadier General William Terrill and Colonel John Starkweather. Prior to that time, the extreme left of the Federal forces were the regiments of Colonel George Webster. Rather than commence the attack against Webster's Federal brigade and possibly risk a counter-attack in flank, Polk chose to let the enemy force begin its deployment and strike it while in the act of deploying. Colonel Wharton's Rebel cavalry was still on the west side of Chaplin River and could report the enemy's whereabouts with ease. There was only one location that these supporting forces would naturally occupy. This was the extension of the ridge line that ran east toward Walker's Bend. Two unoccupied hill tops occupied the space that was south of Wilson's Creek and west of Chaplin River. The first—from east to west—was the wooded hill, followed by Open Knob a little further west. It was clear that this is where any additional enemy forces would deploy for tactical purposes. From the evidence, it appears that Polk did intend to allow these forces to begin their deployment—but strike them before they were completely in place.

Apparently, historians Hafendorfer and Noe believed that the Confederate high command was unaware of the arrival and deployment of these enemy troops on the field due to Wharton's "failed" reconnaissance. Thus, without knowledge of the arrival of this enemy force and its location on the battlefield, Donelson's brigade stepped off in an attack against Webster's Federal brigade which had suddenly become the center of the enemy line rather than the flank. However, General Polk's words do not reflect this understanding. Polk wrote that he "waited until the re-enforcements got into position. The attack was then ordered."[110] Both historians of the battle fail to recognize that Polk's next statement and supporting statements from Maney's report clearly reveal that Wharton's cavalry *then* conducted the charge to clear the hill west of Chaplin River and nearest Open Knob of any enemy forces. "This movement placed in our possession a skirt of woods and an eminence of great importance to our success on our right. It was quickly followed by the brigades of General Cheatham…"[111] Even if Donelson's (possibly) poor eyesight or misunderstanding of the field started him on the wrong axis of advance, it is made clear by other reports that the correction to the axis of advance was made, and the assault on Open Knob against Terrill's brigade and Parsons' battery was successful. From the reports, it seems *most probable* that the extreme flank of the enemy was in fact recognized as Parsons' Federal battery and Terrill's brigade arriving atop "Chaplin's Hill" or Open Knob. Additionally, this misconception of the battlefield by modern historians was certainly concluded due to the lack of knowledge of the Hafley Cabins that were situated on the eastern slope of Open Knob and visible from the Rebel attack position.

[107] Noe, *Perryville: This Grand Havoc of Battle*, p. 193.

[108] Noe, *Perryville: This Grand Havoc of Battle*, p. 193.

[109] Lt. Gen. Leonidas Polk, Report of the Battle of Perryville (*OR*, p. 1110.)

[110] Lt. Gen. Leonidas Polk, Report of the Battle of Perryville (*OR*, p. 1110.)

[111] Lt. Gen. Leonidas Polk, Report of the Battle of Perryville (*OR*, p. 1110.)

WHO IS IN COMMAND?

It's apparent that the point Colonel John H. Savage tried to make in his autobiography was not convincing to modern historians. Savage made several corrections while trying to rectify the story of his regiment at the battle at Perryville. In volume ten of *Confederate Military History*, Savage pointed out that several statements were wrong. First, Savage tried to clarify that it was erroneously reported that he was temporarily in command of the brigade. Savage related that "there is no truth in this statement." Interestingly, there was *some* truth to the statement according to at least one member of the Sixteenth. On September 28, General Bragg left the army to conduct business in Frankfort. Bragg had been superintending the actions of both Kirby Smith's forces and his own Army of the Mississippi from a distance. Initially suspecting an attack on Kirby Smith's forces, the morning of the fight found Bragg a dozen or more miles from the scene of action at Perryville. When Bragg departed the Army of the Mississippi, his absence had caused a temporary shift in the leadership. Lieutenant General Leonidas Polk was temporarily in command of all the forces of the Army of the Mississippi. This had temporarily elevated Cheatham from division command to command of the right wing. Likewise, Brigadier General Donelson was elevated to division command and Colonel Savage—as the senior colonel in the brigade—assumed the First brigade's command. Private Thomas Hooper recorded the events the day after the battle. Hooper made it clear that at some point—at least prior to the fight—Colonel Savage had assumed another position.[112]

Hooper explained "when General Bragg came up and taken *[sic]* command in person," that "General Cheatham[,] Donelson and Col. Savage all come back to their respective commands."[113] Although Savage denied being in command of the brigade *at the time* of the battle, he never actually denied being in command of the brigade in the hours preceding the fight. Savage stated that he "never had command of Donelson's brigade for a moment at the battle of Perryville."[114] The way Savage viewed the accusation was that he could be blamed for the high casualties taken by his regiment and the brigade. Although Hooper related that Savage was back in command of the regiment when the fight commenced, we can see from the commanders' reports that there may have actually been some confusion as to who commanded what. In the end, Donelson wrote a *brigade* report that was submitted to his *division* commander. Cheatham—likewise—submitted his *division* report to the *wing* of the army under command of Leonidas Polk. However, going to the top, General Bragg's report of Perryville opens up a can of worms in regard to who was commanding which force.

General Bragg wrote his report of the battle on October 12, 1862. Interestingly, Bragg related that when he arrived at Perryville and after consulting with General Polk, he *[Bragg]* "declined to assume command, but suggested some changes and modifications of his *[Polk's]* arrangements, which he *[Polk]* promptly adopted."[115] This sentence is confusing, but it seems unmistakable that Bragg indicated that Polk retained command of the troops on the battlefield. This suggestion is further corroborated when later in his report Bragg commended "Major General Polk, commanding the forces."[116] Although Hooper reported that Savage returned to command of the regiment and Savage seconded that fact, it's apparent that General Bragg never assumed command of the forces on the field. This would have left Cheatham in command of the right wing, Polk in command of all the forces and Hardee in command of the left wing of the army. That means that Donelson should have retained command of the division and Savage—command of the First brigade. Since all these commanders were aware of the arrival of Bragg, was it simply assumed that each commander should return to their former commands?

---

[112] John H. Savage, *Life of John H. Savage* (Nashville, TN: John H. Savage, 1903) 117.

[113] Thomas R. Hooper, *1862 Diary* (Copy on file at Stones River National Battlefield) p. 74.

[114] John H. Savage, *Life of John H. Savage* (Nashville, TN: John H. Savage, 1903) 117.

[115] Lt. Gen. Braxton Bragg, Report of Battle of Perryville (*OR*, p. 1087.)

[116] Lt. Gen. Braxton Bragg, Report of Battle of Perryville (*OR*, p. 1088.)

Another implication that the commands had not changed as of the morning of the battle is in Polk's report. He notes the divisions commanded by Generals Buckner, Anderson and *Donelson*. Clearly then as of that morning, Donelson was still in command of Cheatham's division.[117] Although Cheatham would have retained command of the right wing under the circumstances, *his division* was the only one that was present that was included in the right wing of the army. Thus—while still assigned as commander of the right wing, Cheatham truly only commanded his own division during the fight. The fact is that General Withers' division composed the other half of the right wing—but had been sent to the support of Kirby Smith the day before. Regardless, Cheatham is still *credited with command of the right wing* in Polk's report of the battle.[118]

The question is: did the failure of Bragg to assume over-all command cause a misunderstanding of which commander was in charge of a particular command? Even if Cheatham was aware that he would command only his own division, was this obvious to General Donelson? Was Donelson actually informed that he would only command his brigade during the engagement? It's apparent that Donelson eventually understood that he was only commanding the First brigade in his report of the battle, but he may have opened the action under a different belief. In Savage's record of the events, it's clear that Savage believed Cheatham and Donelson ordered his regiment forward in the attack without waiting for the remaining regiments or brigades to close up to his support. Donelson's recollection of the commencement of the action differed somewhat. He recalled that when he realized that the brigade wasn't advancing on the enemy flank as supposed, he ordered Savage to *halt after attaining the proper direction* and to await support. He later learned that Savage had been ordered immediately forward after changing direction by a staff officer under General Cheatham. This may suggest that at the commencement of the action, Donelson believed that he was still in command of the division. Donelson's orders to attack—that he gave to Savage at the outset—may have been issued with the *misunderstanding* that *Savage* was commanding the brigade. In reality, Savage had returned to command of his regiment following the arrival of General Bragg that morning. Unaware that Bragg would *not* assume over-all command, Savage returned to his regiment, while Donelson *may have been* aware that Polk was retaining field command. Thus, in Donelson's eyes—at least at the outset of the action—Savage still commanded the brigade and he—*Donelson*—was still commanding the division. This is supposition, but it may also help to explain the narrative of the battle in *Confederate Military History*. This deserves deeper study.

---

[117] Lt. Gen. Leonidas Polk, Report of the Battle of Perryville (*OR*, p. 1110.)

[118] Lt. Gen. Leonidas Polk, Report of the Battle of Perryville (*OR*, p. 1112.)

ARGUMENTS REGARDING OLD AND NEW EVIDENCE.

"Historiography is the writing of history based on scholarly disciplines such as the *analysis and evaluation of source materials.*"

  After several email correspondences with authors and historians, it became clear that none were willing to delve deeply into the newly discovered evidence that would not only challenge, but change their complete perspective as to the chronology of events and position of units at the battle. In the first of several emails with one of the oppositions, he insisted that he liked to be challenged with new material in order to keep him "humble." However, after overwhelming evidence had come to light, he still refused to accept that *his* interpretation of the fight doesn't coincide with the *chronology* of the actual *historical records.* Over the course of numerous email exchanges, he adamantly argued against the *possibility* that current interpretations were wrong. Now, comparisons and arguments against the new interpretation will be addressed. It should be noted that at the end of his last exchange, it was made clear that further correspondence would be a waste of time.

  The basis of the opposition's argument was that he was *convinced* that it was Maney's brigade—and Maney's brigade alone—that took Parsons' Federal battery and broke Terrill's brigade atop Open Knob. His argument was based on *his interpretations* of both Donelson's and Cheatham's reports *(a report that he apparently still has not read as of this date)*—as well as the testimony of other participants. I found this odd, as his transcribed records of reports that included all the Confederate reports he had on hand—and had shared with me—did not include Cheatham's actual report, but only Cheatham's reminiscence of the battle that was published in *Southern Bivouac.*[119] At any rate, he declared that the Sixteenth Tennessee simply "took off too early, which is why their casualties were so high." "If," said the opposition, "the 16th went up toward Parsons, then the 15th and 38th were soon to follow."[120] I certainly agreed with that concept. The brigade *did* advance against Parsons' guns, and the Sixteenth Tennessee *was* in advance of its two supporting regiments. However, it wasn't simply that the Sixteenth was alone for a few minutes taking fire from infantry and artillery, but rather, I argued that it was the proximity of the Sixteenth Tennessee to Parsons' guns that led to the exceptionally high casualties. The Sixteenth led the advance as the right-most regiment of the brigade, and thus acted as its guide. When the regiment changed direction, but failed to comply with Donelson's order to await the formation of the Fifteenth and Thirty-eighth regiments—per Cheatham's messenger, the regiment raced ahead and was initially engaged with the main line of the enemy atop Open Knob. Parsons' guns—per the firsthand accounts of the men in the Sixteenth Tennessee—were between forty and one hundred yards to their right-front. Thus, as the supporting regiments came into line on their left under cover of woods, it was the Sixteenth that absorbed the brunt of canister and grapeshot from the Napoleons of Parsons' battery along the edge of the wood and in the field south of the Hafley cabins. Keep in mind that the opposition still fails to believe that the Hafley cabins existed—or was on this site. Oddly enough, the Perryville Battlefield Park's *"Owners of the Battlefield"* document proves that Joseph Hafley was a tenant farmer for Squire Bottom in 1862, and that Bottom owned the land that comprised Open Knob. That fact coupled with the Ruger/Kilp survey of 1862 seems to be too much to accept.

  The next argument used by the opposition was that it was Captain Sam Harris' Federal battery that fell to Donelson's brigade and the Sixteenth Tennessee. The opposition wrote that, "Liddell specifically puts General Cheatham at the recently captured Harris' Battery and has a conversation with him, asking instructions as to where to deploy his brigade." He added that, "Liddell also gives credit to the capture of Harris' battery to "Cheatham's Men."[121] This argument makes perfect sense if one believes that the guns captured by Donelson's brigade and the Sixteenth Tennessee were those of Harris' battery; however, what if those guns that Liddell referenced actually belonged to Captain Stone or Bush and had been captured on Starkweather's Hill or even

---

[119] Benjamin Franklin Cheatham, "The Battle of Perryville." *Southern Bivouac*, April 1886, p. 704-5.

[120] Email correspondence, July 2, 2015.

[121] Email correspondence, July 2, 2015.

Open Knob? In fact, when one reads the portion of *Liddell's Record* in reference to the battle at Perryville, nothing is made *clear* by Liddell's own words. As a matter of fact, Liddell's words actually suggest a different battery than the one that the opposition supposes Liddell was referring to. Liddell had just crossed his brigade over Doctor's Creek and was given orders to "go where the *fire is hottest.*"[122]

I crossed the creek, my command following, when suddenly it struck me to attempt the capture of a heavy battery I had seen from the ridge firing over its own lines *from the rear of the Union left wing*. I now ordered the men to move rapidly and did not call a halt until I had reached *nearly the extreme right of Cheatham's Division*.[123]

As can be seen in the foregoing paragraph—in Liddell's own words, his direction of march took him to attack a battery on the enemy's *left* wing and nearly abreast of Cheatham's divisions' *extreme right*. That route would have taken him to the former location of both Stone's and Bush's batteries atop the hill that Starkweather's brigade had recently abandoned. On this hilltop, the remaining guns that were either disabled or unmanageable had been left behind by the retreating Federal forces. The remaining guns of the two batteries had been withdrawn several hundred yards and continued firing from a position that was ten to fifteen feet higher in elevation than their previous position that could easily have been identified as the Federal left—and would certainly be nearer Cheatham's extreme right flank. Liddell's next statement was less concise but it still implies that the guns he passed were likely those of Bush and Stone since he had already noted moving to "nearly the extreme right of Cheatham's Division."

As we neared the front *passing through a battery captured by Cheatham*, the roar of firearms rendered it difficult to be heard. At his moment, General Cheatham, pipe in mouth, rode up to me, waving very excitedly and loudly, "General, you can save the fight! Go on and save it."[124]

Clearly, if Liddell had passed through the abandoned guns of Harris' battery as suggested, Liddell would not be abreast of the Union left, or especially near Cheatham's extreme right. This misunderstanding—of Liddell's very own words—contradict what Liddell's precise words say. This misunderstanding of Liddell's location would have placed Liddell's brigade on the *extreme left* of Cheatham's division. As stated earlier, S. A. M. Wood's brigade was initially responsible for the capture of the four guns of Harris' battery. William Preston was a member of Company B, Thirty-third Alabama infantry in Wood's brigade. He explicitly stated that his regiment and the Thirty-second Mississippi regiments comprised a line—be it the first or second line is unknown—that captured a battery. In one of the final attacks of the day, Wood's brigade had advanced and crossed the dry bed of the intermittent stream that emptied into Doctor's Creek in the long valley running west to east. It was in this "valley" that the corn-crib, Widow Gibson's cabins and a small cemetery were located. Preston related that, "…we rushed their line which broke after our getting near the muzzle of their guns. Co. B on the left of the regiment passed between some of their four or more brass 12-pounder guns and pushed over the ridge, down the slope and into some timber where we met a line behind a fence."[125] There was only one battery in the Federal center that lost a gun that bloody evening. Captain Harris' Federal battery had been so hard pressed—that when they were nearly overrun—they could only manage to limber up two of his guns and make an escape. The remaining four guns fell into the hands of Wood's Alabama and Mississippi Rebels. Later in Liddell's narrative after a close call with enemy infantry in his front, he described that he still intended to take "the heavy battery, which I knew to have been withdrawn from its first position and was then in the edge of the

---

[122] St. John Richardson Liddell, *Liddell's Record*, Edited by Nathaniel Cheairs Hughes, 1985, LSU Press, 1997, p. 92. (*Emphasis* is in original text.)

[123] Ibid. (*Emphasis added*.)

[124] Ibid. (*Emphasis added*.)

[125] William E. Preston, *Diary of William E. Preston and History of the 33d Alabama*, Alabama Department of Archives and History, SPR393.

woods in advance of the skirmish line." However, General Polk objected to that idea with the darkness and confusion swirling about.[126]

Another opposition argument made was concerning Lt. Col. Oscar Moore—commanding the Thirty-third Ohio. As described in earlier text, it is highly unlikely that the Thirty-third Ohio even confronted the Sixteenth Tennessee. However, owing to the fact that Captain Womack informed Colonel Savage that he had sent a prisoner and one of his own men to carry the wounded colonel to the rear, the opposition could not let go of the idea that this is absolute evidence that the Sixteenth Tennessee engaged the Thirty-third Ohio. That would certainly be a case of jumping to conclusions. He insists that, "all sources have those fighting two units fighting together all through the battle."[127] Unfortunately, he doesn't cite any of the *sources*. In fact, three sources imply that idea. The first source was Thomas Head who wrote the first regimental history of the Sixteenth Tennessee. The second source was Colonel Savage himself. The third source was that by Angus Waddle—a member of the Thirty-third Ohio. His concept of the two regiments fighting one another was based off the same suppositions that Head and Savage made. He—like Savage and Head—was aware that Moore was taken captive by Colonel Savage's regiment. However, this is not proof that they fought one another. This was only proof that late in the evening he was found wounded on the field by a member of the Sixteenth Regiment.

The only other sources that suggest this myth were written by modern historians in the last forty years—and in light of recent discoveries, they are hardly reliable. While the opposition willfully accepts the idea that the two regiments fought each other "all through the battle," he adamantly denies the statement by members of the First Wisconsin who state they captured the flag of the First Tennessee regiment in a hand-to-hand engagement atop Starkweather's Hill. This is another example of picking and choosing rather than taking all accounts into consideration. He is unwilling to accept the statement of the men of the First Wisconsin—yet willing to accept the *assumption* of Colonel Savage, Angus Waddle and Thomas Head. Interestingly, it is certain by *all* Federal and Confederate accounts that the First Tennessee fought in hand-to-hand combat for the guns of Bush's battery. But based on only three *assumptions*, the opposition insists that the Sixteenth Tennessee engaged the Thirty-third Ohio. Still, the fact that the First Wisconsin engaged the First Tennessee on Starkweather's Height is not proof that the flag captured by the First Wisconsin belonged the First Tennessee.

In fact, the men of the First Wisconsin were quite possibly in error themselves. In the later part of the nineteenth century, a controversy arose as to whose colors had been captured by the First Wisconsin. The members of that regiment claimed it was the Polk's corps flag of the First Tennessee. Members of the First Tennessee adamantly denied the charge that the flag that was captured belonged to their regiment. So, what regiment did this Polk's corps flag belong to? General Cheatham reported that the Fourth Tennessee fought over the same ground as the First Tennessee during the battle.[128] Now, newly discovered sources explain that the First Tennessee's flag staff had been shot off within eighteen inches of the colors. Sergeant J. W. Carter—of the First Tennessee—had taken out his knife and whittled the staff to fit into the barrel of his rifle to hold aloft. As the Fourth Tennessee took over the assault against Bush's battery after the second repulse of the First Tennessee, portions of the First Tennessee—including the color bearer—once again joined in the attack. Sergeant Carter was mortally wounded in this attack and Private Lewis White—of the Fourth Tennessee—grabbed the colors from Sergeant Carter believing them to be the colors of the Fourth Tennessee. This mistake was apparently realized after the battle. Thus, it is quite possible that the colors believed to have been captured from the First Tennessee were actually the colors of the Fourth Tennessee Infantry.[129] Just as the men of the

[126] St. John Richardson Liddell, *Liddell's Record*, Edited by Nathaniel Cheairs Hughes, 1985, LSU Press, 1997, p. 94.

[127] Email correspondence, July 2, 2015.

[128] Maj. Gen. B. F. Cheatham, *Report of Battle of Perryville* (William P. Palmer Collection, WRHS Collection, Box 1, Folder 6)

[129] "The Battle of Perryville – The Charge of the Fourth Tennessee Regiment." *Memphis Avalanche* (Memphis, Tennessee) Apr. 29, 1888, p. 15. (newspapers.com)

First Wisconsin believed they had captured the flag of the First Tennessee, Thomas Head, Angus Waddle and Colonel Savage supposed that they had engaged the Thirty-third Ohio during the fight. In all probability, chronology of the battle and source information, the Sixteenth Tennessee didn't pass over ground that the Thirty-third Ohio had been engaged on until their last attack near dusk on ground hundreds of yards south of their initial attack.

The opposition also insists that the Sixteenth Tennessee originally stepped off in the attack against Simonson's Federal battery, but the axis of attack was corrected to direct them against Harris' battery. He states that, "…there was no infantry contact against the 16th before they turned…since Moore was found near that little farmstead…we are back to the Widow Gibson farm, because it is impossible that Oscar Moore could have been a hundred yards SE of Parsons' position."[130] That statement again jumps to conclusions without considering all the source material available. True, there was no infantry contact before they corrected their axis of advance; however, when the Sixteenth Tennessee did become engaged with infantry, it was engaged with the *main battle line* and not skirmishers. The Thirty-third Ohio had been deployed as *skirmishers*. This is made clear by all accounts of the members of the Sixteenth Tennessee. He also asserts that Moore was "found near that little farmstead."[131] Not *one single account* exists that claims to even suggest *where* Moore was found wounded. This is mere *assumption* as well. By his interpretation, all mentions of cabins by members of the Sixteenth Tennessee *must be* in reference to Widow Gibson's residence. But even in light of the newly discovered Hafley Cabin site— that practically cements the concept that the Sixteenth Tennessee and Donelson's brigade did in fact attack Parsons' battery, he is unwilling to accept a more reasonable theory. We can agree—however—that it was impossible that Oscar Moore was captured a hundred yards southeast of Parsons' guns. Evidence clearly suggests that Moore and his regiment were over a quarter of a mile south of the area at which the Sixteenth Tennessee was initially engaged near and around the Hafley Cabin site on the eastern slope of Open Knob.

The opposition then argued that since the only two guns taken off the field by Confederate forces were engraved with the names of two members of the First Tennessee that it was Maney's brigade alone that took Parsons' battery. First, that did not happen. The two guns that were eventually engraved with their names were captured at Murfreesboro. His assumption is again voided by the fact that all the regiments *involved* in the capture of Parsons' battery wanted to claim rights to the capture of *Parsons' guns*. That is to say, all the regiments of Maney's brigade including the Sixteenth Tennessee of Donelson's brigade. The fact is that the First Tennessee was barely even involved in the assault against the guns belonging to Parsons' battery. Their real baptism at Perryville came in their ferocious and heroic attempts to seize the guns of Bush's battery on Starkweather's Hill. Not a single account by members of the First Tennessee relates an actual attack by their regiment against Parsons' battery—other than firing a volley and the enemy running away. So how does the fact that two guns were engraved with the names of two men of the *First Tennessee* provide evidence that Maney's brigade took Parsons' battery alone? It doesn't. The simple fact is, Cheatham observed his division attacking from the northern most flank and couldn't even see the attacks of Donelson or Stewart until the battle progressed to—and beyond—Starkweather's Hill. All of Cheatham's accolades about Maney's brigade was owing to the fact that he observed the fight from the extreme right flank; he could not observe the progression of Donelson and Stewart. Additionally, only a fraction of the correspondence and reports written during the war were retrieved and placed in the Official Records. Another correspondence *may* have been sent to Donelson requesting names to be placed on the two captured guns of Parsons' battery; but that is speculation. Although Turner's report mentions the retrieval of two cannon that evening, these two guns were not the ones that were engraved. It appears that two guns that were captured at *Murfreesboro* were eventually engraved with the names of two men from the First Tennessee.

---

[130] Email correspondence, July 2, 2015. (This statement is verbatim.)

[131] Email correspondence, July 2, 2015.

To further this argument, the opposition attempted to use Colonel Savage's own testimony against him. As stated earlier, Savage's autobiography was partly an attempt to prove that his regiment was responsible for the capture of Parsons' battery. In Savage's chapter on the battle, he included a letter from General Maney who personally attested to the fact that Savage's regiment was engaged in action for "not less than thirty minutes before my command came to your assistance by attacking at your right..."[132] In order for the opposing arguments—Noe's, Hafendorfer's or the park's interpretations—to make sense, Maney's brigade would have to destroy Terrill's brigade, capture Parsons' guns, capture Bush's guns and force the retreat of Starkweather's brigade in *less than thirty minutes* in order for Maney's brigade to come abreast of the Sixteenth Tennessee by attacking to the right of Donelson's brigade. According to those interpretations, the Sixteenth Tennessee *and* Maney's brigade would have to be at the Widow Gibson cabin only *thirty minutes* into the engagement. It's this twisted chronology of events that all three of these students of Perryville have managed to fall into—primarily based on the mention of the cabins by members of the Sixteenth Tennessee. Without knowledge of the Hafley Cabin site on the slope of Open Knob, they had nothing else to conclude other than Donelson's brigade had to have been at Widow Gibson's cabins. Opposing arguments, Noe's and Hafendorfer's interpretations then had to hinge on the idea that the Sixteenth Tennessee and Donelson's brigade seized Harris' battery—which fell at about six p.m. by all accounts. This was their conclusion, but it was one that did not reflect the time-tables explicitly stated by members of the Sixteenth Tennessee or others. Even considering the discovery of the Hafley Cabins, none appear to be willing to rethink their interpretations.

To further his argument even more-so, the opposition claimed that the two captured guns of Parsons' battery "were all associated with Maney's brigade...no mention of any other brigade... all Maney... Maney's sources say they captured two batteries unassisted."[133] If one reads only the official reports of the *regiments* of Maney's brigade, they will not find mention of any other brigades involved in the attack on Parsons' guns. That is within the regimental reports; but, Maney—the brigade commander—is clear in his report of the battle. As pointed out earlier, Maney noted that *before* he came into action, "General Donelson had become hotly engaged and was in great need of reinforcements. The action seemed but *a short distance to my front and appeared to be fiercely waged*, both with infantry and artillery."[134] This description by the brigadier-general clearly stated that he was coming to the direct support of Donelson's brigade. By all accounts, the Sixteenth Tennessee was the right-most regiment of that brigade. General Maney was clear when he stated that the enemy battery that he was about to assail was "actively engaged" at "short range" on Donelson's command—i.e. the Sixteenth Tennessee.

> Facing my approach and slightly to the right of General Donelson's command was a strong battery placed on a hilltop in an open field and less than 120 yards from the nearest edge of the woods, in which I was. The battery was actively engaged, partly on Donelson's command at *short range* and partly in firing into the woods through which I was approaching.[135]

Maney's statement that the battery was engaged at short range on Donelson's command implies that *his own force* was *further* from the battery than Donelson's right-most force. That statement also conforms to primary sources in Wharton's cavalry as well as the members of the Sixteenth Tennessee. So, there is—in fact—mention of Donelson's command in the report of Maney himself. To supplement this fact, there were also Marcus Toney's two accounts from his memoirs and his articles in the *Nashville Banner* which tell us a very different story. As noted earlier, Marcus Toney—*a member of the First Tennessee in Maney's brigade*—tells us that the charge was made in conjunction with Colonel Savage and the Sixteenth Tennessee. This is seconded by the two accounts

---

[132] John H. Savage, *Life of John H. Savage* (Nashville, TN: John H. Savage, 1903) 119.

[133] Email correspondence, July 2, 2015. (This statement is verbatim.)

[134] Brigadier General George Maney, Report of the Battle of Perryville, *Supplement to the Official Records of the Union and Confederate Armies.* (Broadfoot Publishing Co., 1999) Part 2, Volume 3. (*Emphasis added.*)

[135] Brigadier General George Maney, Report of the Battle of Perryville, *Supplement to the Official Records of the Union and Confederate Armies.* (Broadfoot Publishing Co., 1999) Part 2, Volume 3. (*Emphasis added.*)

from Stewart's brigade. Was this a post-war conspiracy designed to strip glory from Maney's brigade? Clearly, the answer to that question is no. It was merely five men—not associated with the Sixteenth regiment—describing what they knew and saw.

> Our regiment, after crossing the stream, nearly dry, climbed the steep bluff and *came up in rear of the Sixteenth Tennessee* commanded by Colonel John H. Savage, which he called "the Panthers." The *Sixteenth was engaged in a hot contest to capture the Parrott guns* which were supported by a brigade of Illinois soldiers and Ohio soldiers commanded by General Jackson, from Hopkinsville, Kentucky. As we were moving by the right flank *in the rear of Colonel Savage* and endeavoring to uncover from his right, several of our men were shot before we got into action.
>
> While laying down awaiting orders, General Leonidas Polk rode up and asked: "What Regiment?" The reply: "First Tennessee." He ordered Colonel Fields as soon as he uncovered from Colonel Savage to move by the left flank and assist Colonel Savage to capture that battery.
>
> When we got into line of battle, the firing was furious, but as soon as we fired the Ohio troops fled and we captured the Parrott guns.
>
> … When we charged the Ohio brigade *with Colonel Savage of the Sixteenth Tennessee* and Colonel George C. Porter of the 6th Tennessee, General Jackson, with sword drawn, attempted to rally his men but he was killed and his body fell in the line of company F, Captain Jack Butler (which was known as the Nashville and Chattanooga Railway boys).[136]

It seems that the opposition again attempts to use Colonel Savage's own words against him again to discredit his account. This opposing viewpoint declares that, "Savage himself says Maney's Brigade captured batteries (plural) on his right (North), not to be confused with the Battery his guys took."[137] Ignoring the fact that *direction is relative to a person's orientation* on the field, he continues, "Parsons was the far northern US Battery… there were no other batteries on the CS right past Parsons. Also, Savage, because of his wound, got no further that [sic] the Gibson farm and, did not witness the battery capture personally."[138] Still grasping at straws that the Sixteenth Tennessee was engaged at Widow Gibson's, the opposition forgets that there are many recorded accounts of the battle from members of the Sixteenth Tennessee. Captain J. J. Womack—commanding Company E of the Sixteenth Tennessee—observed the field in their front and recorded their position in his diary the very next day.

> We now occupied ground about three hundred yards from where the enemy lay concealed in an enclosed wood, about one quarter of a mile in length north and south. At each extremity of this wood they had placed a battery. The one at the northern extremity, of 7 guns, that at the southern about the same.[139]

That description of the Federal artillery fails to identify which batteries (by name) of artillery Captain Womack was observing, but he did note that a quarter of a mile separated the two—north to south. This could easily be reference to the separation between Parsons' guns on Open Knob and Stones' and Bush's guns on Starkweather's Hill. Those guns were separated by just over four-hundred yards—approximately a quarter of a mile. The relation in *distance from their position to the enemy guns* fits more appropriately as well. Even Colonel Savage stated that the guns he was initially facing were "some two hundred yards out in the field."[140] The

---

[136] "Fifty Years Ago Tuesday The Battle Of Perryville Was Fought." Marcus B. Toney. *Nashville Banner* (Nashville TN) October 12, 1912. (*Emphasis added.*)

[137] Email correspondence, July 2, 2015. (This statement is verbatim.)

[138] Ibid.

[139] Jamie Gillum, *The Battle of Perryville and the Sixteenth Tennessee: A Reevaluation: 2nd Edition*, Spring Hill, TN, 2015, p. 148.

[140] Email correspondence, July 2, 2015. (This statement is verbatim.)

opposition believes this quote to be in reference to Harris' guns and Simonson's guns that were actually located about eight-hundred yards or more—further west of Donelson's attack position. From the first finger of terrain (Donelson's attack position), Parsons' guns would be only about three-hundred and fifty yards away. From the same terrain feature, Harris' or Simonson's batteries would have been nearly eight-hundred yards away. Both Womack's description of the field and Savage's description are closer to the approximate distance than before believed. If the guns referred to *were* those of Parsons as the evidence supports, Savage's two-hundred-yard distance is more accurate than previously believed. Additionally, Womack's approximated three-hundred yards distance is *nearly* on the money. The fact is that when the Sixteenth Tennessee (on the right of the brigade) and Donelson's brigade stepped off in the attack, they *were* the northern most rebel unit in the attack. Womack verified this in his account.

> The Regt. to which I belonged (Col. Savage's) was on the extreme right of Gen. Bragg's army, and was directly in front of the seven-gun battery before spoken of.[141]

Combined with the earlier mention of the two batteries Womack observed, it is clear that his regiment confronted the northern most enemy battery. Additionally, if one were to get picky, Parsons' battery was comprised of eight guns, but only seven were placed into firing position and thus captured. If one takes Womack literally, there was *no other Federal battery on the field* that was comprised of seven or eight pieces of artillery—or any other battery that lost seven guns.

Regarding Colonel Savage's statement that the guns that Maney took were "on his right," Savage probably did not have a compass on him, and if he did, it is highly improbable he would take it out to orient himself under fire. The sun sets further to the south in October; thus, north-south orientation could be thrown off as much as twenty degrees by the time of the battle in early October. Additionally, if Savage was approaching Parsons' guns from the southeast, Maney would have in fact appeared about a hundred yards to his right—or north—as Savage states. In Savage's perspective of the fight, his regiment was responsible for the capture of Parsons' guns while Maney was responsible for the seizure of Bush's and Stone's guns. Again, direction was relative to the perception of the individual. The reality was that Savage *could never* claim the sole capture of Parsons' battery by his regiment alone—although he would try. All corroborating sources and evidence indicate that his regiment may have been completely destroyed if not for the sudden arrival of Maney's brigade on his immediate right. Together, the Sixteenth Tennessee and Maney's first three regiments (Sixth and Ninth Tennessee and Forty-first Georgia) were responsible for the capture of Parsons' battery within the first forty-five minutes of the commencement of action at the Battle of Perryville. It appears that it is highly unlikely that *either* force (Maney's or Donelson's brigade) alone would have been able to destroy Terrill's brigade and capture the guns without the assistance of the *other* force.

The opposition's argument continues with the declaration that, "Both sides mention/describe the fight at Widow Gibson farm… no one mentions anything about any structure on the slope of Parsons' Hill, even though more soldiers, both North and South, wrote about that piece of ground more than any other on the field."[142] With simple assumption yet again, he *assumes* that all mentions of cabins are relative to Widow Gibson's home site. Once again, the facts reflect a different picture than the one that he has painted. When he suggests that both sides "mention/describe the fight at Widow Gibson farm," that statement is an assumption itself. The only mentions of a cabin or cabins by Federal soldiers or officers that *may be* in reference to Widow Gibson's farm are made by Private Erastus Winters—who authored *Serving Uncle Sam in the 50th Ohio*—and Lieut. Ellis E. Kennon of the Ninety-eighth Ohio.[143] Both of these regiments were in Colonel George Webster's brigade. Not a single participant on the field attributed the cabins that the Fiftieth Ohio or Webster's brigade fought near as belonging to *any specific family or name*. Evidence does suggest that the Fiftieth Ohio was engaged near "an old log

[141] Jamie Gillum, *The Battle of Perryville and the Sixteenth Tennessee: A Reevaluation: 2nd Edition*, Spring Hill, TN, 2015, p. 148.

[142] Email correspondence, July 2, 2015. (This statement is verbatim.)

[143] Erastus Winters, *Serving Uncle Same in the 50th Ohio*, p. 20: Lt. Ellis E. Kennon, Report of Webster's brigade, OR, p. 1066-68.

building."[144] But it's unlikely this was a reference to the Widow Gibson site, as they were moved to the left—or north—near Benton Road along the ridgeline. Lieutenant Kennon's report of the battle seconds the fact that the Fiftieth Ohio would have been moved away from the Gibson homesite. He stated that the Fiftieth Ohio was placed in rear of and to the left of Harris' battery and after a short time was "reformed about 300 yards farther to the left, advancing to the crest of the hill in the woods near a small log cabin."[145] The presumed location of the Widow Gibson homesite is at the head of the valley near the headwaters of "Donelson's Run." This— however—is based off the assumption that the Widow's cabin is where modern historians suppose it to be. Even the opposition has made it clear that the corn-crib has been located, but the actual home-site itself is still illusive and its *precise* location is unknown.

On the Confederate side, we find that only members of the Sixteenth Tennessee made mention of any cabins or structures: that is—the Sixteenth Tennessee and their superiors (Donelson and Cheatham). None of these accounts of the cabins suggest who owned the property on which they were engaged, thus the suggestion that this is in reference to Widow Gibson's property is yet another mere *assumption*. It is the blatant *failure to recognize* the discovery of the Hafely Cabin site that allows this fallacy to persist. Apparently, too many people have become too deeply entrenched in the notion that all mentions of cabins are *only* in reference to Widow Gibson. This failure to recognize new evidence and ground-breaking revelations of the battle may prevent the site from ever interpreting the battlefield in a more comprehensive and accurate manner. Until the leadership is willing to clear their minds of these misconceptions and reevaluate the new evidence without bias, sources and material on hand, *inaccurate* and expensive markers will continue to interpret the battle *incorrectly* on the field of battle at Perryville.

It was pointed out that only two known Federal accounts mention a cabin in the vicinity of Webster's brigade. When the opposition suggests that there was more written by participants about Open Knob than any other part of the field, he fails to recognize that individuals only make reference to the area that was *inclusive* to their experiences. Thus—if the Sixteenth was engaged *at* the Hafley cabins—*exclusive* of other Rebel regiments, they would naturally be the only ones to reference that site or their experiences there. However, there has been the discovery of another Federal account that described the battlefield and *did make mention* of at least a stable or barn on Open Knob within yards of Parsons' battery. Writing thirty-two years after the battle, one Federal veteran still had vivid memories of the battlefield burned into his mind. He was a member of Carlin's brigade. The evening after the battle, he wandered to the extreme Federal left.

…the further I got to the left the more dead I saw. In one place it looked like I could walk the length of a regiment on dead bodies. I came to an orchard, where a battery had been literally demolished, and men and horses lay about thick. It was in an orchard, *near a stable*. The guns were all lying on the ground and the wheels all chopped down. I learned that it was Parson's eight-gun battery, presented to him by the ladies of Cincinnati, and that the confederates, who had captured it, being unable to take it off when they retreated, for want of battery horses, chopped it down with axes.[146]

Although there would likely be an attempt to discredit this evidence by the opposition in some shape or form, it's clear that this soldier was well aware of the location of Parsons' guns and the fact that the carriages of the guns were indeed chopped down and destroyed by Lieutenant Wm. B. Turner's men.[147] Confederate accounts corroborate the fact that the carriages of Parsons' guns were in fact destroyed, and members of the Sixteenth Tennessee related that they had shot almost all of the battery horses and gunners before Maney arrived. This mention of a "stable" is even more eyewitness testimony of a structure on Open Knob. Why did this soldier write about it and other Federal troops didn't? As he walked the field, it certainly played into his

---

[144] Erastus Winters, *Serving Uncle Same in the 50ᵗʰ Ohio*, p. 20.

[145] Lt. Ellis E. Kennon, Report of Webster's brigade, *OR*, p. 1066-68.

[146] "Hot Work at Perryville." *Perrysburg Journal* (Perrysburg, OH) October 19, 1895, p. 7. *(Emphasis added.)*

[147] Report of Lieutenant William B. Turner, Smith's (Mississippi) Battery. *OR*, Vol. 16, Pt. 1, p. 1156 – 1157.

experiences that weren't distracted by the zipping of bullets and screams of comrades nearly a day after the fight. Why aren't there any other mentions of the Hafley Cabins by other Federal soldiers? Who is to say? Could it be because the cabin was not inclusive to many individuals' experiences? As big a role as Widow Gibson's played in the battle (according to Noe, Hafendorfer and Holman), why didn't any of the Federal soldiers mention that site? The answer lies with the soldier of the 105th Ohio when he stated, "One's own view is very limited at best, and few see more than the movements of their own company, or possibly, their regiment." Soldiers wrote about what they personally saw or experienced. Outside of their line of sight or view, they were practically unaware of events. Additionally, of all the sights that are observed on the battlefield, only a fraction of those scenes was actually recorded. Of the recorded materials, only a tiny fraction survived being lost, destroyed or placed in private collections. Thus, we have only seen a tiny fraction of what little was seen, recorded, survived and has been made available.

The final statement made by the opposition was that by his comprehension of the sources, "Each individual point may be able to be isolated, quarantined, and a different interpretation put on it, but on the whole, the outcome is getting more obvious to me the more I look into it." That statement would make sense, except for the fact *that each and every source states the same record of events* which are *at odds* with his own interpretations. There is no "spin" in *this interpretation* by the numerous primary sources that describe the battle on the Rebel right and how it played out. In fact, the "spin" on the primary sources was unintentionally played by these historians of the battle in the first place. This spin was created by failing to use all the sources *in their entirety* or *editing the sources* to conform to their conclusions. It struck me as odd after a trip to Perryville in the late Spring of 2014 that the leadership had agreed that there were discrepancies with the chronology of the battle. I thought that I had certainly made some ground in getting them to reevaluate that portion of the field. It seemed important to me to be there in person or by email as often as possible to act as a balance, suppress bias or entrenched understanding of the field—to act as an objective, yet fact-based tool for them. In the end, it was suggested that he had spent a "ridiculous amount of time on this" and suggested that we should "agree to disagree." I could not and would not let this go on being incorrectly interpreted. I had reached out to Noe, Hafendorfer, Sanders and Holman with the belief that they were still willing to delve into subjects that were thought to be of such importance in their lives. None, in the end, were willing to research to the micro level in order to gain a deeper understanding of the field.

In an email of May 23, 2014 with Professor Noe, he suggested that the evidence did not support the newer (or original) interpretation due to the lack of evidence of a structure on Open Knob. He suggested that deed records and archeological evidence may help support the theory, but in light of what was known—he could not support my interpretation. When I sent him an email informing him of the discovery of the Hafley site in 2014, it garnered no response. In the Spring of 2015, the University of Kentucky at Lexington was contacted. The suggestion of a new project for the university was exciting to the point of contact I made within the archeology department. After Mr. Holman agreed to fill out various forms for the project, my point of contact went to the Perryville battlefield herself. When she was shown the approximate vicinity of the supposed cabin site, she was somewhat discouraged when it was allegedly suggested that the ground had been disturbed by earthmoving equipment in the preceding years and modern trash likely hampered the area even more. Although it was unlikely that a dig would take place due to funding anyway, the nail was put in the coffin when it was suggested it was unlikely that any evidence of a home-site would be found. Nearly every action that was taken was countered by a reluctance to reconsider the chronology and development of the battlefield at Perryville.

THE PERRYVILLE BATTLEFIELD'S "OFFICIAL STATEMENT" ON THE REEVALUATION

Interestingly the Park's management was so concerned by the threat that their interpretation may be seriously questioned, they released an "official statement" in 2015 that attempted to rebut the *new* interpretation of the battlefield. The following points that are made in the statement have—in some cases—already been rebutted or will be in following text. The "official statement" appears strong, but a rebuttal of every point made follows this statement.

Statement on Jamie Gillum's The Battle of Perryville and the Sixteenth Tennessee Infantry Regiment: A Re-evaluation

Perryville Battlefield State Historic Site (2015)[148]

In 2011, author Jamie Gillum self-published a book entitled The Battle of Perryville and the Sixteenth Tennessee Infantry Regiment: A Re-evaluation. Gillum's thesis is that historians have ignored evidence and erred in not giving the 16th Tennessee Infantry proper credit for capturing (or helping to capture) Capt. Charles Parsons' Federal battery at the top of the Open Knob, now more popularly known as Parsons' Hill. After an extensive re-evaluation of all the available evidence, we conclude that the traditional evaluation presented at the battlefield park is in fact the correct one. Col. John Savage's 16th Tennessee fought south of the Open Knob at the Widow Gibson farm against elements of Col. Leonard Harris's Brigade. Col. George Maney's Confederate brigade properly received credit for the capture of Parsons' Battery. The argument is presented below in four broad categories.

REPORTS: After the battle, reports from significant Confederate commanders and other writings invariably pointed to the conclusion that Savage fought Harris and that Maney took Parsons' Hill. Savage himself specifically reported recognizing during the fighting his friend and former colleague from the U. S. Congress, Lt. Col. Oscar Moore, who lay wounded on the field near the Gibson cabin. Savage personally ordered his men to attend to his old friend. Moore's 33rd Ohio was never on Parsons' Hill. Thomas Head of the 16th Tennessee later confirmed in the 16th Tennessee's regimental history that the 16th Tennessee was opposite the 33rd Ohio and the "7th Ohio," which can be no other than 2nd Ohio, since all sources have those two units fighting together all through the battle, and the 7th Ohio served in Virginia. Head in contrast writes nothing about Col. William Terrill's regiments on the Open Knob. It is impossible that Oscar Moore was on or near Parsons' position.

Brig. Gen. Daniel Donelson, Savage's brigade commander, wrote that his brigade (excepting the 8th Tennessee and 51st Tennessee) were together. The 16th Tennessee did attack too early, which is why its casualties were so high. Contrary to Gillum, it was never detached from the brigade. Had the 16th Tennessee moved toward Parsons, the 15th and 38th would have followed, yet evidence from those regiments shows that they did not.

In his memoir, Gen. St. John Liddell specifically puts General B. F. Cheatham (Donelson's wing commander) at Capt. Samuel Harris' captured battery near the Gibson cabin and reported a conversation with him, asking instructions as to where to deploy his brigade. Liddell also gives credit to the capture of Harris' battery to "Cheatham's Men."

JOHN SAVAGE AND THE "THE RIGHT TURN": After some narrative confusion about timing and events at the beginning of the battle, Gillum assumes that Savage initially drove to the west and then turned right under orders from his superiors, which would have taken him northwest to Parsons' Hill. Savage indeed describes turning to the right while under heavy fire. But the available evidence reinforces the traditional interpretation that Savage started out moving to the southwest, and so his right turn took him west toward the Gibson cabin. Crucially, the

---

[148] The "official statement" was retrieved from the "Reviews" on Gillum's book located at: https://www.amazon.com/gp/customer-reviews/R14MNZJSLSA3AG/ref=cm_cr_dp_d_rvw_btm?ie=UTF8&ASIN=1466345799#wasThisHelpful

only Union battery that could have been visible to Savage at the outset was Capt. Peter Simonson's. It also was the only U. S. battery firing at the time. That is why the initial attack was directed towards this battery. The 45 degree turn to the right faced the 16th Tennessee to the west, into "the valley of death," not northwest to the Open Knob. Gillum's interpretation instead requires Savage to intentionally expose his flank to Simonson's fire while initially attacking a battery (Capt. Samuel Harris's) that had yet to be seen or open fire.

Savage himself reinforces the traditional interpretation in his own words:

"There was running up from Chaplain Creek a long hollow about half way between the battery and where the regiment was in line. I thought as soon as I moved into that hollow I would be out of reach of the battery and that I could come up on the other side within sixty or seventy yards of the battery." Note that topographically, there is no "hollow" that would take the 16th Tennessee to Parsons' Hill.

"There was no reason why the battery should not have fired upon the regiment while it was in line, except that a fire would pass through the line and only do a little damage. Marching in the new direction indicated by Cheatham's aide, I was soon in an open beech forest on the top of the hill. I was riding in front expecting a surprise, the left of the regiment was at the edge of the forest and the field, when the battery, about one hundred and fifty yards from the regiment, fired, enfilading it, sweeping the whole length of the line, killing a captain, a lieutenant and many privates. I was riding in front of the regiment; a grape shot passed through the head of my horse below the eyes." This description reinforces the conclusion that the battery was Simonson's, and that the right turn took the regiment to the Widow Gibson farm.

"The men at the battery had been killed or wounded or had fled before Maney's brigade appeared in the field to my right, some hundred yards or more distant, and the battle had ceased at the battery." If this was not Harris's battery, but instead Parsons', what was Maney attacking? Remember that there was no Federal battery north of Parsons' to be assaulted by Maney.

"None of General Maney's brigade was nearer than one hundred yards of this battery. The batteries taken by General Maney's brigade were half a mile or more to the right of this battery." Again, if Savage took Parsons' battery, what batteries could Maney have taken?

PARSONS' GUNS: All of the guns taken from Col. John Starkweather's brigade were recovered and accounted for by Federal troops on October 9, 1862. Only two captured Federal cannons left the field (and the state) after the battle. Based on the reports of Union Gen. Alexander McCook and Confederate battery commander Lt. William B. Turner, (and others) there can be no doubt that the guns in questions are Parsons'. Sources from Maney's brigade invariably assert say they captured two batteries unassisted.

Savage himself wrote that Maney's Brigade captured batteries (plural) on his right (to the north), and were not to be confused with any guns his regiment took. There were no other batteries on the Confederate right past Parsons, so Savage clearly states here that Maney took Parsons' battery. It is worth nothing as well that Savage, because of a wound, did not witness the capture of any battery personally.

Also notable is the correspondence that ensued between Gen. Braxton Bragg's Chief of Ordnance and Col. Maney about whose names should be engraved on those captured guns as honors. Note that Bragg gave Maney, not Donelson, the honor of choosing the names. Maney replied that at Perryville, along with his four Tennessee regiments, there also was the 41st Georgia, led by Col. Charles A. McDaniel. Maney asked that McDaniel's name be engraved on a gun and it presented to a Georgia Battery. Never mentioned was any thought of adding the 16th Tennessee to the list of regiments to be honored. In the end, the two Napoleons were engraved with the names of color bearer A.T. Mitchell and Lt. Col. John Patterson, both of the 1st Tennessee of Maney's Brigade. The Napoleon engraved to Mitchell later was seen in Germantown, Pennsylvania, by a former Confederate who wrote a letter to the Confederate Veteran for its January 1914 issue.

WHERE ARE THE CABINS? Sources from Savage's brigade invariably describe fighting around log buildings. Savage famously wrote that "There was a fence and a field on my right running up to two cabins at the line of the enemy's forces. There were skirmish lines along this fence which fired on our rear as we advanced. The Sixteenth had no protection except a few trees in the forest. I ordered a charge. We drove the enemy from behind the fences, killing many of them as they fled. The right of the regiment was at the two cabins. There was a battery in the line of battle to the right, about thirty or forty yards from these cabins, between which cabins there was an entry, or space, of ten or fifteen feet. The battery opened fire upon us, killing many men, and at the same time a fire of small arms from the line of battle was directed upon these cabins. The battery fired obliquely into this space."

Based on this description, that battery mentioned can only be Harris's. No soldier ever mentioned anything about any structure anywhere on the slopes of Parsons' Hill, even though more soldiers, both North and South, wrote about that piece of ground more than any other on the field. In his book, Gillum concludes without any evidence that there still must have been a structure on Parsons' Hill, it simply hasn't been found yet by archeologists. In his book he also points hopefully to areas where trees later were removed and suggests that those depressions might comprise the remains of a house structure.

More recently, after publication, Gillum pointed in several online venues to an 1877 map of the battlefield that shows a "Hayflay" cabin southeast of the Open Knob. He has concluded that this must be the missing cabin, and thus this map confirms his interpretation. There are two obvious problems, however. First, the cabin is in the wrong place for his narrative. The map places the cabin near the modern outdoor pavilion and playground, nowhere near where it would support the Gillum narrative. It is much too far to the east.

Second, and more importantly, the map clearly depicts 1862 troop movements on an 1877 landscape. Notably, Squire Bottom's cemetery constructed after the battle also is shown on the map. All the map really establishes is that a man named Hayflay (probably Hafely) lived on the battlefield in 1877. There remains no evidence of a cabin there in 1862. It is not on the more familiar "Work Map" of the battlefield. The history of the Sleettown site also demonstrates that in terms of structures, the battlefield looked quite different by 1877. An 1877 map says little then about the state of the battlefield in October 1862. The most logical conclusion is that the structure was built in the mid-1870s.

CONCLUSION: Historical inquiry and revision is always welcome at the park, and over the years we have indeed altered several interpretations based upon new evidence. Mr. Gillum, however, has not proven his case to our satisfaction. Instead, our inquiry reconfirms the traditional interpretation of these events as currently depicted at the park.

THE REBUTTAL OF THE PARK'S STATEMENT

First, it will be noted that the arguments that the park used are not valid. The unknown author of the "statement" used a "Strawman argument" to discredit the reevaluation of the battle. "A *strawman* is a fallacious argument that distorts an opposing stance in order to make it easier to attack. Essentially, the person using the strawman pretends to attack their opponent's stance, while in reality they are actually attacking a distorted version of that stance, which their opponent doesn't necessarily support."[149] Now, the entire statement will be rebutted with actual evidence. The first point of contention is regarding the capture of Colonel Moore of the Thirty-third Ohio. The argument that the Sixteenth Tennessee did not engage the Thirty-third Ohio has already been made, but a few points may still be made. The park's statement is **emboldened** with rebuttals in [brackets]. There was no author attributed to the Park's official statement. Almost all the following arguments had been made in emails to this author.

REPORTS: After the battle, reports from significant Confederate commanders and other writings invariably pointed to the conclusion that Savage fought Harris and that Maney took Parsons' Hill. Savage himself specifically reported recognizing during the fighting his friend and former colleague from the U. S. Congress, Lt. Col. Oscar Moore, who lay wounded on the field near the Gibson cabin.

[None of the "writings" of any of the commanders suggest that Donelson's brigade engaged the Federal center as will be seen in the reports of the commanders later in another section. In fact, none of the reports even suggest the idea that "Savage fought Harris," although there is no argument that Maney's men participated in the action on Open Knob against Parsons. The "writings" that invariably pointed to that idea were *created and perpetuated by modern historians*. There is **no** source or evidence that even suggests where Lt. Col. Moore was found. Savage did not "recognize" Moore "during the fighting." His capture was brought to Savage's attention after the fight. Savage never even admitted to personally seeing the man.[150]]

Savage personally ordered his men to attend to his old friend. Moore's 33rd Ohio was never on Parsons' Hill. Thomas Head of the 16th Tennessee later confirmed in the 16th Tennessee's regimental history that the 16th Tennessee was opposite the 33rd Ohio and the "7th Ohio," which can be no other than 2nd Ohio, since all sources have those two units fighting together all through the battle, and the 7th Ohio served in Virginia. Head in contrast writes nothing about Col. William Terrill's regiments on the Open Knob. It is impossible that Oscar Moore was on or near Parsons' position.

[The reevaluation never suggested that the Thirty-third Ohio fought on or near Open Knob or Parsons' battery. Clearly, another assumption was made by Thomas Head when writing the regimental history—after all, he had learned this second hand himself. When Moore was taken prisoner, the natural assumption would be that the regiment fought the unit Moore commanded. However, it is made clear by Savage's statement, that Moore was *found* and carried to the rear "about dusk." The Sixteenth Tennessee had been relieved and reengaged at about 5:45 P.M., and it's far more probable that in their last advance over different ground Colonel Moore was discovered. At that point, Donelson's brigade was advancing on the left of Stewart's brigade and would not have been traversing the same field on which they had fought earlier—but much further south of where they were first engaged.[151] Additionally, the park's statement falsely declares that "all sources" have the 2nd Ohio and 33rd Ohio "fighting together all through the battle." This is a misstatement, as the Chief of staff for the Tenth Division states that—for a large portion of the fight—the 2nd and 94th Ohio came into their lines between Bush's and Stone's batteries to help support the left. Additionally, a member of the Thirty-third Ohio claimed that their work was

---

[149] https://effectiviology.com/straw-man-arguments-recognize-counter-use/

[150] John H. Savage, *Life of John H. Savage* (Nashville, TN: John H. Savage, 1903) 125.

[151] Maj. Gen. B. F. Cheatham, *Report of Battle of Perryville* (William P. Palmer Collection, WRHS Collection, Box 1, Folder 6): Brig. Gen. D. S. Donelson, *Report of Battle of Perryville* (William P. Palmer Collection, WRHS Collection, Box 28, Folder 9)

"short and sharp" resulting in the majority of their casualties "in less than ten minutes." This caused the regiment to "fall back upon the main body, leaving their dead and wounded upon the field."[152]]

Brig. Gen. Daniel Donelson, Savage's brigade commander, wrote that his brigade (excepting the 8th Tennessee and 51st Tennessee) were together. The 16th Tennessee did attack too early, which is why its casualties were so high. Contrary to Gillum, it was never detached from the brigade. Had the 16th Tennessee moved toward Parsons, the 15th and 38th would have followed, yet evidence from those regiments shows that they did not.

[As will be seen in Donelson's report—later in this work, Donelson never suggested that the Sixteenth Tennessee "attacked too early."[153] Additionally, the reevaluation never suggested that the Sixteenth Tennessee was "detached" from the brigade. The writer states that the 15th and 38th Tennessee "would have followed" the Sixteenth if they had moved towards Parsons, "yet evidence from those regiments shows that they did not." It would be interesting to see the "evidence" that "they did not" follow the Sixteenth wherever they went. The Sixteenth was the guide regiment, and in fact, all evidence presented—old and new—supports the fact that they did follow the Sixteenth. While the Sixteenth concentrated their attacks on the 123rd Illinois and Parsons, the Fifteenth and Thirty-eighth regiments engaged the enemy forces to the Sixteenth Tennessee's left—namely the Twenty-fourth Illinois and Eightieth Illinois.]

In his memoir, Gen. St. John Liddell specifically puts General B. F. Cheatham (Donelson's wing commander) at Capt. Samuel Harris' captured battery near the Gibson cabin and reported a conversation with him, asking instructions as to where to deploy his brigade. Liddell also gives credit to the capture of Harris' battery to "Cheatham's Men."

[The argument concerning Liddell was made in depth earlier in the narrative. The Thirty-third Alabama and Thirty-second Mississippi of Wood's Brigade may have been responsible for the initial capture of Harris' Battery which was covered in depth on page 24 of this manuscript. A member of the Thirty-third Alabama (Wood's brigade) specifically related the capture of that battery.]

JOHN SAVAGE AND THE "THE RIGHT TURN": **After some narrative confusion about timing and events at the beginning of the battle, Gillum assumes that Savage initially drove to the west and then turned right under orders from his superiors, which would have taken him northwest to Parsons' Hill. Savage indeed describes turning to the right while under heavy fire. But the available evidence reinforces the traditional interpretation that Savage started out moving to the southwest, and so his right turn took him west toward the Gibson cabin.**

[The above statements are very misleading. First, the "narrative confusion about timing and events" may well be confusion on that writer's behalf. He suggests that Donelson's brigade commenced the attack to the southwest in the direction of Simonson's battery over a half mile away. This axis of advance would have placed them marching obliquely in front of the aligned regiments of Jones' brigade that had occupied the front line after Wood's brigade had forced the 33rd Ohio into the woods to their front. The alignment of Confederate divisions and brigades had already been completed when Cheatham's division was the last to file into line. Donelson and Savage were certain to observe Jones', Wood's and Brown's brigades to their left—just north of Doctor's Creek. No commander would march his force in front of—or across the frontage—of its supporting forces. It is the park's erroneous belief of the exact location that Donelson's brigade began its advance that leads him to this unsubstantiated conclusion.]

---

[152] Capt. Percival P. Oldershaw, Report of Battle of Perryville, *War of the Rebellion: Official Records of the Union and Confederate Armies*, Vol. 16, Pt. 1, p. 1059-62: "The Thirty-third Ohio" *Portsmouth Daily Times* (Portsmouth, Ohio) Sept. 4, 1886, p. 3. (newspapers.com)

[153] Brig. Gen. D. S. Donelson, *Report of Battle of Perryville* (William P. Palmer Collection, WRHS Collection, Box 28, Folder 9)

Crucially, the only Union battery that could have been visible to Savage at the outset was Capt. Peter Simonson's. It also was the only U. S. battery firing at the time. That is why the initial attack was directed towards this battery.

[According to the above statement, the writer's understanding of where Donelson's attack position was located west of Chaplin River is critical in *his belief of how the battle played out*. He believes that the starting point for the brigade was on a hilltop in the bend of Chaplin River only 100 yards south of the Dug Road. Only from that specific location can his interpretation make sense, but even then, it discounts the fact that the regiment and brigade would be advancing in front of and overlapping Wood's and Jones' brigades. Additionally, while the terrain has remained the same, the landscape has changed. Woods—that once covered the approaches between Mackville Pike and Chaplin River—have largely been cleared. The trees present at the time would have added an additional 25 to 35 feet or more in elevation concealing the observation of Simonson's guns. But—most importantly, the Tenth Division's Chief of Staff once again dispels the belief that Simonson's battery was the only one firing. In his testimony during the Court of Inquiry for General Buell, he testified that previous to seeing rebel infantry approach, "we were firing at long range from two batteries."[154] Which battery was the second battery? We know that Stone's battery had already been firing at cavalry in the deep valley to the north as stated in other Federal reports. Additionally, Captain Percival Oldershaw reported that Parsons' battery was in position and had already commenced firing before the rebel advance was detected.[155]]

The 45 degree turn to the right faced the 16th Tennessee to the west, into "the valley of death," not northwest to the Open Knob. Gillum's interpretation instead requires Savage to intentionally expose his flank to Simonson's fire while initially attacking a battery (Capt. Samuel Harris's) that had yet to be seen or open fire.

[Here—yet again, the writer misinterprets the reevaluation. The reevaluation does not in any way suggest that Savage ever saw or advanced in the direction of *Harris' battery*. Nor does it suggest in any way that Donelson's brigade received fire from Simonson's battery. Simonson's battery directly confronted the brigade of John C. Brown and three brigades of Buckner's division. The new interpretation—instead—suggests that the Sixteenth Tennessee changed direction to the northwest to attack Parsons' battery after possibly beginning their advance in the direction of Stone's Battery atop Starkweather's Heights. Additionally, "the 45-degree turn" is fabricated by the writer of the statement. The most accurate information that can be had regarding the direction of the turn came from a soldier in the Sixteenth Regiment that stated the regiment was reformed "at right angles to the line when marching to charge the battery in the field."[156] In the following paragraphs, the writer attempts to use Savage's "own words" to support his version of events.]

Savage himself reinforces the traditional interpretation in his own words:

"There was running up from Chaplain Creek a long hollow about half way between the battery and where the regiment was in line. I thought as soon as I moved into that hollow I would be out of reach of the battery and that I could come up on the other side within sixty or seventy yards of the battery." Note that topographically, there is no "hollow" that would take the 16th Tennessee to Parsons' Hill.

[It's interesting that the writer states that there is no "hollow" topographically that would take the Sixteenth Tennessee to Parsons' position. In fact, there is only one terrain feature that separated the two forces at the commencement of the action. It was one deep hollow that separated the first finger of terrain from the second finger upon which Parsons' battery and Terrill's brigade was deploying. (See the map on page 131.) If Savage advanced up the "Valley of Death"—as

---

[154] Capt. P. P. Oldershaw, Buell Court of Inquiry, *War of the Rebellion: Official Records of the Union and Confederate Armies*, Vol. 16, Pt. 1, p. 293-96.

[155] Capt. P. P. Oldershaw, Report of Action near Perryville, *OR*, Vol. 16, Pt. 1, p.1059 – 1062.

[156] John H. Savage, *Life of John H. Savage*, Nashville, TN, 1903, p. 126,

the writer states—there would be NO hollows in which to avoid enemy fire (see map page 59). His interpretation suggests that they would have advanced up the length of the valley in the bottoms of what is currently called "Donelson's Run."]

> **"There was no reason why the battery should not have fired upon the regiment while it was in line, except that a fire would pass through the line and only do a little damage. Marching in the new direction indicated by Cheatham's aide, I was soon in an open beech forest on the top of the hill. I was riding in front expecting a surprise, the left of the regiment was at the edge of the forest and the field, when the battery, about one hundred and fifty yards from the regiment, fired, enfilading it, sweeping the whole length of the line, killing a captain, a lieutenant and many privates. I was riding in front of the regiment; a grape shot passed through the head of my horse below the eyes."** This description reinforces the conclusion that the battery was Simonson's, and that the right turn took the regiment to the **Widow Gibson farm.**

[Here, the writer has *somehow* translated the above to support his version of events. The fact is that Savage doesn't state which direction the fire from the enemy battery came from. He simply states that the battery was "about one-hundred and fifty yards from the regiment" when it fired and enfiladed the regiment. How does this "reinforce" any idea that the battery was Simonson's or that the "right turn" took the regiment to Widow Gibson's? Additionally, his interpretation would have the regiment engaging the Tenth Wisconsin of Lytle's brigade that supported the left of Simonson's battery. The only battery that members of the Sixteenth Tennessee mention being in very close proximity to them is located on the regiment's *right flank* as is seen in Savage's account as well as those of his men.[157] If the fire did come from the right, it would rule out the possibility of the fire coming from Simonson's guns—as those guns would have been located on the regiment's left. Colonel Savage, Captain Womack and Thomas Head all related that it was the Sixteenth Tennessee that had caused the death of General James Jackson commanding the Federal army's Tenth Division. Captain Oldershaw of the Tenth Division staff reported that Jackson was killed very early in the action just after the 123rd Illinois had advanced to the north-south fence—fired a volley and fallen back.[158]]

> **"The men at the battery had been killed or wounded or had fled before Maney's brigade appeared in the field to my right, some hundred yards or more distant, and the battle had ceased at the battery."** If this was not Harris's battery, but instead Parsons', what was Maney attacking? Remember that there was no Federal battery north of Parsons' to be assaulted by Maney.

[Again, it appears that the writer cannot get past the *fact* that direction is relative to an individual's orientation and perspective of the field. The above assertion would indicate that Harris' battery was defenseless and fell to the Confederates only thirty minutes into the fight. However, it is stated in Federal and Confederate reports that Harris' battery fell around 6 p.m. The Confederate attack commenced around 2:00 p.m. All accounts of the participants claim that Maney came to their assistance thirty minutes after the Sixteenth became engaged—including General Maney himself.[159] That would mean that in less than thirty minutes, Maney had crushed Terrill, captured Parsons' guns and caused the retreat of Starkweather and advanced astride Donelson's brigade at Harris' battery. Impossible. When Savage stated that the "battle had ceased at the battery," he was implying that his regiment was more responsible for its capture than Maney's men. Did that mean that the Sixteenth Tennessee was more responsible for the capture? Not necessarily, but the role played by the regiment in the attack on Parsons' guns was pivotal in the outcome of the attack. The facts absolutely support the idea that the battery Maney was attacking was the same one that Savage's regiment had been fighting for thirty minutes as is seen in Marcus Toney's account as well at Maney's own report of the battle.]

---

[157] John H. Savage, *Life of John H. Savage*, Nashville, TN, 1903, p. 122: J. J. Womack, *The Civil War Diary of Capt. J. J. Womack* (McMinnville, TN: Womack Printing Company, 1961) p. 62-4: Thomas R. Hooper, *1862 Diary of Thomas R. Hooper*, (Photocopy on hand at Stones River National Battlefield, Murfreesboro, TN) p. 76.

[158] Capt. P. P. Oldershaw, Report of Action near Perryville, *OR*, Vol. 16, Pt. 1, p.1059 – 1062.

[159] John H. Savage, *Life of John H. Savage*, Nashville, TN, 1903, p. 119, 124, 127.

"None of General Maney's brigade was nearer than one hundred yards of this battery. The batteries taken by General Maney's brigade were half a mile or more to the right of this battery." Again, if Savage took Parsons' battery, what batteries could Maney have taken?

[This was Savage's attempt to claim capture of Parsons' guns. Savage believed that his regiment was RESPONSIBLE for the capture of Parsons' battery, while Maney was responsible for the capture of the remaining guns of Bush and Stone on Starkweather's Hill. Direction is relative to the individual. From Savage's perspective, it is quite possible that it appeared that another battery was further right, when in reality it was directly in the Confederate attack's front. It's highly probable that Parsons' battery could not have been captured without the assistance of *both* units.]

PARSONS' GUNS: All of the guns taken from Col. John Starkweather's brigade were recovered and accounted for by Federal troops on October 9, 1862. Only two captured Federal cannons left the field (and the state) after the battle. Based on the reports of Union Gen. Alexander McCook and Confederate battery commander Lt. William B. Turner, (and others) there can be no doubt that the guns in questions are Parsons'. Sources from Maney's brigade invariably assert say they captured two batteries unassisted.

Savage himself wrote that Maney's Brigade captured batteries (plural) on his right (to the north), and were not to be confused with any guns his regiment took. There were no other batteries on the Confederate right past Parsons, so Savage clearly states here that Maney took Parsons' battery. It is worth noting as well that Savage, because of a wound, did not witness the capture of any battery personally.

Also notable is the correspondence that ensued between Gen. Braxton Bragg's Chief of Ordnance and Col. Maney about whose names should be engraved on those captured guns as honors. Note that Bragg gave Maney, not Donelson, the honor of choosing the names. Maney replied that at Perryville, along with his four Tennessee regiments, there also was the 41st Georgia, led by Col. Charles A. McDaniel. Maney asked that McDaniel's name be engraved on a gun and it presented to a Georgia Battery. Never mentioned was any thought of adding the 16th Tennessee to the list of regiments to be honored. In the end, the two Napoleons were engraved with the names of color bearer A.T. Mitchell and Lt. Col. John Patterson, both of the 1st Tennessee of Maney's Brigade. The Napoleon engraved to Mitchell later was seen in Germantown, Pennsylvania, by a former Confederate who wrote a letter to the Confederate Veteran for its January 1914 issue.

[The argument above—regarding Savage's claims—was rebutted in detail earlier in the narrative. The fact is that just because a captured gun had the names of members of Maney's brigade engraved on them does not mean they were solely responsible for the capture of the guns. Two guns were eventually engraved with the names of two members of the *First Tennessee* that played NO role in the capture of *Parsons' battery*. What the writer ignores is that the correspondence which he refers to is in regard to the capture of guns at the *Battle of Murfreesboro*. The request for names to inscribe was made in reference to *that* battle. Maney's reply to the correspondence stated, "it would be a profound gratification to me to be allowed the privilege of inscribing the name of Colonel McDaniel on one of the guns captured by my brigade *at the battle of Murfreesborough*, the gun to be presented to some Georgia battery…"[160] Maney clearly had great respect for the man. He made no other suggestions. General Ed Walthall and many other brigade commanders were asked the same question regarding guns captured at Murfreesboro in the Spring of 1863. Walthall did submit four names.[161] Conversely, when an inquiry came after the Battle of Murfreesboro to attain a list of names to add to the Confederate Roll of Honor, Colonel Savage declined stating that he could not name a few when so many were so courageous. If such was asked of Savage after Perryville, his response would have certainly been the same. The following argument made by the park shows how an argument can be made from nothing at all.]

---

[160] *OR*, Vol. 16, Pt. 2, p. 1003-04. (*Emphasis added.*)

[161] https://www.fold3.com/image/271/75442331

WHERE ARE THE CABINS? Sources from Savage's brigade invariably describe fighting around log buildings. Savage famously wrote that "There was a fence and a field on my right running up to two cabins at the line of the enemy's forces. There were skirmish lines along this fence which fired on our rear as we advanced. The Sixteenth had no protection except a few trees in the forest. I ordered a charge. We drove the enemy from behind the fences, killing many of them as they fled. The right of the regiment was at the two cabins. There was a battery in the line of battle to the right, about thirty or forty yards from these cabins, between which cabins there was an entry, or space, of ten or fifteen feet. The battery opened fire upon us, killing many men, and at the same time a fire of small arms from the line of battle was directed upon these cabins. The battery fired obliquely into this space."

Based on this description, that battery mentioned can only be Harris's.

[Nowhere in the above description did Savage say "Harris' battery." Nor did anyone else in the regiment or brigade. How can one CONCLUDE that based on THAT description that the battery "can only be Harris's"? Additionally, the park's management insisted that Harris' battery was located about three-hundred yards further northwest of the only archeological evidence of a corn crib that they allege belonged to Widow Gibson. Savage and other members of the regiment state that the enemy battery they faced was within "thirty or forty yards" of their right flank.]

No soldier ever mentioned anything about any structure anywhere on the slopes of Parsons' Hill, even though more soldiers, both North and South, wrote about that piece of ground more than any other on the field.

[That is easy to believe if one *believes* that Savage's regiment did not attack Open Knob. As was noted in earlier narrative, there is a federal source that mentions a structure on Open Knob.[162] If the writer of the official statement is wrong—as the wealth of evidence suggests—then the only cabin structures mentioned by Confederate commanders and privates in the Sixteenth Tennessee speak *only* of the Hafley cabins on the slope of Open Knob. Additionally, the fight against Open Knob was recorded no more than the participants of the fight in front of—and against—Lytle's brigade near Squire Bottom's house and Burnt Barn.]

In his book, Gillum concludes without any evidence that there still must have been a structure on Parsons' Hill, it simply hasn't been found yet by archeologists. In his book he also points hopefully to areas where trees later were removed and suggests that those depressions might comprise the remains of a house structure.

[The writer states that "Gillum concludes without any evidence" that there were cabins on the east slope of Open Knob. In fact, all of the evidence *supports* that the Hafley cabins were indeed on the slope of Open Knob. The evidence includes census data, participants' accounts, two maps drawn from war-time surveys, and even the Park's own "Owners of Battlefield" document that admits Hafley lived on Bottom's land from 1858 to 1862. Additionally, the park has not conducted any sort of dig in the area of the Hafley cabins—as they do not believe it existed. How can one find archeological evidence of a structure when one is unwilling to conduct a scientific dig? Finally, since the introduction of earth moving machinery to make the park look closer to what it may have looked like in 1862, a wealth of potential archeological evidence has been destroyed or dispersed.]

More recently, after publication, Gillum pointed in several online venues to an 1877 map of the battlefield that shows a "Hayflay" cabin southeast of the Open Knob. He has concluded that this must be the missing cabin, and thus this map confirms his interpretation. There are two obvious problems, however. First, the cabin is in the wrong place for his narrative. The map places the cabin near the modern outdoor pavilion and playground, nowhere near where it would support the Gillum narrative. It is much too far to the east.

---

[162] "Hot Work at Perryville." *Perrysburg Journal* (Perrysburg, OH) October 19, 1895, p. 7.

[The writer's declaration that the cabin is "in the wrong place for his narrative" is false. In fact, if one observes the actual map and observes the north seeking arrow, the cabin site is located due north and slightly west of the symbol for the Confederate cemetery. This position is actually 300 yards from the playground and is less than 100 yards from the known position of Parsons' battery. It is in the precise vicinity that the cabins were supposed to have been.]

Second, and more importantly, the map clearly depicts 1862 troop movements on an 1877 landscape. Notably, Squire Bottom's cemetery constructed after the battle also is shown on the map. All the map really establishes is that a man named Hayflay (probably Hafely) lived on the battlefield in 1877. There remains no evidence of a cabin there in 1862. It is not on the more familiar "Work Map" of the battlefield. The history of the Sleettown site also demonstrates that in terms of structures, the battlefield looked quite different by 1877. An 1877 map says little then about the state of the battlefield in October 1862. The most logical conclusion is that the structure was built in the mid-1870s.

[In the Library of Congress, the description of the 1877 Ruger/Kilp map states:

"Authorities: surveys by Edward Ruger and Anton Kilp [and] official reports of officers of both armies." Map gives "position of General Gilbert's corps on the evening of October 7th" and the positions of both the Union and Confederate troops "on the 8th before being brought into action," "while engaged," and "after dark on the evening of the 8th." Roads, the railroad from Lebanon to Stanford, drainage, vegetation, relief by hachures, houses, and the **names of residents** are also represented.[163]

In fact, nearly all the names associated with the map are found in the 1860 census, but not in following censuses. That fact—coupled with the two maps, "Owners of Battlefield" document, eyewitness testimony and census data from 1860 and 1870—points to the "most logical conclusion:" that there was a home-site occupied by Joseph Hafley on the southeast slope of Open Knob in 1862. The only family named Hafley living in Boyle County in the 1870 census is the same Joseph Hafley that lived miles south of Perryville with a Mitchellsburg post office. Additionally, *not one* "Sleettown" resident or structure is identified or located on the 1877 battlefield map—more indication that the map was compiled from the 1862 survey. The primary reason that there is no archeological evidence of a structure is due to the fact that no archeological survey has been conducted on that site location. Lastly, the writer mentions the "more familiar Work Map." This is supposed to be the J. B. Work map. It is hard to believe that the J. B. Work map is considered reliable. That map was published in 1900 and was "compiled by the records and other sources."[164] It is possibly the *least* reliable map of all of the known maps. A more reliable map might be the one included in *The Official Military Atlas of the Civil War*. That map was also compiled by Ruger and Kilp's surveys taken in 1862 and can be found on Plate 24, number 2. Another more credible map is from *History of the Army of the Cumberland* which was compiled from Ruger and Kilp's survey of 1862 as well. Why would two of their maps contain a symbol for a home-site and the name Hayflay (Hafley) while other maps don't? It may simply be the fact that the map became over-crowded with superfluous information and troop dispositions. To this author's knowledge, there are only four well-known and reliable maps in existence. All four are compiled from the Ruger and Kilp map. Two of them include the Hafley name and home-site. Only one of those two has troop positions superimposed on it. Of the remaining two maps that were also published from surveys by them, both have troop dispositions but no reference of the Hafley name. The map from *History of the Army of the Cumberland* does not include the Hafley name, but neither does it include the H.P. Bottom House or barn, Widow Gibson's Cabin nor the Russell House. Similarly, the more familiar map from *The Official Military Atlas of the Civil War* does include the Gibson, Russell and the Bottom House, but no mention of Hafley.]

CONCLUSION: Historical inquiry and revision is always welcome at the park, and over the years we have indeed altered several interpretations based upon new evidence. Mr. Gillum, however, has not proven his

---

[163] https://www.loc.gov/resource/g3954p.cw0227000/?r=0.631,0.481,0.388,0.247,0 (***Emphasis added.***)

[164] Work, J. B. *Map of the battle-field of Perryville, Ky., October 8th 1862.* [Chicago, Ill, 1900] Map. Retrieved from the Library of Congress, https://www.loc.gov/item/99447187/. (Accessed June 04, 2017.)

case to our satisfaction. Instead, our inquiry reconfirms the traditional interpretation of these events as currently depicted at the park.

[Sadly—if an archeological dig ever did take place and turn up homesite artifacts at the location of the Hafley Cabins, the "straw man" argument would be that it only proved that a cabin existed there—but only long after the battle. Let the reader be the judge.]

IMAGERY OF THE BATTLEFIELD –
THE THOMAS HEAD BATTLEFIELD ENGRAVING.

Thomas Head was the first historian of the Sixteenth Tennessee Infantry Regiment. He published *Campaigns and Battles of the Sixteenth Regiment Tennessee Volunteers* in 1885. The first part of the book is dedicated to the regiment's history during the course of the war. On page 240 of the book, there is an engraving of the Battle of Perryville that was *specifically commissioned* for his history. The engraving was made by Crosscup and West and is followed by the letters PIHLA. Crosscup and West was an engraving firm out of Philadelphia, Pennsylvania ran by George W. Crosscup and William R. West. They were both Union veterans of the Civil War.

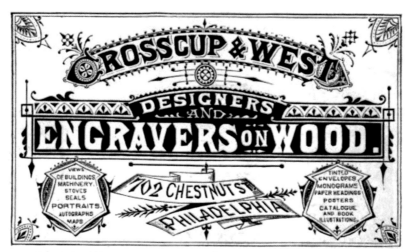

(http://alphabettenthletter.blogspot.com/2016/09/lettering-crosscup-west-engravers.html)

The engraving in Head's book is interesting for several different reasons. The perspective is from the Confederate viewpoint and is oriented as if the observer were on the hills just south of Walker's Bend on the Chaplin River. Probably on a hill near the Goodnight House. It appears that the engraving was probably made from a battlefield sketch—but that is speculation. Regardless, the engraving shows many recognizable features. The following engraving is from Head's history of the Sixteenth Tennessee. Running across the map from right to left—is Chaplin River. The bottoms where there were pools of water is clearly visible at far right. Doctor's Creek continues from that point across the engraving to the extreme left of the engraving. The artwork shows the opening moments of the fight when Donelson's brigade began the attack and the Sixteenth Tennessee was the extreme right force for the Confederate Army. The title of Head's engraving is "PERRYVILLE—OPENING ATTACK." Many members of the Sixteenth Tennessee state that they were the first Rebel unit in action on the extreme right of the army and that they fought near and around a cabin or cabins and within very close proximity of a battery of cannon that fell to their assault approximately thirty minutes into their attack with Maney's assistance.[165]

---

[165] Ten men in the regiment mentioned cabins or shared the same recollection of the fight. These men included Carroll H. Clark (Co. I), Isaac Mercer (Co. C), Capt. Fisher (Co. G), Jesse Walling (Co. E), Thomas Head (Co. I), James C. Biles (Co. C), E.S. Rowan (Co. C), Huel Moffit (Co. E) and William H. White (D) from Savage's biography. This is a total of ten men from the regiment representing five different companies and the regimental commander.

Hartz

1920

Parsons' Battery

Hafley

Bush

Casualty collection

Dug Road

New Maysville Road

Stone

Trevis

Visitor's Center

Harris' Battery

Widow Bottom

Battlefield Rd

Simonson's Battery

This is a birdseye view of the same terrain as the Head engraving for the regimental history.(Image Courtesy Google Earth Pro.)

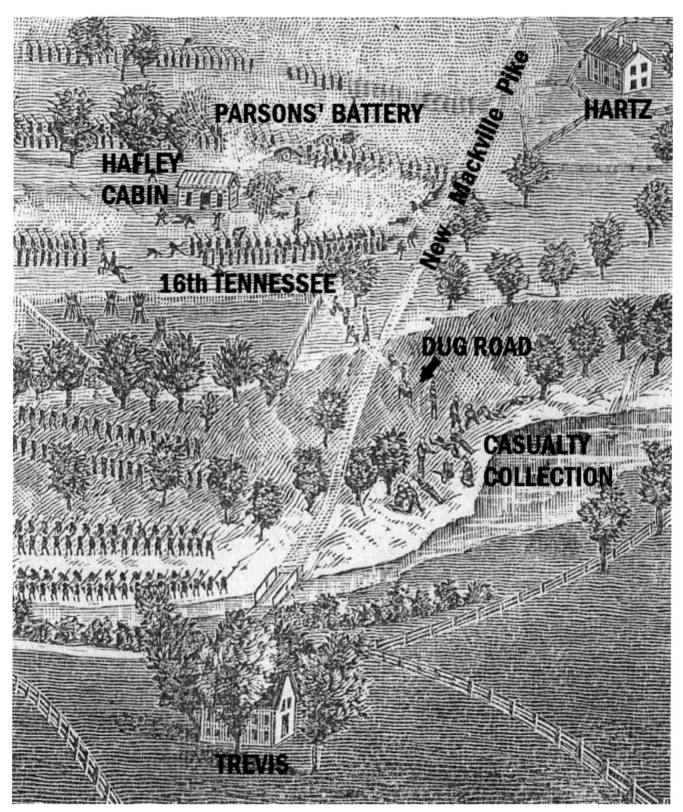

This close-up of the engraving shows detail of the fight on the right as it was meant to be understood. The Sixteenth Tennessee is clearly engaged at the Hafley Cabins and in short range of the deadly fire of Parsons' battery.

This close-up of the engagement between the Sixteenth Tennessee and the battery and its supports at and near the Hafley Cabins shows the havoc wreaked in the regiment's ranks. This engraving was made prior to 1885—the year in which the publication of the book was made. What argument can be made that a cabin did not exist on the battlefield at that time if a contemporary observer of that time had clear recollection of it—as well as numerous eyewitnesses in the regiment? The illustration clearly shows whatever unit that is represented at the cabin structure was the extreme right unit of the Confederate forces at that time. Additionally, this image was ***specifically produced*** to be included in a history of the Sixteenth Tennessee Regiment. What the image relates is backed up by all of the members of the regiment in their descriptions of the battle—as well as both Generals Donelson and Cheatham.

One of the most well-known contemporary sketches was in the November 1, 1862 issue of *Harper's Weekly*. It was sketched by H. Mosler and shows the attack on Harris' battery not far from the Widow Gibson corn-crib. The orientation would have been looking from the Federal lines behind the battery to the east-south-east. From the drawing's perspective, the Widow Gibson cabin would have been just out of view down the hill to the far right. This image has often been attributed to the Sixteenth Tennessee's attack at the Gibson homesite. As noted earlier, it is likely that they did participate in the capture of these guns with the Eighth and Fifty-first Tennessee later in the evening as stated by a member of the Eighth Tennessee.

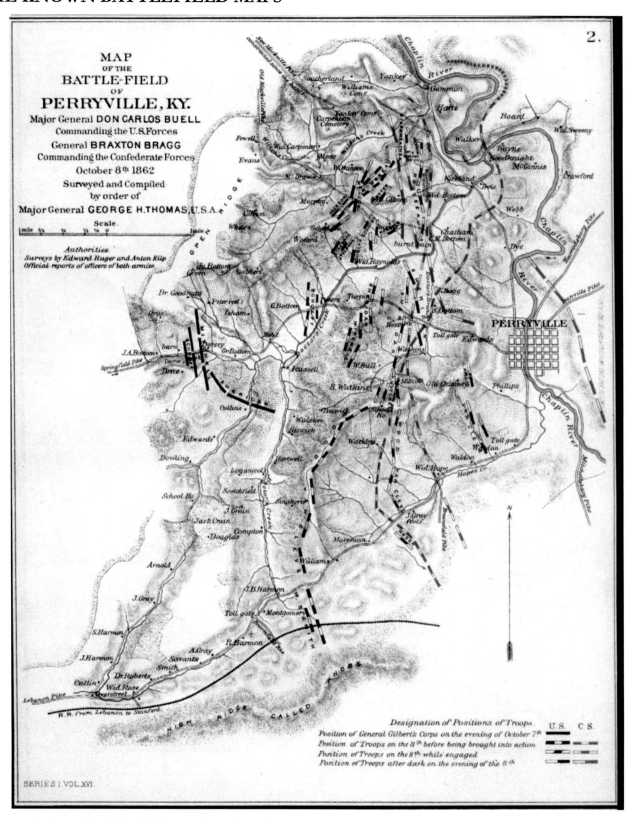

This map is from *The Official Military Atlas of the Civil War*. It was sold as a supplement to the *Official Records of the Union and Confederate Armies*. It is plate 24, map number 2. This is one of the most well-known maps of the battlefield simply because it is included in the Atlas. The information used in this map regarding terrain and families was compiled by Ruger and Kilp in 1862. This map has many of the names from the original survey, but it *does not* include Hafley.

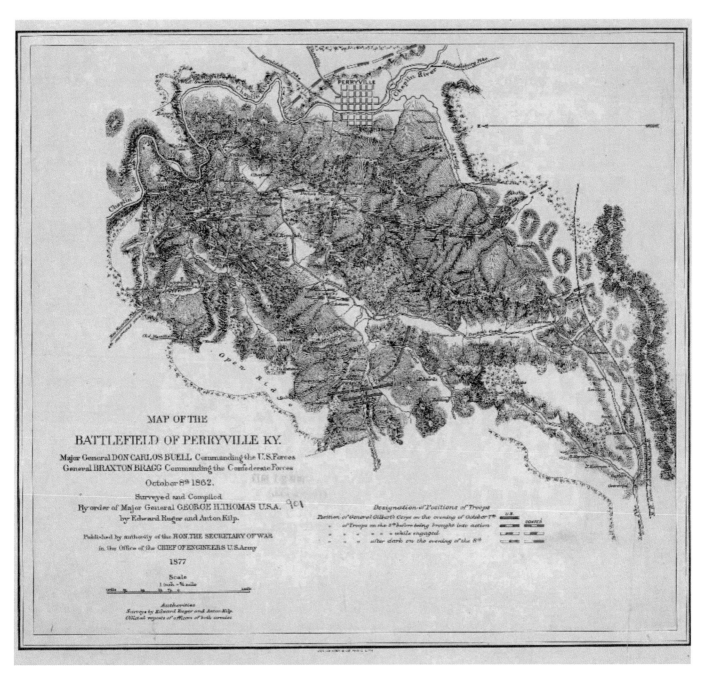

This is probably the most well-known map of the Perryville battlefield. It is the 1877 map. This map was created from the same Ruger and Kilp survey taken in 1862. This map was not included in *The Official Atlas of the Civil War*. It appears that the primary purpose of this map was to be sold in the post-war market as a souvenir. This map lists most of the names from the original Ruger and Kilp map and *does* include the site and name of the Hafley Cabins on Open Knob. The map also has a symbol that indicates the site of the Confederate cemetery. Credit: Library of Congress, Geography and Map Division.

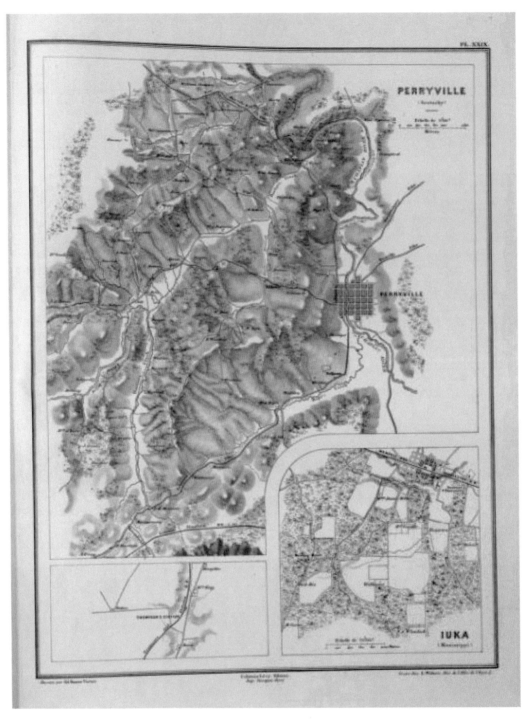

This is the plate from *Histoire de la Guerre Civile en Amerique*. This unique map is most likely the closest to the original Ruger and Kilp survey that would have only included the aspects of terrain and home-sites from 1862. This map includes every name from the rural vicinity of Perryville that Kilp was able to determine. It *does* include the Hafley cabin-site as well as a star that represents the location at which General Jackson fell. The Confederate cemetery was not indicated on this map. The publication of this work was done in 1873—making it the earliest map of the Perryville battlefield. This map does not contain any troop dispositions, as they were later added to remakes of the original after reviewing the Official Records. The map was copied and hand-drawn by Ed. Dumas Vorzet. The publication of this particular atlas was completed in 1883.[166]

[166] Paris, Louis-Philippe-Albert D'Orléans, Comte De. *[Histoire de la guerre civile en Amérique Atlas. 1874-90]*. [Paris: Michel Lévy, 1890] Map. Retrieved from the Library of Congress, https://www.loc.gov/item/2009581129/. (Accessed June 04, 2017.)

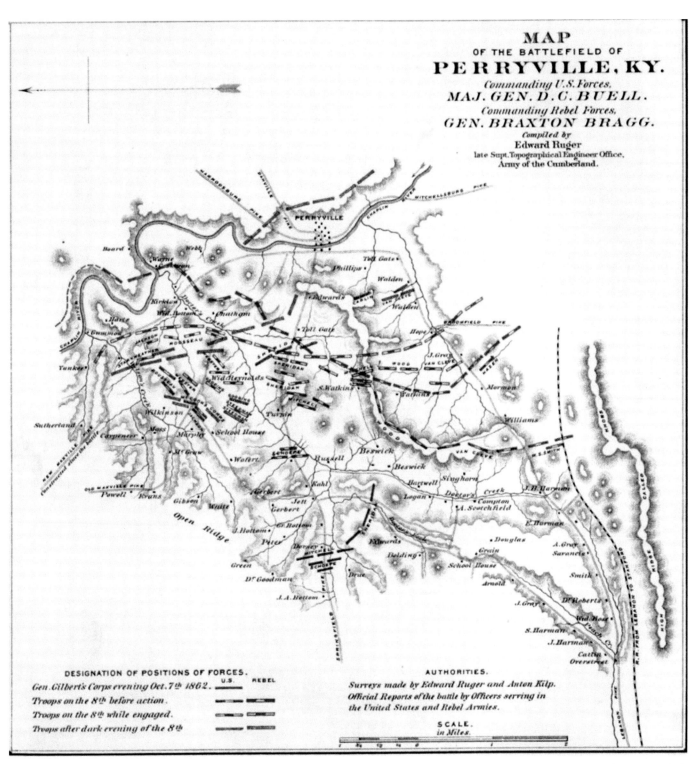

MAP
OF THE BATTLEFIELD OF
PERRYVILLE, KY.
Commanding U.S. Forces.
MAJ. GEN. D. C. BUELL.
Commanding Rebel Forces,
GEN. BRAXTON BRAGG.
Compiled by
Edward Ruger
late Supt. Topographical Engineer Office,
Army of the Cumberland.

DESIGNATION OF POSITIONS OF FORCES.

U.S.   REBEL

Gen. Gilbert's Corps evening Oct. 7th 1862.

Troops on the 8th before action.

Troops on the 8th while engaged.

Troops after dark evening of the 8th

AUTHORITIES.

Surveys made by Edward Ruger and Anton Kilp.
Official Reports of the battle by Officers serving in
the United States and Rebel Armies.

SCALE.
in Miles.

This map was also compiled from the Ruger and Kilp 1862 survey. It was included in the *History of the Army of the Cumberland* and was published in 1875. This map does not include the Hafley name; but, neither does it include the Russell, Widow Gibson nor H.P. Bottom's names.

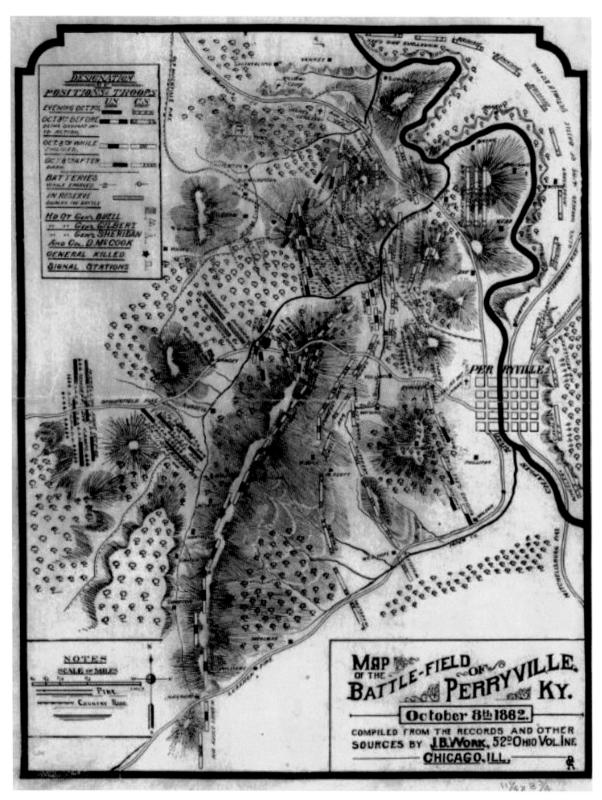

This final map was created and published in 1900. It does not include the Hafley site nor the Widow Gibson, Chatham or Widow Bottom sites. Its accuracy is very poor and was created for sales purposes. This map was compiled by J. B. Work of the 52nd Ohio. This is the "Work Map" that the battlefield park refers to in its statement on Gillum's reevaluation.[167]

---

[167] Work, J. B. *Map of the battle-field of Perryville, Ky., October 8th 1862.* [Chicago, Ill, 1900] Map. Retrieved from the Library of Congress, https://www.loc.gov/item/99447187/. (Accessed June 04, 2017.)

IRREFUTABLE FACTS

1. There are some very important facts that tend to be over-looked by historians of this battle. First and foremost is the *fact* that the first two forces to become heavily engaged in this fight—in line of battle—were the 123rd Illinois for the Federal forces and the Sixteenth Tennessee for the Rebel forces. Neither of these forces was deployed as skirmishers. Additionally, all the accounts from both of these units reinforce the fact that they were the first units to come into heavy contact with the opposing force's main line. Thus, if they were the first opposing units to come into heavy contact, they had to have engaged one another. We also know that the Confederate attack was commenced from right to left, and that the Sixteenth was initially the furthest north or right-most Rebel unit. All Federal reports also recognize that the initial heavy action was on the Federal left, and that the 123rd Illinois was the first unit engaged in line of battle on the left.

2. From all accounts in the Sixteenth Tennessee, the regiment seized a battery in the first thirty to forty minutes of action.

3. From all Federal accounts, Parsons' battery fell in the first thirty to forty minutes of action.

4. All accounts that relate the capture of the guns insist that it was taken with Maney's assistance.

5. No other unit claims the capture of a battery so early in the action other than Maney's brigade.

6. No Federal battery—other than Parsons'—was lost in action so early in the fight.

7. Maney admits that he came to Donelson's assistance on his right after being ordered forward by Cheatham.

8. Maney confirmed in a letter to Savage that he did come to his assistance by attacking at his right after Savage's regiment was engaged for not less than thirty minutes.

9. Joseph Hafley and his family were living on Squire H. P. Bottom's property at the time of the battle.

10. H. P. Bottom owned the land encompassing the Confederate cemetery and Open Knob.

11. Federal topographical engineer officers Edward Ruger and Anton Kilp surveyed the field following the battle.

12. The information from their 1862 survey was compiled and published on a map printed in 1877 by authority of the Secretary of War and the Office of the Chief of Engineers in the U.S. Army.

13. Ruger and Kilp identified a family on the south-east slope of Open Knob that they labeled as "Hayflay."

14. The 1860 census of Boyle County, Kentucky lists only one Hafley in the county. Joseph Hafley had a Perryville P.O.

15. Joseph Hafley did not live in Perryville in either the 1870 or 1880 censuses. That proves that the name was not labeled there on a later map.

16. Modern historians credit the Sixteenth Tennessee with the capture of Harris' battery. Harris' battery fell to the Rebels at about dusk—near six p.m. This time frame is completely inconsistent with all accounts of the men in the ranks of the Sixteenth Tennessee that state they captured their battery in the first thirty plus minutes of action.

17. The 123d Illinois was engaged *before* Starkweather's right was engaged, but Starkweather states that his right two regiments were struck by Donelson's brigade. If Maney came into action *after* Donelson was engaged—as Maney states— the Sixteenth Tennessee would *have to be* the unit engaging the 123d Illinois and Parsons' guns. They were engaged *before* Starkweather.

18. Before commencing his attack—from a personal reconnaissance, Maney observed Parsons' battery engaged at "close range" with Donelson's right-most unit. From his assault position, he would not have been able to observe any portion of Donelson's brigade if it were in the vicinity of Widow Gibson's owing to terrain and vegetation. This can only support the fact that Donelson's right and the Sixteenth Tennessee were within one or two-hundred yards of Maney's line of sight.

19. The Sixteenth Tennessee was the right-most unit in Donelson's brigade.

20. Marcus Toney—a member of the First Tennessee—described in detail (in **four** separate accounts) the Sixteenth Tennessee *engaged with Parsons' battery directly in his front* and the *charge to capture the guns* with that regiment.

21.   T. J. Wade's account—Company I, First Tennessee—concurs with Toney's account of the attack in that the First Tennessee *came up in rear of* Donelson's brigade.

22.   At least two members of Stewart's brigade relate either Donelson's brigade or the Sixteenth Tennessee attacking a battery on a hill. This was *before they went into action* observing from their assault position. Stewart's brigade only went into action *after Parsons' guns fell* to the Confederates.

23.   The Crosscup and West engraving of the Battle of Perryville was specifically commissioned for Thomas Head's History of the Sixteenth Regiment Tennessee Volunteers. The engraving is true to the words of the men that were in the ranks that day and includes the unidentified Hafley Cabin on the extreme right flank of the Rebel attack.

These facts can stand alone in the determination as to what battery the Sixteenth Tennessee engaged that day. They are irrefutable. Not one of the statements can be intelligently argued.

THE PRIMARY SOURCES:
CONFEDERATE ACCOUNTS

To better understand each of the primary sources in the conduct of the battle, the sources are now related in their *entirety* for clarity and perception in context of each source. The reports are indented. *Notations are made in brackets* but do not interrupt the chronology of the reports. All parentheses are original to the text. The reports are given in their entirety from start to finish in relation *to the combat* at Perryville. The beginning and ends of reports have been edited out to keep the text true to the action only. The following reports have been copied exactly as they were written—with run-on sentences, superfluous commas, abbreviations and capitalizations.

Major General Frank Cheatham's report is important for many reasons. First, it appears that *very few* have ever seen the report in its entirety, or recognized the significance of it. Secondly, taken as a whole, it's clear that Cheatham's report reflects a different chronology than the one presented by current historians of the battle. Third, it is also helpful in identifying the newly discovered Hafley home-site. Frank Cheatham's report was written on November 19, 1862 while at Tullahoma, Tennessee. This report was only cited in Hafendorfer's book and has not been cited in any other book about Perryville to this date. Unfortunately, the guts of the report fail to be cited in that work.

MAJ. GEN. BENJAMIN FRANKLIN CHEATHAM'S REPORT[168]

Just before the formation of my lines in order of battle, the Field Battery attached to the Brigade of Brig. Gen. Donelson, under command of Capt. Carnes was halted and placed in position on an eminence by order of General Bragg, and two Regiments of the same Brigade, the 8th Tennessee, Col. Moore, and the 51st Tennessee, Col. Chester, were placed in position, as a supporting or protecting force to the Battery. Capt. Carnes immediately opened fire upon one of the Enemy's Batteries posted on a ridge in his front, which proved to be a Battery of rifled pieces. He reported to me that his guns (which are smooth bored Six Pounders) could not attain the range necessary to reach the Battery of the Enemy with effect, & I at once ordered his Battery to be withdrawn and relieved by the three inch Rifled Battery of Capt. Stanford, attached to the Brigade of Brig. Gen. Stewart.

This being done, an artillery conflict began between Capt. Stanford's Battery and that of the enemy, which was kept up vigorously and with but slight intermission for an hour and a half. It was soon evident that the well directed fire of Capt. Stanford was taking effect on the Enemy, who several times changed his position, and at last retired from the contest, nearly if not quite all of his guns having been silenced. About two O'clock I received orders from Maj. Gen. Polk to move my command forward, and at once engage the Enemy, whose lines were distinctly visible across the open field and about three fourths of a mile to my front, directly fronting me was a precipitous bluff bounding the western side of Chaplin's Creek, which had to be passed in making the movement, this being accomplished, the first Brigade under command of Gen. Donelson, consisting of the 16th Tennessee Regiment, Col. Savage, the 38th Tennessee Regiment, Col. Carter and the 15th Tennessee Regiment, Col. Tyler, (the 8th and 51st Tennessee Regiments having been previously detached) moved forward in admirable order and most gallant style, this command was followed by the Brigade of Brig. Gen. Stewart.

[The initial assembly area for Cheatham's division was several hundred yards east of Chaplin's Creek not far from the Walker House on the hillside overlooking Chaplin's Creek. From that position, the enemy line was visible around three-quarters of a mile away. That placed the enemy line visible in a north-south orientation that stretched from near Open Knob to the site of the burnt barn of Squire Bottom's property.]

---

[168] Maj. Gen. B. F. Cheatham, *Report of Battle of Perryville* (William P. Palmer Collection, WRHS Collection, Box 1, Folder 6)

I (in the mean time) having directed Brig. Gen. Maney to move his command to the right, and attack and press the left flank of the Enemy. Gen. Donelson's Brigade moving steadily and rapidly forward was soon engaged under a heavy fire from the Artillery and infantry lines of the Enemy, who were discovered posted under protection of a skirt of woods and also protected by a fence and some buildings, without hesitating for a moment, although under a most terrible fire of grape, canister and musketry, and having a command of three Regiments only in hand—this gallant leader gave the order to charge, the order was repeated rapidly along the line, and with a cheer which rang through all the surrounding woods, these brave men rushed forward with a determination and impetuosity which not even superior numbers or advantage of position could resist, the Enemy was driven back into the woods, leaving his former lines thickly strewed with dead and wounded.

[During the foregoing advance, Cheatham does not mention the correction that was given to Colonel Savage in his advance on the enemy. But after changing direction, the Sixteenth Tennessee assailed the first of the enemy lines that were in the act of forming on Open Knob. Savage fought his regiment to the buildings that Cheatham referred to—now recognized as the Hafley Cabins. The two supporting Rebel regiments raced to form on the Sixteenth's left flank but found themselves primarily engaged in the woods opposing Starkweather's right-most regiments.[169] Savage's regiment absorbed the concentrated fire from Parsons' guns and Terrill's infantry only yards away.]

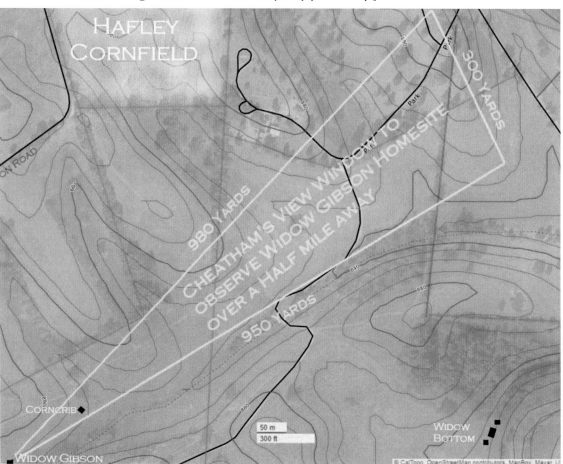

[Note the window of view that Cheatham would have had to Widow Gibson's was extremely small as well as the fact that the homesite was over three hundred yards behind Federal lines—not at them. In the next image, note the close proximity that Cheatham and Donelson would have to view the Hafley homesite and the large window of nearly 600 yards that they would have to view the enemy line "protected by a fence and some buildings" only a short distance to their front. These measurements were also taken using 3D line on Google Earth Pro as well.]

---

[169] Col. John C. Starkweather, Report of Battle of Perryville, *War of the Rebellion: Official Records of the Union and Confederate Armies*, Vol. 16, Pt. 1, p. 1155-6.

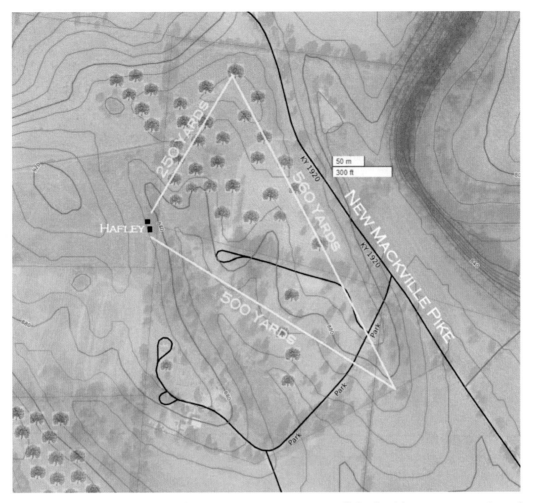

This daring and desperate charge however was not accomplished without most serious loss. Over one third of the men engaged were killed or wounded, among whom were some of the most valuable officers in the command. Col. Jno. H. Savage, commanding the 16th Tenn. Regiment, received a serious wound from a minnie ball in his left leg, and was painfully bruised by the fragment of a shell, and had his horse shot while gallantly leading his men against the enemy's lines.

[Clearly at this point of the battle, neither Maney's nor Stewart's brigades had entered the fight. Cheatham then described the addition of Maney's brigade to the fight.]

Just at this time Maney with his Brigade, which had been moved across the creek to my right, came forward in the woods from which the Enemy's skirmishers had been driven a few moments previously by a furious and gallant charge of Col. Wharton's Cavalry, and under shelter of a slight ridge, commenced forming his command for action, in two lines, three Regt.s in his front line, and two in his rear as a reserve. I here gave Genl. Maney orders to move rapidly through the woods and attack and carry a Battery of Eight Guns (12 lb Napoleons) of the Enemy, planted on an eminence in an open field some three hundred yards to the front and about one hundred yards beyond the edge of the woods, which was fiercely opposing my advance, and had almost destroyed Genl. Donelson's Command on my left.

[If Donelson's command had been almost destroyed by Parsons' battery, they would not be found at—or even near—Widow Gibson's cabin which was located no less than eight-hundred yards south and west of Parsons' position on Open Knob (nearly half a mile). Additionally, it is noted that Cheatham referred to Parsons' eight guns as "12 lb Napoleons." This is another indication that—even though written only forty-two days after the battle—Cheatham's testimony stands in question according to some historians' historical methodology. Using Noe's argument against Marcus Toney's testimony, Noe must believe that Cheatham cannot be referring to Parsons' battery either—due to incorrect identification of the guns. Federal Captain Percival Oldershaw stated in his report that the right guns of Parsons' battery had turned and opened on the initial rebel forces attacking his position at not more than ninety yards. That the fire had initially stymied the rebel attack, and that soon, they were confronted by another force that threatened their opposite flank. This is undeniably Maney's arrival.[170]]

Leaving a Staff Officer to form and bring up his reserve, Maney led forward his three Regts already in line, and here commenced one of the most desperate conflicts I have ever witnessed. The Battery's attention was immediately turned to meet this new attack, but notwithstanding, its heavy fire of shot and shell, our line pressed onward rapidly and in fine order, until it reached the fence which separated the woods and open field, in which the Battery was situated, here the entire Eight guns together with their strong support poured their fire with deadly and crushing effect full upon it. For a moment the line is staggered and halts. Maney's horse was knocked from under him, but passing along this line on foot, he urged and cheered his men forward, this was all that was needed, the gallant line responded with a cheer, and with desperate courage again rushed rapidly forward, silencing the Battery and driving the gunners from the pieces, but the danger and trial was not yet over, as the summit of the hill was approached, the Battery's support (a full brigade) sheltered measurably from sight and injury by the crest of the hill, delivered their fire with such deadly severity that the entire line was again checked, but kneeling and lying on the ground, responded with an incessant fire, preventing the Enemy from retaking his guns or using them upon us,— but the moment was indeed an anxious one, reduced and shattered by the terrible fire and conflict under which it had advanced, and fearfully outnumbered by veteran troops in advantageous position, it seemed that it could not be otherwise than that the noble line should be forced back in spite of all its daring courage and the gallant efforts which had been made to carry it forward. At this critical moment, the Battery of Capt. M. Smith (my Chief of Artillery) but under command of 1st Lieut. Wm. Turner, attached to Maney's Brigade, and which had fortunately been ordered to follow him, came up, and having myself discovered a point at the edge of the woods and field about two hundred yards to the right of the Enemy's left and somewhat on his flank, I instantly caused two 12 lb Howitzers to be placed in this position, under the superintendence of Capt. M. Smith, and opened a sudden and destructive fire upon the force supporting the Enemy's Battery, throwing it into confusion and literally cutting it to pieces. The Howitzers were served with great activity, and in a few moments their effect could be plainly seen in the broken and disordered condition of the Enemy's ranks. It was while he was being staggered by this galling flank fire of our Howitzers that Maney's line again moved forward, captured the Battery, and drove the Enemy in confusion from the field.

[The above description related the events unfolding as Maney led his brigade to the crest of Open Knob and seizure of Parsons' guns. As related by the participants of the Sixteenth Tennessee, this action took place in the first thirty to forty minutes of the engagement. Cheatham observed this action from the extreme right (or northern) edge of the rebel lines. In the following paragraph, Cheatham continues his description of the fight with the assault of the First Tennessee on Starkweather's Hill and the attempt to seize the guns of Bush's battery. He also mentioned the relief—not retreat—of Donelson's brigade.]

The Battery having fallen, I rode forward to order the reserve into action, and on reaching the fence, met Genl Maney returning from the hill top, over which his front line had just passed in the same mission. The first Regt was promptly placed in line a little to the right of the Battery just captured, and moved forward with direction to attack another Battery (Loomis') which about this time had opened on Maney's front line, and that of Gen. Stewart which had come up and relieved Gen. Donelson's Brigade, which latter I ordered to reform in a ravine about one hundred yards to the rear. The first Regt. crossed a piece of woods and continued its advance to a hill-top in a cornfield about five hundred yards beyond the Battery just captured, when it met the Enemy's third line, and charged his 2nd Battery, driving the men from their guns, but having not support was compelled to fall back to the foot of the hill, where it was reformed, advanced again, and a second time took possession of the Battery, but the Enemy, here his three

---

[170] Capt. Percival P. Oldershaw, Report of Battle of Perryville, *War of the Rebellion: Official Records of the Union and Confederate Armies*, Vol. 16, Pt. 1, p. 1059-62.

lines having been driven together, was too much odds, and it was compelled to fall back to the woods, two hundred yards when the 3ʳᵈ Brigade (Maney's) was reformed to protect my right, and remained until dark.

[The preceding paragraph related the attempts to seize the guns of Bush's battery and the twice capture of those guns; however, if Donelson's brigade and the Sixteenth Tennessee were still at Widow Gibson's as related by previous interpretations, Maney would still not have been abreast of the regiment. Bush's and Stone's guns were located nearly five-hundred yards north and slightly east of Widow Gibson's supposed cabin site. Additionally, Cheatham made it clear that Maney's brigade took no further part in the action that day and remained in place in the woods separating Starkweather's Heights and Open Knob.]

I must here say of Gen. Maney and his noble Brigade, that I have never seen a command more promptly engaged, or one which fought with more desperate determination. It has fallen to the lot of few if any of their numbers to render more signal service in any field, for the capture of the Battery was absolutely necessary to our success. The attack upon it was skillfully conducted, and the dashing, headlong courage on the part of the troops before which it fell, I do not believe could be excelled.

[At this point of Cheatham's report, he had to revert in time to the moment at which Parsons' battery fell in order to explain the exploits of Stewart's brigade. The following paragraph clearly explains that Stewart went into action immediately after the fall of Parsons' guns and that Donelson reformed in the ravine. Stewart continued in action eventually forcing back the Federals of Starkweather's brigade. If current interpretations are correct, this would have put **Stewart** abreast of Donelson's men at Widow Gibson's *instead of Maney*. That would be in direct conflict with current histories of the battle and primary sources in the Sixteenth Tennessee.]

Brig. Genl. Stewart with his veteran Brigade, many of whom had encountered the Enemy at Belmont & Shiloh, moved up on the left of Gen. Maney, and to the relief of Gen. Donelson at the point of time when Gen. Maney's front line had charged and captured the Eight gun Battery. The Regiment on the extreme right of Gen. Stewart's command, the 4ᵗʰ Tenn. Col. Strahl, the 5ᵗʰ Tenn. Col. Venable, the 24ᵗʰ Tenn. Col. Bratton, 33ʳᵈ Tenn. Col. Campbell, and 31ˢᵗ Tenn. Col. Jenkins, and entered the action in the order here named from right to left. They entered the fight under charge of their cool and valiant Leader, in admirable order, and pressed forward under a most galling fire, with a coolness and yet impetuosity that could not be surpassed, driving the Enemy before them until they reached the crest of a ridge, which terminated on the right in a cornfield, when they were compelled to halt and fall back to the foot of the ridge for want of ammunition.

[The next paragraph mentions the probable position of Captain Sam Harris' battery that would have confronted Stewart's left front after they forced Starkweather back. This account shows that Stewart's right fought on the same ground on which the First Tennessee fought for Bush's battery.]

The ground over which a large portion of this Brigade moved was covered with a dense forest, and filled with the Enemy's Sharpshooters, and the force encountered was a prolongation of the Enemy's second and third lines. It was also exposed to a terrific enfilading fire from a Battery of four guns on the left, which was afterwards captured. Notwithstanding the heavy odds against them, the brave men of this Brigade drove the Enemy steadily for three fourths of a mile, suffering a very heavy loss, but sustaining the reputation and adding to the laurels that its men and its General had achieved on other fields. The 4ᵗʰ Tennessee Regiment, Col. Strahl, who was on the right of Genl. Stewart's Brigade, fought through the same field with the 1ˢᵗ Tennessee Regiment—of which mention has heretofore been made, and captured a gun which had been withdrawn from the Battery of Napoleon pieces, making the eighth gun of the magnificent Battery, the other seven having been captured by Gen. Maney's Brigade.

[In the following paragraph, Cheatham changed his chronology of events—reverting to before the capture of Starkweather's Heights. He mentions the artillery fire of Carnes' battery forcing the eventual retreat of Starkweather in combination with Stewart's attack.]

The Battery of Capt. Carnes which opened the engagement on our right, after being relieved by Capt. Stanford's rifled Battery, reported to me at about half past three O'Clock, accompanied by the 8ᵗʰ and 51ˢᵗ Tennessee Regiments of Gen. Donelson's Brigade. I ordered Capt. Carnes to place his Battery in position at a point which had been selected by Maj. Martin of Genl. Donelson's staff and Col. Wharton of the Texas Rangers, and directed the two Infantry Regiments to form on it as a supporting force, the position chosen was on an elevation beyond and nearly in line with the left flank of the Enemy. The Battery having been placed in position opened a spirited enfilading fire upon the Enemy's left flank with shell and canister, causing his left to give way and take shelter behind a ridge, and causing the withdrawal of Loomis' Battery, which had twice been captured by our brave troops.

[According to Cheatham, the preceding events began around 3:30 p.m. In the following paragraph, he explained that at approximately 5:45 Donelson's brigade—now joined by the Eighth and Fifty-first Tennessee regiments—again advanced on the left of and over the ground that Stewart had just crossed. This final attack is probably the one that helped capture Harris' battery in conjunction with Wood's attack on their left.]

About half an hour by sun, the 8th Tenn. Regiment, Col. Moore, and 51st Tenn. Regiment, Col. Chester, having rejoined Gen. Donelson, they were by him moved forward, together with the 38th Tenn. Col. Carter, accompanied by Maj. Genl. Polk, to the relief of Brig. Gen. Stewart, and fought and drove the Enemy in front of and on the same ground passed over previously by the first and second Brigades, although the Enemy had been heavily reinforced here, he was driven by this attack more than a mile from his line, suffering terrible slaughter, and was finally routed and driven from the field, and this advanced position was held by our troops until half past two O'clock on the morning of the 9th, at which time it was ordered to withdraw from the field and move my Division to the Harrodsburg road.

[It's likely that during this advance, General Webster was mortally wounded and resulted in the falling back of his brigade. Reports of his regiments suggest that the brigade didn't actually break, but were ordered to fall back due to the withdrawal of Starkweather on their left and the heavy attacks causing the withdrawal of Harris' brigade on their right.]

Brigadier General Daniel S. Donelson's report was written on October 26, 1862 at Knoxville, Tennessee. Just as in the case of Cheatham's report, the chronology of the text is undisturbed. Only the end of the report has been edited out for space. His report is full of run-on sentences, absence of punctuation and numerous grammatical errors. This report supports Cheatham's in substance and sheds even greater light on the experiences of his brigade. *Brackets and italics* are used to identify errors in the text and relate the narrative to the battlefield.

BRIG. GEN. DANIEL S. DONELSON'S REPORT[171]

In compliance with orders I have the honor of submitting the following report of the participation of my command in the 1st Brigade, 1st Divn Rt Wg Army of the Miss in the engagement against the Enemy at Perryville Ky on the 8th Inst. About light my command was drawn up in line of battle South of Perryville and remained in this position until about 9 o'clock when I was ordered with it to the extreme right – supposed to be about two miles north of Perryville and ½ mile west *[east]* of Chaplin Creek. I should here state that my Command consisted of the 16th, 38th and 15th Tenn Regts the 8th - 51st Tenn Regt and Capt Carnes Battery having been detached as I understand by order of Genl Bragg to fill up a gap in Genl Hardee line at this point.

This 2nd position was occupied for more than an hour under a constant firing of the Enemy's Battery, in position about a mile distant. From this point I was ordered to move my command forward and take position on the right of Genl Hardee's command. This order was promptly executed. Remaining in this position ~~for more than an~~ *[this was struck through]* about ½ an hour, I dispatched my A A Genl to get if possible the 8th and 51st Tenn to the Brigade. He soon reported that he had obtained Genls Cheatham, Polk and Bragg's consent to do so, and he was sent after them just as the order was given to move rapidly in the direction of the Enemy.

[Although Donelson sent his AAG to bring the Eighth and Fifty-first regiments back to the brigade, they were not returned until much later in the afternoon. The brigade moved through the fields west of the Walker House and down to Chaplin River.]

On reaching the Creek having passed over stone walls I was directed to form a line of Battle immediately on a bluff on the west creek *[sic]* of Chaplin's Creek. This position was taken with some difficulty owing to the impracticability of ascending the Bluff in line of battle. The movement however was accomplished with great promptness and the line formed in an open field just at this time the order was received to move forward and attack the Enemy. For the execution of this order proceeding in the direction of the Enemy. *[copied verbatim]*

[In the following paragraph, Donelson describes the advance of his brigade. He admits that he did not have the proper direction when he ordered the advance. An enemy battery further to his right had opened fire on his command. He then directs the change of direction further to the right.]

In the execution of this order proceeding in the direction of the Enemy battery, I soon ascertained from the fire of another Battery of the Enemy's further on our right that I did not have the proper direction. I accordingly gave orders for a change of direction further to the right, in making this move I sent forward a staff officer to order Col Savage Comdg Regt on the right to halt when in the proper direction, until I could bring up the other two Regts in line of battle.

[As noted earlier—the preceding sentence gave two "orders" to Colonel Savage. The first order was to change direction and the second order was to wait for the Fifteenth and Thirty-eighth regiments to close up on his line. It is now clear that it was the second order that Savage did not obey. The Sixteenth Tennessee is identified as the right most regiment in the brigade.]

This order was not obeyed because as I have since learned one of Genl Cheatham's Staff ordered said Regts to move forward rapidly. The consequence was when this Regt came within range of the Enemy's

---

[171] Brig. Gen. D. S. Donelson, *Report of Battle of Perryville* (William P. Palmer Collection, WRHS Collection, Box 28, Folder 9)

small arms, they received the first shock of the Enemy's fire. The other two Regts ~~came within range~~ the 38th and 15th came as rapidly as possible.

[As noted above, the Sixteenth advanced rapidly toward the battery and was the first Rebel regiment to become engaged with the Federal's main line. This initial line is now recognized to be at the cornfield and Hafley Cabins on the southeastern slope of Open Knob where Parsons' battery was still being deployed. The 123rd Illinois had just reached the field at nearly the same time the Sixteenth Tennessee was arriving near the knob. The extreme right of Starkweather's brigade engaged the Fifteenth and Thirty-eighth regiments as they belatedly swung into position on the Sixteenth's left flank.]

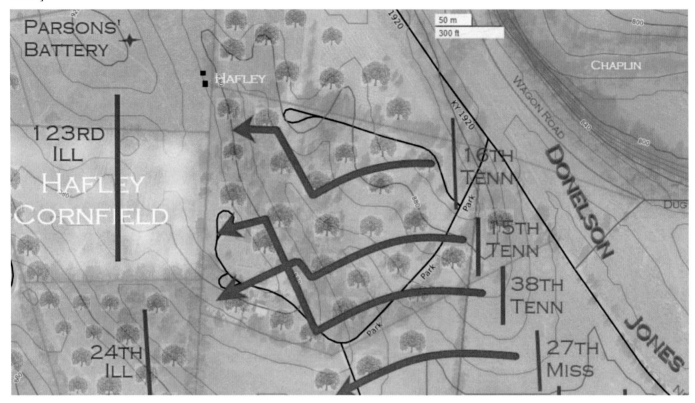

The Enemy was near a small farm House and Cornfield from which point they opened fire upon the 16th Tenn Regt and upon the other two Regts as they came into line on the left. The fight here was obstinate and warmly contested. Col. Savage received a flesh wound in his leg and an injury to his back.

It is proper that I state that in making through the open field for more than ½ mile the Brigade was subjected to the cross firing of two of the Enemy's Batteries killing and wounding several although shot and shell fell in profusion there was no faltering on the part of men or officers. The three Regts moving forward at a double quick step amid yells and cheers at every step.

[As noted above, the brigade was fired on by at least two batteries. In the current interpretations, these batteries were thought to be Simonson's and Parsons' guns. It is highly unlikely that Simonson's guns were turned to engage an enemy that was fully 80° to the *left* of their "front." Simonson's battery had extensive Rebel lines advancing at a distance in its front fully visible at that time. It is more probable that Simonson was engaging either enemy batteries in his front or the enemy infantry lines advancing in the distance in his direct front. Although we know Parsons was the "right" battery that confronted the Rebels, it may never be determined which was the battery on the left that was cross firing on the brigade— although existing evidence supports that it was most likely Stone's battery.

The following lines explain that the initial contact that was made was at the Hafley Cabins and eastern most fringes of the cornfield. Donelson makes it clear that the battery was in exceptionally close proximity of the house.]

The charge was made at a House and small cornfield some 100 yards from the Enemy's Battery. There *[their]* infantry soon fell back to the battery the command following in hot pursuit. At this point the Cornfield was exceedingly hot and obstinately contested.

[Note that Donelson mentions the enemy's "battery." His next lines will still be in reference to the same battery. While Donelson's report lacks detail regarding the initial combat at the Hafley cabin and edge of the cornfield, Savage's report and other eyewitness testimony give a clearer picture of the combat there. Clearly, the combat was fierce and short lived at this point. Next, Donelson describes the arrival of Maney's brigade on his immediate right.]

At his critical moment the 3rd Brigade came to the rescue. The contest for the battery lasted but a short time causing great loss of life on both sides before the Enemy retreated leaving the field and battery in our possession.

[Donelson's own words make it clear that the initial combat conducted by his brigade "lasted but a short time… before the enemy retreated leaving *the battery* in our possession." Contrary to historians suggesting that Donelson's brigade retreated to "almost its starting point," Donelson makes no mention of a withdrawal. This is hard evidence that the battery that fell into Rebel hands was Parsons' guns which were only yards from the right flank of the Sixteenth Tennessee. The third brigade was in fact commanded by Maney. Other testimony shows that Donelson's brigade and the Sixteenth Tennessee were engaged for about thirty minutes when Maney's brigade arrived and helped to seize Parsons' battery.]

The enemy retreated to the next hill when he made an obstinate stand. At this opportune moment Genl Stewart Comdg 2nd Brigade until now not in the fight, came to the rescue, causing the Enemy still to retreat further. All our forces being now in the fight, and the major part for an unusual time showed exhaustation *[exhaustion]*.

[In the above text, Donelson related the "obstinate stand" made by Starkweather and his batteries. It was described in detail by General Cheatham. He also relates the committal of Stewart's brigade and recommitted his own brigade in the fight. In the following lines, Donelson relates that when the forces under Starkweather finally retreated on the Rebel right, firing slackened and the fight on the right took pause.]

The consequence was a general falling back to the rear took place, and for a time the almost cessation of infantry firing. When the fact was reported of the want of ammunition not knowing where the supply had been placed, I directed the men to get their supplies as far as practicable from the cartridge boxes of the wounded and dead men. This done I sent two of my aids in search of and if possible to bring up the two detached Regts the 8th and 51st fortunately I afterward learned Genl Polk had ordered them forward. My Aids met and conducted them double quick time placing these two Regts in line and gathering up the fragments of other Regts and putting them also in line the order for a forward movement upon the Enemy was given and with yells and cheers most promptly obeyed.

[With the two fresh regiments returned to his brigade, Donelson then conducted his last attack—that Cheatham related to have taken place around 5:45 p.m. In the following lines, Donelson describes the Federals moving a force forward—in all likelihood—to retake Harris' battery that had just been captured by Wood's brigade. The Federal forces had consolidated and were attempting a counter-attack. It is highly probable that during this advance Lt. Col. Moore was found and captured by the Sixteenth Tennessee.]

I would here remark that the Enemy were at this time making a forward movement in the direction of the captured Battery evidently with a view to retake. The Command moved rapidly coming in range of the Enemy the firing commenced moving forward all the time. The Enemy gave way in a short time to what I supposed to be their ~~third~~ *[struck through]* 2nd line of battle. They were driven back with great slaughter for more than a mile. The evidence were *[sic]* to plainly be seen to admit of any mistake, that we had committed sad havoc in killing and wounding large numbers.

The fight lasted till sometime after dark say near 8 o'clock when there was a cessation on either side. This last line of battle moved forward about ½ hour by sun, the effects and consequences resulting there-from were most fortunate and most gallantly performed. Officer and men performed their parts nobly. Too much credit cannot be given them. The firing having ceased at the time mentioned, my command occupied the field of battle until order to retire about 2 o'clock on the morning of the 9th inst. I bivouacked on the ground in person had fifty men detailed in bringing forward and taking care of the wounded.

Brigadier General George Maney wrote his report from camp near Knoxville on October 29, 1862. His report supports the testimony given by both Cheatham and Donelson. Maney's report contributes hard evidence that his brigade came to the assistance of Donelson's brigade within a short time of the engagement's commencement. The very beginning and end of his report has been edited out. The end of Maney's report is comprised of commendations of his subordinate officers and tally of casualties in his brigade. This portion of his report begins with his brigade on the east bank of Chaplin River.

BRIG. GEN. GEORGE MANEY'S REPORT.[172]

The opposite bank of this creek directly in front of our approach was a precipitous bluff from twenty to forty feet high, the ground beyond it woodland, not more than ordinarily undulating and extending forward to open fields. To ascend the bluff directly in front in anything like order would have been impossible, and in approaching it I was instructed by staff officers of both Major-Generals Polk and Cheatham to move my command by the right flank past the creek by a crossing at the lower point of the bluff and take possession of the woods in the highlands beyond. This crossing was perfectly practicable for a movement by the flank, but the general ruggedness and irregularity of the ground on either side rendered the passage impracticable to any extended front of line, and in a strong degree imparted to it the character of a defile.

[Maney's Brigade did not climb the embankment, but crossed Chaplin River on the north side of Walker's Bend which had a much easier ascent.]

About the same time I commenced my movement by the flank a gallant dash was made by COL. Wharton's cavalry command through the woods to which I had been directed, and while this was going on I received orders from Major-General Cheatham in substance as follows: 'To advance as rapidly as practicable through the woods toward the enemy; attack, drive, and press him.' There had been considerable firing, but the movement of our cavalry appeared a success in clearing the woods, and deeming it important to appropriate the advantage of any confusion which might exist with the enemy, in consequence, I pressed on with all rapidity practicable, turning to the left after crossing the creek bed and following the sound of the action. In passing through the wood, I encountered much of our cavalry, which had been engaged in the dash just made, and knowing that when deployed my command was to constitute the extreme right of our infantry line, and being unable at the moment to find the commanding officer, I instructed the cavalry whether in squads or companies to pass rapidly to the right, so as not to enfilade my infantry movement, and to take position for the protection of my right flank. Meeting COL. Wharton a few moments afterwards, I mentioned my action and wishes with respect to his cavalry and requested his personal efforts in carrying them out, which was promptly given. During my movement by the flank, to avoid delay so far as possible, my staff were kept almost constantly passing to the rear to deliver necessary orders and keep the command closed up. My own time was occupied in directing the cavalry to my right and examining the ground forward with the view of advantageous movement.

After proceeding several hundred yards through the woods in the course I had first taken, I was informed General Donelson had become hotly engaged and was in great need of reinforcements. The action seemed but a short distance to my front and appeared to be fiercely waged, both with infantry and artillery.

[At this point, Maney's statements clearly reflect that his brigade had not been in action as of yet. He was informed that Donelson's brigade was heavily engaged and required his support. From Maney's perspective, this fight was taking place "but a short distance" to his front and being "fiercely waged, both with infantry and artillery." The only enemy force in Maney's front at that time was Terrill's brigade and Parsons' battery on Open Knob. Clearly, this is indicative that the same force in his front was confronting Donelson's right flank—only a short distance ahead.]

---

[172] Brig. Gen. George Maney, *Supplement to the Official Records of the Union and Confederate Armies*, Part 3, Vol. 2, Broadfoot Publishing Co., Wilmington, NC, p. 667.

A depression in the ground, protected in front by a slight ridge and extending some distance to my right, afforded shelter for and favored the convenient formation of line of battle by filing to the right, halting and fronting when proper space was attained. My line was here and by this movement commenced, and in a few moments I ascertained by a personal reconnaissance the position of the enemy. Facing my approach and slightly to the right of General Donelson's command was a strong battery placed on a hilltop in an open field and less than 120 yards from the nearest edge of the woods, in which I was. The battery was actively engaged, partly on Donelson's command at short range and partly in firing into the woods through which I was approaching. General Stewart's Brigade, which was to form between General Donelson's and mine, had not yet arrived, but my instructions as well as the immediate assistance needed by General Donelson's command committed me to engagement without delay and my preparations to attack the battery were made forthwith.

[As Maney explained, he had yet to make contact with infantry but had formed his lines and personally observed the battery in his front engaging Donelson's brigade at short range. Canister shot was most effective at ranges under 400 yards. Maney clearly states that his position was just over 100 yards from the enemy battery. He also notes that the battery was only "slightly to the right" of Donelson's command. This implies that Donelson's right flank—the Sixteenth Tennessee—was even nearer the battery than Maney's own force was. This also coincides with members of the Sixteenth Tennessee that state that they were within forty or fifty yards of a battery on their right flank. About half of the guns were turned on Maney's force as they were observed moving into position in the tree line.]

Colonels McDaniels, Porter's and Buford's Regiments were fronted into line for the immediate attacking force (these constituting as much front as could be brought to bear advantageously against the battery) and a staff officer sent back to direct Colonels Frierson and Field, so as to form in rear of and as a supporting line to the three first regiments. These arrangements being made without waiting for the supporting line to get into position, I commenced the advance of the attacking line, directing it so as to reach the open field at the nearest point to the battery. From the nature of the ground the right of my line first emerged from the shelter of the ridge under which it had been formed, and immediately the enemy's fire was opened upon it. Steadily and rapidly, however, the advance was continued to the fence dividing the woodland from the field, about an average of 120 yards from the battery. Here the enemy's battery of eight guns, six of which were 12-pound Napoleons, together with his entire infantry support concentrated a most terrific and deadly fire upon it. For a moment the line seemed to halt, before uncovering in the open field in front and instantly at the halt commenced firing. This was unfavorable; the enemy's battery together with his entire infantry force (a full brigade) were pouring destruction upon us, casting more shots and to better advantage than ourselves.

[From Maney's statements above, it is clear that the Sixteenth Tennessee had been hit so hard and suffered so terribly, that the enemy battery and its support was able to turn much of its fire on Maney's command at the fence. Next, Maney describes—at length—the attack on the battery by his command. It was when Maney's men reached the aforesaid fence that Colonel Savage and members of his regiment relate that Maney had come to their support.]

Our only chance of success was to move rapidly forward, carry the battery, and break and drive the support. I was at the moment on the extreme right of my line and became dismounted by the falling of my horse, and as an additional embarrassment, my entire staff had been sent to deliver necessary orders to other portions of the command. Passing, however, down the line with as much rapidity as possible on foot, I urged it forward, and aided by the gallantry of its officers and courage of the men, by the time I passed the Sixth Tennessee Regiment, the center of my attacking line had succeeded in having the charge resumed rapidly and with spirit. The brave men seemed only to need know what was desired, and though many had fallen during the unfortunate short halt at the fence, the survivors dashed forward, seemingly reckless of the danger and death before them. Continuing to advance with my front line until its forward move had been well and spiritedly re-established and the guns bearing on it silenced and abandoned by the gunners, and believing it would then certainly go directly over the battery, I turned to remount myself and look after the second line, which I deemed by this time would have arrived. I succeeded in remounting almost instantly, and just then the First Tennessee Regiment (Colonel Field's) came up, advancing under cover of the woods but near to the open field.   At the same moment looking forward I observed to my great surprise and anxiety my front line halted about 100 yards in advance of me and within perhaps forty yards of the battery lying on the ground and hotly engaged in firing against the enemy's battery support which was protected by the crest of the hill, *[where]* the battery had been, and my front line covered it entirely and by active firing prevented the guns being used against us.   But the line, to the extent of my ability, had been impressively instructed, both in its officers and collectively, never to halt until the battery was taken, and though much weakened by the destructive fire it had suffered, I knew it was an instant before dashing forward with all the impetuosity and speed possible.   The halt under these circumstances gave the greatest anxiety, lest the line had been checked by opposition in the battery support, over which it was not possible to pass it in its then shattered condition, and by which it must be soon if not instantly forced back in spite of all its determined courage and every effort that could be made to prevent it.   The enemy in front greatly outnumbered my command, besides his battery; to recoil before such a force unless promptly covered and redeemed was ruin.   To renew the front line's forward movements, it was first necessary to get it up from the ground and establish concert for its advance.   I was not certain that all my efforts could accomplish this, but it was certain that instantaneous preparation of my reserve was imperatively necessary, not only to cover and protect the first line until it could be rallied in case of its recoil, the danger of which at the moment seemed imminent, but also for an immediate second effort against the battery, for from the character of the ground behind us it could not be repulsed under a pressure without most ruinous loss, if not utter destruction.   To hold the field the capture *[of]* the battery was a necessity, and at the moment appeared strongly probably would be the task of the second line.   My knowledge of the field, the location of the enemy, the disposition of our own troops, and, to an extent, our plan of action was necessary for advantageous management of my reserve and rendered my personal presence with it indispensable until my information and instructions on the particulars could be imparted, for should the line in front be borne back and the second become involved in confusion with it for want of proper instruction and preparation, I all without having first engaged and applied all my force.   But whilst the preparation of the reserve was so essentially necessary, it was also important to omit no chance of moving forward the front line, and to neglect this until I could instruct and prepare the reserve might lose the last moment at which it could be advanced and perhaps allow it to recoil before the reserve was prepared to relieve it.   It was an emergency requiring the instantaneous press of every effort and demanding action of both my lines at the same moment.

As yet no staff officer had joined me, but Colonel Field and Lieutenant-Colonel Patterson both being near with a view of omitting no chance of a success, which was vital in importance to us, I deemed it proper to detach Colonel Field temporarily from his command and direct him to bear my orders to the regimental commanders in front to make concerted and all possible effort to carry their line over the hilltop and break the enemy before them, himself to take charge of the line for this purpose.   Whilst I prepared the troops in reserve to relieve it in case of the recoil, I must add at the time of this detachment I was informed that Colonel McDaniel, senior colonel on the front line, had fallen, and knew that the line had lost the good influence of many others of its officers; moreover I had confidence in Lieutenant-Colonel Patterson for the position the detachment devolved upon him.   The information of Colonel McDaniel's loss, though inaccurate at the time, was sadly realized a few moments later.   Colonel Field dashed promptly to the duty assigned him and unwaveringly, amidst its dangers, urged its forward movement.   Lieutenant-Colonel Patterson then in command of the First Regiment by reason of Colonel Field's temporary detachment, my adjutant-general, Captain Malone, joined me, and I sent him to reiterate and urge the order to advance.   Colonel Patterson's attention was directed to the protection of the left flank of the front line against any attempt by the enemy there, General Donelson's line having been too much weakened to secure this by advancing in line with it.

[Again, it is clear by Maney's statement that he was about to forcefully seize the guns of Parsons' battery. He had just instructed Lt. Col. Patterson to have the First Tennessee support his left flank during this effort. This was essential due to the slaughter that had been inflicted on the right of Donelson's brigade—namely the Sixteenth Tennessee. This statement verifies that he had come abreast of Donelson's right flank at that point—prior to the seizure of Parsons' guns. It was at this point that Marcus Toney of the First Tennessee—whose account has already been included—declared that "we charged the Ohio brigade with Colonel Savage of the Sixteenth Tennessee."]

But my main instruction was, in case the front line should give way, to advance his command instantly and rapidly by the right of companies to the front, allow the front line by this movement to pass to the rear, bring his command by companies into line, and immediately charge the battery. I then moved to the right to give like instructions to the Twenty-seventh Regiment. The line in front still holding its positions, now about eighty yards in advance of me and loading and firing from the ground, it seemed impossible in the noise and roar of the action to get it to cease firing and move forward, even with all the gallant exertions I knew were being made for that purpose.

The Twenty-seventh Regiment, by my orders, should have been in line directly on the right of the First Regiment, but through a misunderstanding it had, in coming up to the open field, moved directly forward in the battery, effecting its bodyment in the front line in the thinned ranks of the Sixth Tennessee and Forty-first Georgia, both of which had suffered severely by the destructive fire at the fence. Immediately on learning the Twenty-seventh Regiment was forward I turned to follow it, and at that instant my front line resumed forward movement and pressed over the hill, placing the battery behind it. Moving directly to the hilltop I found, though much broken, my front line was still advancing, fighting with spirit, and the enemy retiring in disorder before it. My conclusion at this moment was the enemy's entire force at hand had been concentrated for the protection of the battery from which he had just been driven, and that vigorous pressing even with one strong and spirited regiment might do much toward his rout. Hastening back to the First Regiment for the purpose of advancing it, I met Lieutenant-Colonel Patterson, who informed me that General Polk had just ordered him forward to take a second battery which showed itself slightly to the right and on a ridge some 500 or 600 yards beyond the one just captured.

[Again, it is evident from Maney's report—as well as Cheatham's—that his brigade had come abreast of Donelson's brigade *before* seizing Parsons' guns. The First Tennessee would now be used to assault Bush's guns on Starkweather's Heights four-hundred yards to their front (or west). Cheatham's report clearly stated that when Parsons' battery fell, he had Donelson reform his brigade in a ravine while Stewart's line advanced as is noted below.]

About the same time this order was reiterated to me by Major-General Cheatham in person, and at the same instant I saw General Stewart's line but a short distance off, coming eagerly forward through the woods, and this strengthened my confidence that the disordered condition of the enemy might be turned to a rout. With these impressions Colonel Patterson was ordered to move by the right flank so as to clear the line in front and then forward, pressing whatever force he encountered. I now moved toward that part of my command which had taken the first battery; it was greatly disordered, but I did not deem it proper to attempt any disengagement at that moment, thinking it might be of some advantage to our fresh troops to keep up the fight as it was and trusting General Stewart's Brigade and my one fresh regiment would in a very short time break and rout the enemy in front, when I would reform the line of regiments first engaged.

The First Tennessee went forward most gallantly and in perfect order, and on reaching the top of the hill next beyond the battery which had been taken a distance as stated of about 500 or 600 hundred yards, encountered immensely superior numbers of the enemy supporting the battery upon which it had been directed. Bravely as ever men fought they rushed upon the foe. His battery was silenced and the ground covered with his dead, but the odds against them were great and after a short but severe and bloody onset in which the gallant Lieutenant-Colonel Patterson and others of the best officers and men of the regiment were lost, it fell back under shelter of the hillside. Meeting the regiment returning from the hilltop, I called on it to reform for another effort. It reformed promptly and with spirit under Colonel Field, who had meantime been directed to return to his regiment and was again moved forward in order to join in the press, which I still trusted would be successfully made by General Stewart's fresh brigade, immediately to my left.   I then commenced reforming the remnants of my remaining regiments where I stood. Advancing again to the hilltop the First renewed the attack upon the immensely superior numbers there fighting with the desperation inspired by the memory of invaded and outraged homes. Numbers could not resist its valor and deadly volleys, and the enemy in front was broken and driven before them, but advance was checked by a heavy and deadly flank fire from the left. The gallant Field looking towards his flank saw the flag of a regiment which had become detached from General Hardee's wing and found its way toward the right, advancing in the direction to relieve his left, and still obstinately held his ground cheering his command with the assurance that the enemy on the flank would be soon dislodged by our troops to the left.[173]   This hope, however, was disappointed; the regiment bearing the flag was forced back and again the fire from the flank renewed, raked by the destructive fire from the left and opposed in front by many times its numbers.   It was sheer madness to attempt to advance further or hold longer the exposed position, and the regiment after perhaps one of the bloodiest and fiercest contests of the war for the numbers engaged was compelled to fall back, which it did in good order, not from the opposition in its front, but because our line to the left was not advanced sufficiently to protect the flank in that direction.

Just before the return of Colonel Field, having learned that General Stewart's Brigade had encountered a severe contest in the woods to my left with an enemy perhaps in larger force than in my immediate front and had not been able to advance so far forward as mine on the right, thus exposing my command to flank fire, I determined to hold my line in prolongation of his.   The First Regiment was joined to the line which I was then forming, and immediately afterwards, I was ordered to retire behind the hill to my rear, there to form line with General Stewart's and General Donelson's Brigades and await orders for further movements.   I did so and this ended my engagement, for when I advanced again I kept on line with our forces to my left and no enemy troubled me in front.

[The above statement by Maney indicates that after the attempts to seize the guns of Bush's battery, he reformed his lines with Stewart on his left—followed by Donelson's brigade. This was the original intended formation of the forces as indicated earlier in Maney's report. As Maney stated, his brigade line moved forward again later, but he had no opposition. In the later advance, Stewart's brigade confronted the remnants of Starkweather after his withdrawal, while Donelson advanced on Stewart's left and engaged portions of Webster's brigade.]

My wounded were brought from the field that night and placed in hospital.   I bivouacked on the battlefield—my advance picket covering it until 2 o'clock next morning, when I was ordered off preparatory to withdrawing to Harrodsburg.   In the capture of the enemy's front battery, which I think may justly be considered one of the most desperate undertakings ending in perfect success of the war, my battery, under Lieutenant Turner, bore a highly useful part—such was the enemy's advantage in position and numbers that all the efforts of as brave a line as ever fought might have failed against him but for its timely assistance.   As soon as I found the ground across the creek practicable for its passage and use, I sent an order for it to follow me and coming forward during the heat of my engagement by direction of Major-General Cheatham at the critical time my first line was halted before the enemy's first battery. Lieutenant Turner was placed in position to enfilade the enemy's infantry support, and the next moment two 12-pound howitzers efficiently served and at short range were sending death and disorder into this force which held us in check.   Torn in flank by our shot and shell and pressed with a desperate and reckless courage on the part of the entire line in front which could not be surpassed, the enemy, nearly three times our numbers, yielded and broke in confusion the line in his front, rushing forward at the same time and delivering its volleys with the most destructive and deadly effect upon his disordered masses. My highest commendation is due to Lieutenant Turner and his efficient officers and men. The captured battery was moved from the field, and finding a supply of ammunition two of the Napoleon pieces were substituted for our two 6-pounders.   It was perhaps mainly due to the enemy's terror of the desperate

---

[173] This was probably the 24th Tennessee which was in Stewart's brigade. They had transferred from Cleburne's brigade only three months earlier and were still carrying their Hardee corps flag. It is also known that the 24th Tennessee was in the center of Stewart's line and its approach would have taken it directly toward the 79th Pennsylvania. This would have placed it on the First Tennessee's left flank.

courage and fighting of our troops engaged that we withdrew from the field at our own time in the face of his immensely larger numbers without in the least being troubled or embarrassed by him.

Colonel John H. Savage wrote his report of the battle in the weeks following the campaign, but the original was apparently lost or misplaced in its ascent to the war department—as was the case with so many reports. Savage's commentary and "report" of the battle come from his autobiography—*Life of John H. Savage*—published in 1903. Much of it was probably taken from a copy of his original report that he had kept for his own records. At that time, Savage was unaware that Cheatham, Donelson and Maney had—in fact—prepared and submitted reports of the battle that had not been included in the Official Records. This account is exceptionally long.

COLONEL JOHN H. SAVAGE'S ACCOUNT.[174]

As a prelude to my report of the battle of Perryville, I will state a few facts, as follows:

Under the orders of Cheatham and Donelson the Sixteenth Regiment charged a battery in front of the main line of the Yankee army, solitary and alone, without any Confederate force in sight. The battery fired upon the regiment, enfilading it—killing a captain, a lieutenant, and many privates, and sending a grape shot through the head of the horse that Savage was riding.

Savage dismounted, took a six-shooting Remington pistol from the holster, and to escape the fire of the battery ordered the regiment forward. At a distance of about forty yards in a beech forest he was fired on by the main line of the Yankee army, formed behind a rail fence. He charged with the regiment, emptying his pistol, and the regiment made three charges upon the Yankees behind the fence before they fled. The battery at which Major-general Jackson was killed was firing on the regiment at short range, say forty yards. There were two cabins near the battery; after emptying his pistol, Savage got between them and would watch the gunner ram home the charge, and then say, "Lie low boys, he is going to fire." While performing this service a minie ball passed through his leg; the wood off a canister shot struck the cabin, rebounded and knocked Savage down, paralyzing him for an hour. He directed Colonel Donelson to take charge of the regiment and the battery at which Major-general Jackson was killed, as, he, Savage, was unfit for service. He was hauled back to Tennessee in an ambulance. He was on crutches from that time until a few days before the battle of Murfreesboro.

[The above prelude to his report of the battle is a much more concise summary than his later narrative gives. The unit was struck by a sudden blast of canister from an enemy battery. They advanced rapidly to try to pass the field of fire of the guns but were struck by the enemy's main line of battle behind a rail fence. They conducted three charges to seize the fence and Hafley cabins. He was aware that General Jackson was killed at this location. As Maney's brigade charged, his regiment made one last effort, and he ordered Lt. Colonel Donnell to take charge.

Following his preface, Savage began accusations against Cheatham and Donelson for what he believed was their failure to prepare and submit reports of the battle to the war department.]

Looking to the "War of the Rebellion" and finding a blank space left for Cheatham's report and no report appearing, knowing that Governor Porter had been upon Cheatham's staff, he wrote him to know why no report was made by Cheatham of the battle of Perryville. Governor Porter in reply, in a letter dated June 18, 1900, wrote as follows: "Perryville was a splendid fight and I will never cease to regret that the men who made it made no report." Cheatham did not want to put all he knew in an official report. Porter makes a very poor excuse for his commander. The soldiers will never cease to regret that he did not let everybody know what important military secret Cheatham desired to conceal.

In the eighth volume of "Confederate Military History," page 52, it is written: "Donelson's brigade sustained a loss of three hundred and forty-seven, killed and wounded, the Sixteenth, under Colonel Savage, losing one hundred and ninety-nine men, more than half the casualties of the brigade." The total loss of Bragg's army was three thousand, two hundred and twelve. It is estimated that Cheatham's division (most all Tennesseans) lost one thousand, two hundred and sixty-two.

---

[174] John H. Savage, *Life of John H. Savage*, Nashville, TN, 1903, p. 116-24.

I think it due to the men of the Sixteenth Regiment and to the Tennesseans who were in Cheatham's division, who now sleep in unmarked graves upon the hills of Chaplain's Creek where the battle of Perryville was fought, to do for them what Cheatham and Donelson, for some unknown cause, failed to do, regardless of their duty as commanders of brave and patriotic men.

[As Savage was unaware that his commanders actually had submitted reports, he believed something was being covered up. Savage's report set out to accomplish two things. First, he intended to prove that his regiment was responsible for the capture of Parsons' battery—though he failed to ever mention it by name. Second, he intended to place the blame of the high casualties suffered by his regiment on the shoulders of both Donelson and Cheatham.]

BATTLE OF PERRYVILLE.

Inasmuch as no reports by General Maney, General Donelson and Major-General Cheatham can be found in the records of the War of Rebellion, or elsewhere, I propose to make a report of this battle in accordance with the facts within my knowledge, and also of the acts and conduct of the Sixteenth Regiment under the orders of Brigadier General Donelson and Major-General Cheatham, so as to correct errors made by those persons who have attempted to write history.

My experience in political contests and in war satisfies me that there is less reliance and less regard for truth in the reports of military officers in regard to campaigns and battles than there is in the reports of parties and leaders in political contests, for the reason that the falsehood or lie of the party leader can be contradicted immediately, whereas the error or falsehood of the military officer cannot be contradicted until after the war is ended. Lord Byron wrote: "Truth is often more strange than fiction itself."

Many strange questions are presented in reference to the conduct of Generals Cheatham and Donelson before the battle, at the battle and after the battle. In the eighth volume of a publication called "Confederate Military History," purporting to give an account of the battle of Perryville, it is written: "General Polk being in immediate command of the army until the arrival of General Bragg, General Cheatham was in command of the right wing, Brigadier-General Daniel S. Donelson taking temporary command of his division." There is no truth in this statement as will be shown hereafter. It was further written: "Cheatham's division was almost exclusively Tennesseans, the First Brigade, Donelson's, being temporarily commanded by Colonel John H. Savage." There is no truth in this statement. Savage never had command of Donelson's brigade for a moment at the battle of Perryville. These false statements as made shift the responsibility for the loss of one hundred and ninety-nine soldiers of the Sixteenth Regiment, from Cheatham's and Donelson's shoulders so as to wrongfully charge it on Colonel Savage, all of which will appear hereafter.

It appears in said volume, page 52, that the Sixteenth, under Colonel Savage lost one hundred and ninety-nine men, more than one-half of the casualties of the brigade, and that among the killed was Captain J. B. Vance. This is an error. It was Captain J. G. Lambert who was killed.

[Captain J. B. Vance was not killed, but he was mortally wounded. Captain Lamberth was killed. This was just another opportunity for Savage—the lawyer—to argue.]

Bragg's total loss in this battle was three thousand two hundred and twelve, of which Cheatham's division lost one thousand two hundred and sixty-two, as estimated. No reports are found in the "War of Rebellion" by Donelson, Maney or Cheatham. General Maney, by his letter January 16, 1901, writes me: "The war records show no report of this battle by General Cheatham, chief of division, or either of the brigade commanders." General Maney also says in his letter: "Assuming always that your regiment, the Sixteenth, was part of Donelson's brigade, I very well remember in conversation having stated to you that it had been engaged for not less than thirty minutes before my command came to your assistance by attacking at your right, and having so stated verbally, of course am willing at your pleasure to place it in writing as I here do. On this point I am persuaded that though wounded, you were still with your command when I went into action, and you had not been borne off the field, so your memory will thoroughly concur with mine, and here again intervening events involving time in occurrence may be relied on as conclusive support." (*General Maney's letter.*)

[In the foregoing, General Maney clearly stated that his brigade came to Savage's assistance by attacking at his right and that this took place only thirty minutes into the action. All three historians—Noe, Holman and Hafendorfer—credit Donelson's brigade with the capture of Harris' battery. By all accounts Federal and Confederate, Harris' battery did not fall until near dark—around 6 p.m. The initial attack began at approximately 2 p.m. according to the primary sources. How can Maney's statement be used to support the idea that Maney assisted Donelson and Savage in the capture of Harris' battery nearly four hours **after** the commencement of the action? Maney made it clear that he was **abreast** of Savage's regiment approximately thirty minutes after the opening attack by Donelson's brigade; this was clearly during the assault against Parsons' battery.]

SAVAGE'S REPORT OF THE BATTLE OF PERRYVILLE, KENTUCKY.

From early in the morning until twelve o'clock the Sixteenth Regiment was in line of battle in the dry bed of Chaplain Creek, its right resting on the road that leads to Harrodsburg. The regiment was then ordered to march down Chaplain Creek. After going a mile or more the cannon balls began to fall among the men but did no harm. At the distance of about two miles the creek widened to something like a small bottom, with water in it, the banks having become forty to fifty feet high, covered by heavy timber and undergrowth. Turning to the left the Sixteenth was ordered by General Donelson to ascend the bluff, through the timber and undergrowth, which was steep and difficult to get up. The path led along the foot of the bluff some fifty or sixty yards to a dug road, up which I rode into an open field and saw a battery of artillery some two hundred yards out in the field.

[Savage's mention of a "dug road" was in reference to a narrow, unimproved road that had been dug out of the western bank of Chaplin River's bluff and ascended nearly sixty feet in elevation from the river bottom. This road—or path—had been constructed long before the battle. By at least one source—an engraving of the battle, the path led northwest to the site of the Hafley cabins. Current interpretations relate that his regiment's attack position was on a hilltop immediately south of the dug road—within less than one-hundred yards of the road. From Savage's testimony—as well as Captain Womack's following statement—it is more likely that their attack position was around three-hundred yards west of the northern most portion of the dug road. This would have placed the regiment on the first long north-south finger of terrain that ran south toward a tributary that empties into Doctor's Creek and terminates right before its junction with Chaplin River. Today, this intermittent stream is called "Donelson's Run," but it should more appropriately be referred to as "Wood's Run." Surveys by Ruger and Kilp made in 1862 show that part of this Dug Road continued north on the west side of the river as far as the Gammon House in Mercer County. Thus, the regiment was probably formed in line on the finger only around one-hundred yards north-west of the park entrance. From that position, Open Knob is visible at about three-hundred and fifty yards west-north-west. In all likelihood, it was from this position that Savage may have observed Parsons' battery just beginning to arrive atop Open Knob. Six-hundred yards west of this supposed attack position is Starkweather's Hill on which Stone's battery was positioned. It may have been either of these batteries witnessed by Savage; however, Parsons' position is more relative to the distance given by Savage.]

Riding to where the men were getting up the hill into the edge of the field, I formed the regiment into line on the edge of the bluff directly fronting the battery.

[Savage stated that he formed his regiment "on the edge of the bluff." This has been taken too literally by previous interpretations. The regiments of Donelson's brigade ascended the bank of Chaplin River in line formation—one at a time. As Savage's regiment was the first to ascend, they had to move forward (west) to allow room for the following regiments—as well as Stewart's brigade that ascended after Donelson. The "edge" of the bluff that Savage refers to is probably the second abrupt ascent of nearly forty more feet in elevation in a distance of about eighty linear yards to the crest of the first finger.]

By this time General Donelson rode up and said, "Colonel, I am ordered to attack," to which I made no reply. He repeated a second time, "Colonel, I am ordered to attack." I again made no reply. He repeated a third time, "Colonel, I am ordered to attack the enemy!" I then said: "General, I see no enemy to attack except that battery over there in the field. Do you mean, sir, that you want the Sixteenth to charge that battery?" He said, "Yes." I replied, "General, I will obey your orders but if the Sixteenth is to charge that battery you must give the order." He raised his voice in a rather loud and excited tone and said, "Charge."

[Much has been made of the reluctance of Savage to initially charge the battery. Savage and Donelson were in fact polar opposites, but in light of the situation at the time—only two other Rebel regiments on the western bank of the river—Savage's reluctance was probably well founded.]

I believed that the battery was supported by a strong line of infantry concealed by a fence, and a forest not more than eighty yards in its rear, and that it had been placed in the field as a decoy to invite a charge. I believed that a charge would end in my death and the defeat and ruin of my regiment, and while I had often disobeyed Donelson's orders, for which he had court-martialed me, I could think of no military principles that would authorize me to disobey such an order in the face off the enemy and at the beginning of such a battle.

[By Savage's description—at that time, the battery had yet to be supplemented by visible infantry supports. This coincides with the reports of Federal commanders that state Parsons' battery was unlimbering before the arrival of the infantry. The first Federal regiment to arrive in support of the battery would be the 123rd Illinois. The report of Jackson's Federal division supports the fact that Rebel infantry could be seen advancing to occupy the same ground—at the same time—in reference to the 123rd Illinois. Savage also mentioned the wooden fence and the grove of woods that was less than 100 yards south and west of the crest of Open Knob at the time.]

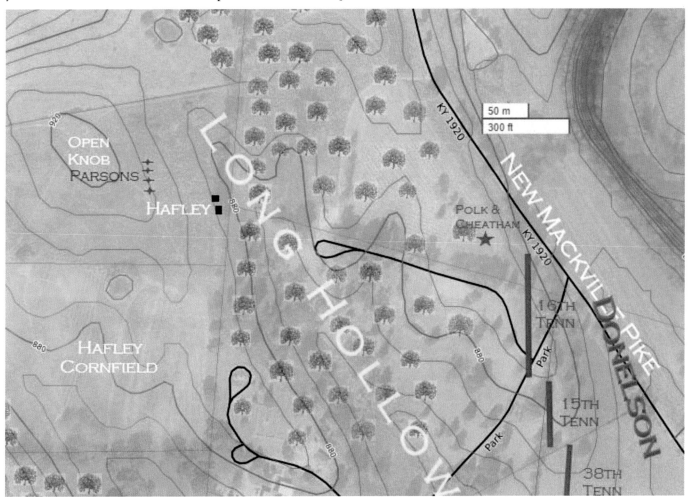

There was running up from Chaplain Creek a long hollow about half way between the battery and where the regiment was in line. I thought as soon as I moved into that hollow I would be out of reach of the battery and that I could come up on the other side within sixty or seventy yards of the battery. I was in no hurry; got in front of my regiment and said, "Forward, march!"

[In the foregoing paragraph, Savage mentioned the "long hollow" that ran from Chaplin's River. Historians have erroneously concluded this to be the valley in which the tributary to Doctor's Creek currently named "Donelson's Run" flows. If Savage's words are taken literally, he is not referencing the valley that contains Donelson's Run, but rather he is referencing the "hollow" that lies parallel to the Federal lines and empties into the valley. This is easily determined by the fact that the length of the valley or "hollow" that encompasses "Donelson's Run" runs east to west and would run perpendicular to the Federal lines. The benefit that Savage saw was that he would traverse the width of the hollow placing his force in defilade just prior to the assault. If he were advancing up the length of the hollow, he would have been in view nearly the entire time by at least **some** portion of the Federal lines. The advance would have been over a much greater distance as well.]

About the time the regiment reached the bottom of the hollow an aide of General Cheatham's came from the woods near the right, saying that the enemy was in the woods at the head of the hollow at the right. I halted the regiment, ordered my color bearers to the front and ordered the regiment to dress on them so as to march in the new direction indicated by Cheatham's order. I was in no hurry, for outside of Cheatham's aide and Donelson there was no Confederate in sight. There was no reason why the battery should not have fired upon the regiment while it was in line, except that a fire would pass through the line and only do a little damage.

[Exactly how Savage lost his direction in the advance on the battery is a debate in itself. He may have seen Stone's or Bush's more distant battery on the heights of Starkweather's Hill. However, his description suggests that he was referencing Parson's battery. It is—however—easy to lose direction when a linear formation is crossing stone and wooden fences. As described in Donelson's report also, Cheatham redirected Savage's axis of advance. This axis would take him to within yards of the cornfield and Hafley cabins where the regiment came under a heavy fire from infantry and artillery. If Savage had been advancing to the Widow Gibson cabin site, they would have been under infantry fire for over four-hundred yards **before** arriving at the site. Additionally, no Federal artillery was in less one-hundred yards of the Widow Gibson site. Oddly, Savage's account of the action—as well as those of his men—fails to mention the effects of artillery fire during their initial advance. Perhaps—since the Sixteenth Tennessee was in advance of the trailing regiments—it was the Fifteenth and Thirty-eighth regiments that were more effected by frontal fire. Donelson did make mention of the destructive fire of artillery during the advance.

The following lines explain what happened when the regiment came under fire. The biggest question raised is which battery Savage had originally observed. It is possible that as he began his advance that *fences* and *terrain* forced his regiment off course as he descended the hill and caused Cheatham's aid to redirect his advance. Or, he may have originally observed Stone's battery on Starkweather's Heights several hundred yards further south and west of Parsons' position. Either way, when his force redirected to the right—or north—he approached the edge of the wood and field just south and east of Parsons' guns.]

Marching in the new direction indicated by Cheatham's aide, I was soon in an open beech forest on the top of the hill. I was riding in front expecting a surprise, the left of the regiment was at the edge of the forest and the field, when the battery, about one hundred and fifty yards from the regiment, fired, enfilading it, sweeping the whole length of the line, killing a captain, a lieutenant and many privates.

[From Savage's testimony it appears that after the redirection, the regiment resumed the advance in a northwesterly direction. As the line crested the hill and the left of the regiment reached the edge of the wood, the right most guns of Parsons' battery opened fire with canister. This fire struck the regimental line obliquely creating immediate mass casualties. His account contradicts any allegation that his regiment could be anywhere near Harris' battery at this point. Harris' battery would still be nearly eight-hundred yards west of this position. In order to be anywhere near Harris' battery, the regiment would have had to bypassed or tip-toed past the Twenty-fourth Illinois, Seventy-ninth Pennsylvania, Thirty-third Ohio, Second Ohio, Fiftieth Ohio and Ninety-fourth Ohio without detection. Additionally, the guns of Harris' battery were fully three-hundred yards *north-west* of the Widow Gibson corn crib.]

I was riding in front of the regiment; a grape shot passed through the head of my horse below the eyes. Remembering to have seen thirty or forty rider-less horses running over the field of Molino del Rey, I threw the bridle of my horse over a snag, took a Remington pistol from the holsters, and ordered the regiment forward to get out of range of the battery. Descending the hill some forty or fifty yards, we were fired on by the main line of the Yankee army, not more than fifty or sixty yards distant, concealed behind a rail fence which was a prolongation of the fence enclosing the field in which the battery was situated.

[As the regiment crested the finger of land—a few hundred yards north of which the visitor center and Confederate cemetery now occupy, they came under the rifle fire of the 123rd Illinois that had just arrived on the field north and west of the Confederate cemetery. This Federal regiment was nearly as green as they get. As they deployed into line, they unfortunately found their rear rank in front. This caused mass confusion in the ranks of the new regiment. Still, they fired a heavy volley that caused the Sixteenth Tennessee to waver momentarily. In all Federal accounts of the battle, it was the 123rd Illinois that was the first unit heavily engaged in combat. Likewise, all Rebel accounts show that the Sixteenth Tennessee was the first Confederate unit heavily engaged in combat. Somehow, historians have thus far been unable to correlate this relationship. Naturally, the first units reported engaged in heavy combat—not skirmishing—were undeniably engaged with each other. The following lines describe the situation at the Hafley Cabins.]

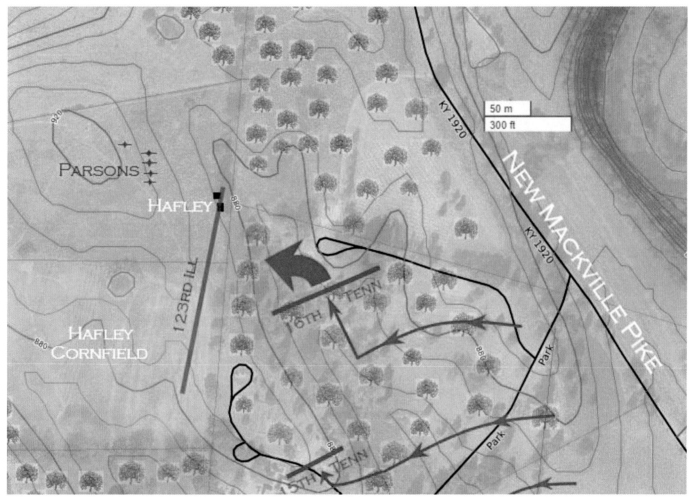

There was a fence and a field on my right running up to two cabins at the line of the enemy's forces. There were skirmish lines along this fence which fired on our rear as we advanced. The Sixteenth had no protection except a few trees in the forest. I ordered a charge. We drove the enemy from behind the fences, killing many of them as they fled. The right of the regiment was at the two cabins. There was a battery in the line of battle to the right, about thirty or forty yards from these cabins, between which cabins there was an entry, or space, of ten or fifteen feet.

[As noted earlier, historians have attempted to associate this mention of cabins with the Widow Gibson home-site. It is clear from Savage's description of the situation that the action had just started. Nearly all historians relate the Seventy-ninth Pennsylvania and Twenty-fourth Illinois' positions as trailing from the western bend in Benton Road (known as modern day Whites Road) toward the south—atop and along the finger of terrain from Starkweather's Heights in a southerly direction. Donelson's brigade would have to have bypassed this heavy enemy force by nearly four-hundred yards

133

to come within any reasonable distance of Widow Gibson's corn-crib. Savage—instead—has clearly related that as soon as they came under fire by the main line of the enemy protected by a fence in their front and a skirmish line along a fence to his right that ran "up to two cabins at the line of the enemy's forces," he ordered a charge. The charge routed the enemy at the fence and gave the right of the regiment possession of the two cabins. Only a short distance away—"thirty or forty yards"—Parsons' battery continued to fire at exceptionally short range.]

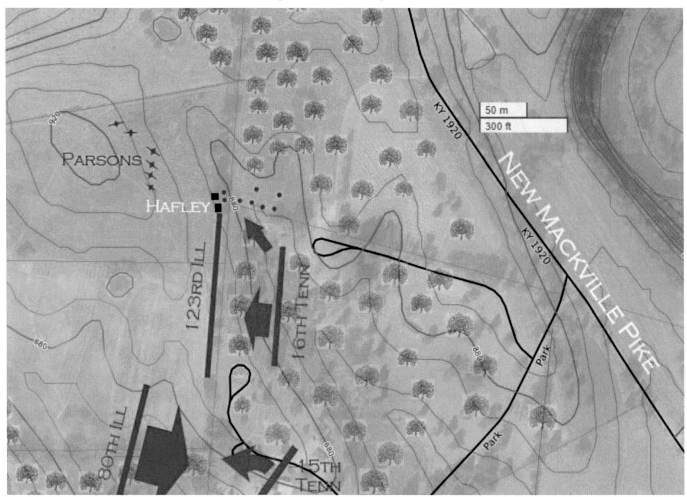

The battery opened fire upon us, killing many men, and at the same time a fire of small arms from the line of battle was directed upon these cabins. The battery fired obliquely into this space. I stood between the cabins, would watch the gunner ram home the charge, and say, "Lie low, boys; he is going to fire," and step for protection close to the cabin nearest the battery. The battle was furious, the men loading and firing as rapidly as possible, falling back and again charging up to the fence.

[Above, Savage has related that the battle along the fence teeter-tottered back and forth a second time. This description corresponds with other members of the Sixteenth in their recollections of the battle.]

A private, Andrew Dow Mercer, said, "Boys, let's take the battery," and started in that direction. At this time I saw a force to my right and in my rear. I countermanded Mercer's order, but he had gone some five or six steps towards the battery to a tree. Seeing that he was not supported, he hugged the tree closely for a short space of time and returned to the cabin without being wounded.

[As Savage mentioned, an enemy force appeared to his right and rear. It's believed that this was the charge of one wing of the 105th Ohio. The scene was doubtful indeed for the bloodied Tennesseans. Next, Savage relates the arrival of Maney's brigade. It was the appearance of this Rebel brigade that forced the enveloping Ohioans to beat a hasty retreat back to the cover of Parsons' guns. Savage—however—attempted to make it clear that the artillerists and their horses had already been disabled to a great degree before Maney's force "appeared in the field to my right" in the midst of their attack on the battery.]

134

While standing between the cabins a Minié ball passed through my leg without breaking the bone, and the wood off of a canister shot struck the opposite cabin, and glancing knocked me down, paralyzing me for a time. The men at the battery had been killed or wounded or had fled before Maney's brigade appeared in the field to my right, some hundred yards or more distant, and the battle had ceased at the battery.

[Savage was aware of Maney's presence—although he would like to have claimed the capture of the guns by the Sixteenth single-handedly. Savage mentioned that Maney appeared "in the field to my right." It is important to note that he states it is a field. If the Sixteenth had been at the Widow Gibson's, Maney would have appeared in the woods. The nearest field would have been north of Benton Road. Had Maney been further than a hundred yards away, it is unlikely Savage or any of his men would have been aware of his arrival.]

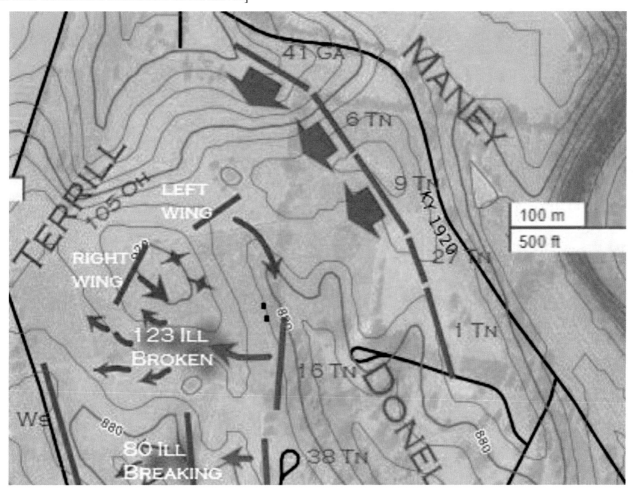

I said to Colonel Donelson: "I am unfit for duty. Take charge. Go to the battery. It belongs to the Sixteenth." There was then no enemy in front or firing upon the regiment.

[The combined fire of the Sixteenth Tennessee and Maney's Brigade—with their charge on the guns—left the enemy retreating toward the lane at Benton Road. Savage's position at the cabins was not receiving fire at this time.

In the following lines, Savage relates that he believed his regiment was responsible for the killing of General James Jackson atop Open Knob. Current interpretations of this suggest that Savage must have been mistaken because General Jackson wasn't killed at Harris' battery. Clearly, Jackson died at Parsons' guns, and all mentions of Jackson's death are in relation to the defense of the Knob and Parsons' guns. So, why is it assumed that Savage is wrong? It's because his statement didn't coincide with the views of late twentieth and twenty-first century historians. That **is** the answer. Who was responsible for Jackson's death is irrelevant. What is relevant is that Jackson's body *was found* near or at the battery that the Sixteenth Tennessee attacked.]

After the battle was over Captain Fisher of the Sixteenth said to me: "Colonel, we killed at that battery the bravest captain we ever saw. We tried to get him to surrender, but he would not surrender and we had to kill him," and I recognized in Captain Fisher's "brave captain," Major-General Jackson, whose body was found among the guns of this battery.

[One of the most important factors to note in Savage's testimony is the fact that he clearly stated that his regiment remained engaged from the initial canister shot until the arrival of Maney's brigade and capture of Parsons' battery. This is related time and again by Maney and several members of the regiment as taking place in as little as thirty to forty minutes. In contrast to how historians have narrated the battle, the evidence clearly shows that Donelson's brigade never "retreated" an inch and was in fact reformed and recommitted almost immediately by the general himself. Some historians have insisted that Donelson's men made it all the way to Widow Gibson's cabin only to retreat to "almost their starting point" nearly a half mile away. Neither Donelson's report nor Savage's reports mention a retreat of any sort, and the action was only momentarily lapsed to reform after the capture of the battery only thirty minutes into the fight.

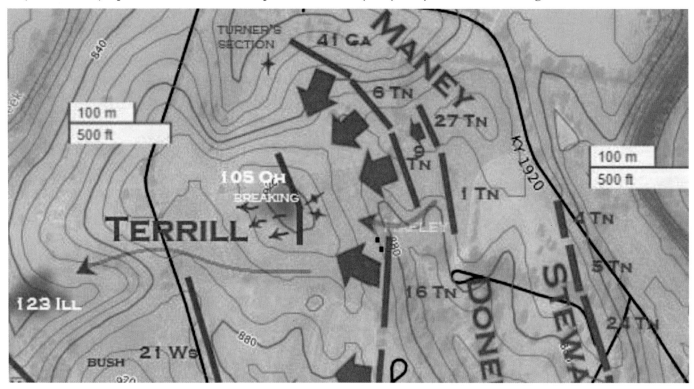

Next, Savage explained the reason why he thought his regiment was responsible for the capture of Parsons' guns. It was his regiment that had faced it single-handedly for around a half-hour before the arrival of Maney. Also, Savage was wounded between the Hafley cabins, and it is likely he wasn't particularly aware of exactly what happened in the following minutes. If nothing else, he certainly believed his regiment was *more responsible* for the capture of the battery than any other force. As will later be seen in accounts of his subordinates, many of the artillerists and infantry defending the guns had already been shot down before Maney arrived. Savage was clearly aware of the fact that Maney's men took another battery, but *it wasn't this one*—at least in his mind. In his perspective of the field, while the guns of Bush and Stone were "a half mile or more to the right of this battery," the reality was that they were four hundred yards due west of his position. But location is relative to one's own *orientation and perspective* of their position on the field. Since Maney arrived on his right, it would be natural for Savage to believe that the guns that Maney took were to the right (or north) of his position.]

None of General Maney's brigade was nearer than one hundred yards of this battery. The batteries taken by General Maney's brigade were half a mile or more to the right of this battery.

[Reflecting back to the fight at the Hafley cabins, Savage again explained that his force had finally captured and remained at a rail fence on the left of the regiment and at the cabins on the right. Savage explained that they couldn't retreat without suffering even worse casualties. Shortly after his lieutenant-colonel came to him, Maney's brigade appeared in the field to his right and the Thirty-eighth Tennessee closed up on his left flank and engaged the enemy line of battle.]

During the hottest of the battle my lieutenant-colonel, Donnell, came to me and said: "Colonel, order a retreat. We are losing all our men and are not supported." I replied: "Protect your men by those trees and that fence and I will protect this wing by these cabins. We were ordered to fight. To order a retreat at the beginning of a great battle is not war. We must hold this position until supported, and it is the duty of our commanding officers to bring us support." The regiment could not then retreat without being brought again under the fire of the battery in the field. Soon after the time that Maney's brigade appeared on the right the Thirty-eighth Regiment belonging to Donelson's brigade engaged the enemy's line of battle on the left. It is stated in this same volume of "Confederate Military History" that the Sixteenth Regiment under Colonel Savage lost one hundred and ninety-nine men, more than half the casualties of the brigade.

[Unaware that reports had ever been penned by his superiors, Savage went on a tirade to place responsibility for his high casualties on the shoulders of his commanders.]

Either Savage or his commanders are responsible to God and their country for this terrible slaughter of brave men. It is difficult to form an opinion as to why this occurred as it did. Was it incompetency or neglect on the part of Donelson and Cheatham, or were there other motives operating to produce this result? There was at the time no good feeling between Donelson, his son and son-in-law upon his staff, and Savage. The friends of Savage claim that by disobeying Donelson's orders at Huntersville in Virginia he saved his regiment from great loss by fatal disease. It was also claimed that by disobeying Donelson's order at Valley Mountain in Western Virginia he saved Donelson's brigade and also General Robert E. Lee from capture next morning.

It appears in the sixteenth volume, page 1022, "War of the Rebellion", that the battle of Perryville has been reported by forty-four officers, twenty-eight of whom are Yankees, and sixteen Rebels. I have carefully read these reports to try to form an opinion as to the truth and fairness of the statements made on each side. I am inclined to treat the statements made by officers as testimony made by a witness in court, whose feelings and prejudice are all on one side. There are certain leading facts on each side that must be credited, because in accordance with reason and in harmony with admission on each side.

[In the following lines, Savage related that he had no less than five members of the regiment recollect the battle as he did. Unfortunately, only one soldier's letter was included in his narrative.]

To corroborate and sustain my report, I have taken the statements of five soldiers of the Sixteenth Regiment, now residing in Warren County—James C. Biles, Jesse Walling, E.S. Rowan, Huel Moffit and William H. White—who all remember the facts as I report them, and they all agree that no regiment of Donelson's brigade or other Confederate force was in sight when Cheatham and Donelson gave the fatal order to the Sixteenth Regiment, solitary and alone, under the fire of the battery in sight in the field, to charge the main line of the Yankee army; and that the regiment was engaged for half an hour before Maney's brigade appeared on the right.

I here state a few facts appearing in the report of General Buell and his officers which corroborate and sustain the recollections of the soldiers of the Sixteenth, whose statements I have taken.

General Buell approached Bardstown with an army of fifty-eight thousand men, at which point Bragg's army was stationed under command of General Polk, who left Bardstown when Buell was approaching. Buell followed Polk, and on the night of October 7, 1862, Bragg determined to five Buell battle at Perryville and ordered Polk to remove Cheatham's division, then at Harrodsburg, back to Perryville to support Hardee, then pressed by the enemy. Bragg directed Polk to attack Buell at daylight, which Polk failed to do. Bragg arrived on the battle field at ten o'clock and made suggestion to Polk, but no battle was commenced until the afternoon, when Bragg in person ordered the attack, Cheatham's division being rapidly removed from the left to the right, under a continuous fire of artillery. The battle was furious until dark.

Buell reports a loss of four thousand, three hundred and forty-three, and names as killed Major-general Jackson, Brigadier-general William R. Terrill, Commanding Brigadier-general Geo. Webster, P. Jonnet, W. P. Campbell, Ales. S. Berryhill and John Herrell. He says the corps of McCook was very much crippled, and the division of General Jackson almost entirely disappeared as a body.

Oldershaw, assistant adjutant-general, and chief of staff, says that General Jackson, while standing on the left of the battery was killed by two bullets entering his right breast; that the battery had been taken and that it was impossible to recover the body of General Jackson. (See War of the Rebellion, vol. XVI, page 1060.)

This statement corroborates and sustains the statements of the men of the Sixteenth, and makes it most probable that Terrill and Colonel Webster were killed by Maney's brigade.

[The above statement related that Savage was aware of his position on the field and that his regiment engaged Parsons' battery. He suspected his regiment was responsible for the death of General Jackson. He may very likely have been correct in his supposition. The Federal accounts all note Jackson's death taking place within only a few minutes after the action commenced. Unfortunately, Savage didn't include the letters of all five of the men in the regiment that responded to his inquiry. Only one letter was included that clearly corroborated his recollection. The others were obviously left out to save space. However, Savage was clear that all of the men corroborated his recollection of where they fought and what happened during the attack.]

General McCook says, "The bloodiest battle of modern times for the number of troops engaged on our side." (Page 1042, vol. XVI, W. of R.)

Colonel Oscar F. Moore, of the Thirty-third Ohio, was wounded and taken prisoner. Captain I. I. *[J. J.]* Womack directed a Rebel and a Yankee soldier to carry Colonel Moore to the Rebel hospital, about dusk.

General Hardee reports his loss in this battle at two hundred and forty-two killed, one thousand, five hundred and four wounded—including three brigadier-generals, Cleburne, Wood and Brown—with a quartermaster and commissary killed and three colonels wounded, next in rank to brigadier-generals.

[The following paragraph relates that in light of Savage's belief that Donelson and Cheatham failed to write reports, they conspired to kill him at the battle. What follows is an attempt to incriminate Donelson and Cheatham over the next several pages. This rant is all based on Savage's conspiracy theory but has been included for the few important facts that are related in his text.]

Yet it is remarkable and strange to say that in all these reports, Yankee and Rebel, nothing appears from Cheatham, Donelson, Stewart or Maney, nor any officer in Cheatham's division except the reports of the commanders of regiments in Maney's brigade. This taken in connection with Governor Porter's letter and General Maney's letter is conclusive proof that Cheatham and Donelson willfully, wrongfully, violating military law, suppressed all reports. Common sense makes it plain that they pursued this course because of some guilty conduct which they dared not disclose for fear of dismissal from the service and punishment.

[Savage never learned of the actual reports that his commanders had made, and he went to the grave still blaming them.]

First. It is proven beyond doubt that no regiment of Donelson's brigade or any Confederate force was present or in sight when Cheatham and Donelson gave the fatal orders, or appeared until after Maney's brigade appeared on the right.

[The Foregoing appears to be supported by all Rebel sources that participated in the fight. Donelson had even admitted that Savage's regiment raced ahead of the other two regiments without waiting. The evidence also suggests that the supporting regiments of the brigade became engaged before reaching the left flank of the Sixteenth. For this reason, the Thirty-eighth Tennessee didn't appear on their left until the appearance of Maney's brigade on their right.]

Second. J. C. Biles, clerk and master of the Chancery Court at McMinnville, in his written statement says that after the regiment had been formed in the edge of an old field, with a battery in its front, General Donelson rode up, and after some talk between him and Colonel Savage, Donelson rose up in his stirrups and gave the order to charge; that the regiment moved as if to charge the battery and was halted after moving a short distance, and was formed in line of battle at right angles to the line when marching to charge the battery in the field.

[In the following letter, note that Biles states the regiment was formed "in the edge of an old field, with a battery in its front." Biles, Savage, Donelson, Cheatham, Womack, Hooper and Clark (as will be seen) all stated this battery was visible in their front. From their supposed attack position north of the park entrance, the battery commanded by Parsons would have been between three and four-hundred yards to their west on Open Knob. This is after they had ascended the bank of the river and moved forward to allow room for following units. Additionally, note that he states that the regiment moved "as if to charge the battery" but was halted "after moving a short distance." Biles then stated that the line was reformed "at right angles to the line when marching to charge the battery in the field." This statement could imply that the guns they saw initially were actually Stone's battery atop Starkweather's Heights further west. They then changed direction to the north-northwest to move on Parsons.]

The letter of Jesse Walling, now president of the National Bank at McMinnville, is given and is in accordance with the statement of Biles and the others.

"COLONEL JOHN H. SAVAGE:

DEAR SIR: In reply to your inquiry as to what I remember about the part your regiment took in the battle of Perryville, Ky., I would state that we were encamped near a creek when orders were given to break camp and move forward.

[The following lines reveal that they ascended the bank, formed line and moved "southward" a half mile. This suggestion that they moved "southward" has been taken too literally by historians as well. First, that distance south from Dug Road would have placed the regiment south of Doctor's Creek and within 230 yards of the Chatham House. It also would have placed the regiment within 700 yards northeast of Squire Bottom's and about 430 yards south-southeast of Widow Bottom's residence. To rectify this, historians have decreased that distance to only about 250 yards. However, it's likely that if his distance was that far off, his direction was probably off as well.]

We ascended a very steep embankment, formed line and moved southward, probably one-half mile, when General Donelson appeared, and after talking with you for about a minute or so we were ordered to charge the enemy. The first sight that we had of the enemy was a battery of beautiful cannon. We charged in right oblique course and were met by the grape and canister shot from these guns, which killed many of our men.

[Walling failed to mention the halt and redirection of the regiment, but stated that the regiment charged in "right oblique" toward the enemy guns. This was likely in reference to their change of direction. In the following, he mentions three distinct charges that the regiment made. The initial engagement is supposed to be against the 123rd Illinois. Although that enemy regiment was twice the size of the Sixteenth, the violence of action broke their regiment and allowed the campaign hardened Rebels to seize the fence. Each charge accomplished a little more—finally seizing the guns with the assistance of Maney's brigade. He then added that they continued pressing the enemy—"killing them as they ran." This is further evidence that the regiment—as a whole—didn't stop at the guns, but continued on with the left of Maney's brigade in their assault through the cornfield.]

All at once the enemy raised up from behind a rail fence, pouring a deadly fire into us and killing great numbers of our men. We fell back a short distance, rallied and charged again, meeting the same deadly fire which drove us back for the second time. The third time we went over the fence, driving the enemy before us, capturing the cannon. We continued running them, killing them as they ran. Their dead and wounded lay thick behind the fence and over the field.

[Walling notes that the regiment was unsupported for "at least thirty minutes" before Maney appeared on their right.]

I was in the center of the regiment (Sixteenth Tennessee), and noticed that we were not supported either to the right or to the left. My company went into the fight numbering eighty-four men and next morning we only had sixteen men able for service. You will see that our loss was terrible, but the most surprising thing to me is that every man in your regiment was not killed, as we fought the enemy to the front, left and right flanks unsupported.

The Sixteenth was engaged with the enemy for at least thirty minutes when General Maney's men appeared to our right as we were running the enemy across the field.

[While Walling suggests that they were already running "the enemy across the field," it appears it was—in fact—the combined efforts of Maney's men and the Sixteenth in their final charge that broke Parsons' support and allowed the capture of the guns.]

I could not begin to name over all the dead and wounded as most all our company were in this list, and to name some of our brave and good and leave out others equally as honorable, I could not do.

Why our regiment was ordered to fight this battle alone and on a field where our position was decidedly against us I shall never be able to understand. To look at the great numbers of the enemy in comparison to our little regiment it seemed that we were brought up to be slaughtered.

[In the foregoing, it is clear the men in the ranks were bewildered at the lack of assistance they initially received. Their thirty minutes under fire probably seemed like an eternity.]

One of the bravest men I have ever seen was one of the enemy, who stood upon his fine brass gun, waving his hat over his head after all his comrades had fled. But he too fell in this brave act. I could not hear distinctly his words as he stood there waving his hat.

You will please pardon me for speaking of this brave fellow, but he is always before me when I think of this terrible battle. Yours very truly,

JESSE WALLING, *First Lieutenant.*"

The report appearing in the eighth volume of the so-called "Confederate Military History" does the Sixteenth and Colonel Savage a gross injustice by the suppression of and failure to state important facts. It fails to state that the Sixteenth Regiment killed General Jackson, who refused to surrender at the battery they captured, and that Jackson's body was found among the guns of the battery near the double cabins. It also fails to state that Savage was wounded by a minie ball and was knocked down by the wood off a canister shot, fired by the battery near the double cabins at which General Jackson was killed. It also fails to state that the Sixteenth Regiment under orders from Donelson and Cheatham and without support on the right or the left charged and broke the enemy's line of battle thirty minutes before General Maney's brigade appeared in the open field on the right.

[Savage felt that all of these details should have been included in the history, but clearly, many of these details would be too much to ask for in a sweeping military history. However, it does appear—from the evidence—that Jackson was in fact probably killed by the fire of the Sixteenth Tennessee. Following sources in the Federal section will point out that Jackson was killed just after the opening moments of the action.]

The following lines relate Savage's belief that his regiment engaged and routed the Thirty-third Ohio from behind the rail fence. From foregoing evidence, it is clear that the Thirty-third Ohio was formed as skirmishers and not in line of battle. There is a distinct difference in the two. Lines of battle are two ranks deep and formed shoulder to shoulder. Skirmish formations—in which the Thirty-third was sent out—have open ranks with a distance of several yards between each man. This was so the formation could cover greater lateral distances. Skirmish lines were intended to develop the enemy front and position—not to engage enemy lines of battle. The 123rd Illinois—on the other hand—marched directly into action and was formed in line of battle at a fence. There, they engaged the forces in their front until breaking under heavy accurate Rebel fire.]

It also fails to state that the Sixteenth charged and drove from its line of battle formed behind a fence the Thirty-third Ohio Regiment, and wounded and captured its colonel, Oscar F. Moore, with whom Savage served in Congress, and that Savage directed his doctor to take the same care of Colonel Moore as he would take care of himself if wounded.

[By Savage's own testimony, he was out of action for an hour after being wounded. He was unaware of the ground his regiment later fought over. It is more probable that his regiment later passed over ground on which Colonel Moore had been wounded earlier in the action. Savage even related earlier that Womack discovered Moore on the field and sent him to the hospital "about dusk." At that time, the regiment would have been on the left of Stewart's brigade and was probably falling back after their last attacks in the vicinity of Harris' battery east and south of Dixville Crossroads.]

It fails to state that Savage's horse was wounded by a grape shot, also that Colonel Donelson's *[Lt. Col. Donnell's]* horse was killed at the fence behind which the Yankees had formed their line of battle. Savage charged with the regiment and emptied his Remington revolver, and these were the only shots fired by him during the war.

It is difficult to form a satisfactory opinion as to the reasons and motives that induced Donelson and Cheatham to order the Sixteenth Regiment, solitary and alone, to charge the main line of battle of the Yankee Abolition army. Did it result from excitement and stupidity or dullness on the part of these officers, or was it a purpose to sacrifice a disobedient and insubordinate officer? The last suggestion derives strength from the fact that neither Donelson nor Cheatham made any report of this important battle, but suppressed the facts, which if published might show that they ought to be dismissed from the service or shot by court-martial.

Governor J. D. Porter, in a letter to me the 19th of June, 1900, says: "Perryville was a splendid fight. I will never cease to regret that the men who made it made no report. Cheatham did not want to put all he knew in an official report." The proof is clear beyond doubt that Cheatham willfully failed to report, and suppressed all reports, which constituted a military crime of the highest grade, deserving of the greatest punishment—which should have resulted in the dismissal of himself and Donelson in disgrace from the army.

[When Porter related that Cheatham "did not want to put all he knew in an official report," Savage took this to be regarding the purposeful slaughter of his regiment. But in retrospect, it is possible that Cheatham didn't want to include information that would have cast a poor light on Bragg. Cheatham consistently tried to stay out of the politics that engrossed many officers in the army.]

The charge of the Sixteenth Regiment at the battle of Perryville, under orders of Cheatham and Donelson, was as gallant, brave, dangerous and desperate as the charge of the Light Brigade or six hundred men upon the Russian battery at Balaklava during the Crimean War, under the rash and fatal orders of Lord Cardigan, which has been immortalized by the poets Meek and Tennyson. And the Tennesseans who sleep on the hills of Chaplain Creek, with no stone to mark their graves and with no report by commanding generals to keep in memory their heroic valor, invite the attention of some future unborn poet to present the charge of these brave men as equal in desperate daring to the charge of England's Light Brigade of six hundred. There are many incidents in the charge of the Sixteenth upon the main line of the Yankee army under the fatal orders of Cheatham and Donelson similar to the charge of the Light Brigade of six hundred under the rash and fatal orders of Lord Cardigan, and to show the similarity of these two battles I quote from Tennyson's poem as follows:

> "Forward, the Light Brigade!
> Was there a man dismay'd?
> Not tho' the soldier knew
> Some one had blunder'd:
> Theirs not to make reply,
> Theirs not to reason why,
> Theirs but to do and die:
> Into the valley of death
> Rode the six hundred.
> Cannon to right of them,
> Cannon to left of them,
> Cannon in front of them
> Volley'd and thundered;
> Storm'd at with shot and shell,
> Boldly they rode and well,
> Into the jaws of death,

Into the mouth of hell,
Rode the six hundred."

Bennet Young, of Perryville, said in a speech at Murfreesboro: "The fighting was at close range; and at one time and in one part of the fray, only a rail fence divided those who were thus contesting in deadliest combat." This was the Sixteenth, solitary and alone, for thirty minutes in battle with the Yankee army. Persons who had seen Shiloh and Chickamauga declare that Perryville in many parts was the most dreadful battle field they had ever seen. Yet Cheatham and Donelson made no reports; and the "Confederate Military History" misstates the facts so as to transfer the blunder and crime of Donelson and Cheatham to Colonel Savage.

Many attempt to explain the mysterious and strange conduct of Cheatham and Donelson. I propose to judge of their acts at the battle of Perryville by those universal rules of law and common sense adopted by courts of justice to as ascertain the guilt or innocence of the parties charged with crime. "The law presumes that the party intended that which is the immediate or probable consequence of his act." (Roscoe's *Criminal Law*, page 16.)

The order to charge the battery and the enemy's line of battle without support was equivalent to ordering the death of Savage and the defeat and destruction of this regiment, and law and common sense say they so intended. This fatal and malicious order resulted killing Colonel Donelson's horse, the wounding of Savage and his horse and the killing and wounding of one hundred and ninety-nine men— more than half his regiment. If Cheatham and Donelson were on trial for murder before a jury the verdict would be with malice aforethought. "The law presumes parties guilty of crime who suppress and destroy evidence." (First Greenleaf, page 37). Why is it that no report appears from Stewart or his regimental commanders? Why were no reports made by Cheatham or Donelson? These facts, in connection with the letter of Cheatham's adjutant-general and best friend, prove beyond doubt that Cheatham and Donelson gave the fatal order jointly, and the law presumes they continued to act in conjunction until the contrary is proved.

[Clearly, the contrary was proven in their reports that surfaced many years later.]

Every unlawful act is a criminal act, and every careless act or omission of duty by which life is lost is a crime. It is remarkable that none of the Sixteenth saw Cheatham or Donelson during the battle or when removing the dead and wounded from the battle field. It may be that they dreaded to look on the dead men that they had ordered to certain death and defeat. The proof shows the guilty conduct Cheatham and Donelson beyond doubt, and excludes all other conclusions, except proof that they were drunk. In all prosecution for murder malice is a necessary element which the law says is evidence by antecedent menaces, former grudges and concerted schemes to do another some bodily harm. I propose to show the causes why Donelson and Cheatham entertained hatred and malice for John H. Savage.

[The mention that neither Donelson nor Cheatham were seen by members of the Sixteenth Tennessee after the action started is revealing. Cheatham clearly stated in his report that after the attack commenced, he went to the right and observed the fight from the extreme Rebel right flank. Thus, his lack of presence with the regiment is understood. Donelson's lack of presence is intriguing though. Is this more circumstantial evidence that suggests Donelson believed he was commanding the division and Cheatham the right wing?]

They were both men of no very great knowledge or ability, not above the level of the ordinary soldier they commanded, and without military instinct and with but little knowledge of the art of war, with many soldiers in the ranks who were their superior in brain and business capacity. They were soldiers fit to be commanded and ready enough to obey orders, and believed it a great military offense to disobey orders, and that it deserved the severest punishment. They had never heard or read that Plutarch in writing the history of Lycurgus the great Greek legislator and statesman, had declared it to be a military axiom that "Men are not bound to obey those who do not know how to command." Or the saying of Cyrus, king of Persia, that "None ought to govern but those who are better than those he governs."

142

[With both Donelson and Cheatham dead when his autobiography was published, Savage blatantly disrespected his former superiors with insults regarding their combat leadership and tactical knowledge. This may not have gone over too well with the surviving members of the regiment who were dearly devoted to Cheatham and served under his leadership for the remainder of the war.]

It was well known to Cheatham as well as Donelson that Savage had disobeyed Donelson's orders at Huntersville and Valley Mountain. There were other occasions of smaller import not necessary to be named. The arrest of Savage at Pocatalligo *[Pocotaligo]*, South Carolina, showed the malice and hatred of Donelson; and the facts that Savage held the respect and confidence of Generals Lee and Pemberton, as manifested by his release from arrest, and special instructions to make investigations without consulting Donelson, were calculated to arouse the hatred and illwill *[sic]* and vanity of Donelson. There were other considerations calculated to gain for Savage the illwill *[sic]* of Cheatham and Donelson. It was well known that Savage was in the habit of criticizing severely President Davis and his administration, and his unwise and unfortunate management of military affairs. It was well known that Savage often said that Davis and his administration were a failure, and that unless some change was made the conquest of the Southern people was a certainty; that the Government and the army should be reorganized, from the President down, or the people should make peace on the best terms that could be obtained. Savage came into the army unpopular with President Davis and Isham G. Harris because of his known opposition to the doctrines of secession as taught by them and Calhoun. The proof in this case, if it does not establish beyond doubt that guilty purposed of Cheatham and Donelson, is inconsistent with any other conclusion than that they persuaded themselves that the best thing they could do to maintain the honor and discipline of the army and to secure the triumph and freedom of the Southern people was to bring about by any means possible the death of the disobedient, insubordinate and disrespectful Colonel Savage.

Some persons may think or say that the assumption that the officers intended to commit a crime so enormous ought not to be entertained. Let us see a few examples as to what has occurred in the past. Human nature is now the same as it has been throughout the ages, and what has occurred at one time may occur again, for history repeats itself. The churches in past ages have beheaded, hanged, drawn, quartered and burnt at the stake thousands upon thousands of brave men and good women for heresy, for disbelief in questions which we now consider as of no importance whatever. The Duke of Alva executed twenty thousand good people and banished one hundred thousand more because they could not believe in accordance with the creed of the Church of Spain. The number of victims of the Spanish Inquisition from 1481 to 1801 amounted to three hundred and forty-one thousand and twenty-one. Of these nearly thirty-two thousand were burned. There were twenty thousand officers of the Inquisition, who served as spies and informers. (Spofford's *Encyclopedia*.) Charles II of England caused the bones of Oliver Cromwell, of his mother, and his son-in-law, Ireton, after they had long been buried, to be dug up and cast into a lime pit. The skeleton of Cromwell was hung and his head was put on a pole upon the walls of West Chester Abbey. Lucius Junius Brutus, a Roman consul and general, condemned his son to death for disobedience of orders, and was present and saw his son slain without manifestation of sympathy. It is stated in history that towards the close of the seventeenth century the belief in witchcraft was transmitted to New England and spread far and wide, and that twenty women at Salem and in Boston were tried, condemned and hanged, and hundreds were imprisoned, whipped or branded for this imaginary offense.

Cotton Mather, one of the ablest and best educated men of his day, was the avowed champion of this persecution. It is history that under the decrees and bulls of the Pope of Rome five hundred witches were burned at Geneva in three months, about the year 1515, and one hundred thousand in Germany, the last execution taking place in 1749; and that thirty thousand were put to death in England as witches. It may be assumed that David, king of Judea, was a good a man at heart as Cheatham and Donelson, although a Jew. He had more brains and intelligence than either of them. Yet for less cause of hatred and malice than had Cheatham and Donelson against Savage, he redonciled it to his conscience to send Uriah to certain death by an order to Joab, his general, saying: "Set ye Uriah in the forefront of the hottest battle, and retire ye from him, that he may be smitten, and die."

Cheatham and Donelson ordered Savage to the forefront of the battle and then retired from him as if the earth has swallowed them, and no soldier of the Sixteenth saw them or knew where they were during the battle. Perhaps no human sagacity will be able to determine beyond doubt the motives that caused Cheatham and Donelson to order the Sixteenth Regiment, solitary and alone, without any Confederate force in sight, to attack the main line of the Yankee Abolition army. This was apparently an order for the death of Savage and the destruction of his regiment. It was a strange order given by two strange sort of men. Was it necessary to sacrifice Savage and his regiment for the general success in the battle, or did some other matters cause the fatal order? The proof appears to show that Cheatham and Donelson were drunk, and their reason had been dethroned by looking at the batteries in front of them.

The attempt of Abraham Lincoln and his fanatical abolitionists to give to the negro race equal rights with the Anglo-Saxon white race is treason to good government and a bold defiance to the decrees of an all-wise Ruler of a boundless universe, and is equal in enormity to the cruelties of the Spanish Inquisition, the burning of witches in Germany, England and the United States. It is the history of fanatics that the more unreasonable are their theories the greater the numbers join them and greater cruelties are inflicted upon innocent people.

SAVAGE'S COMMENTARY UPON CHEATHAM AND DONELSON AT THE BATTLE OF PERRYVILLE, KENTUCKY.

Generals Donelson and Cheatham were guilty of a crime or an inexcusable blunder in sending one regiment, solitary and alone, under the fire of a battery to attack the main line of the Yankee Abolition army.

[As noted earlier, it is possible that Cheatham was informed that he would retain command of the right wing when Bragg refused to take command of the troops on the field. Donelson—in turn—may have been informed that he would retain command of the division, but Savage may not have been informed that he would retain command of the brigade. This is only mentioned again to point out their failures that Savage highlights below.]

It was their duty to see that all the regiments were in line of battle in supporting distance of each other. The brigade should have been moved forward as a unit and the attack should have been made by all the regiments at the same time. It was Cheatham's business to see that all the brigades in his division were on hand and in line of battle and in supporting distance of each other, so that his whole division could make a simultaneous attack upon the enemy. Cheatham's aide, changing Donelson's order to attack the battery, came out of the woods near the beech forest and near the Sixteenth Regiment, and Cheatham must have seen the Sixteenth Regiment at the time he changed Donelson's order and must have known that there was no support in sight for the Sixteenth Regiment.

[The above sentence indicates that his order was changed—not to attack another battery, but—to attack the enemy at the head of the hollow. This was likely the leftovers from Wharton's cavalry attack and the infantry supports of Parsons' battery.]

It was his duty to arrest Donelson's march and to order him to form his brigade in the proper place to support the Sixteenth in the charge which they ordered. Savage never saw Cheatham during the battle and does not know whether he was drunk or sober.

[As Savage noted, a very simple tactical blunder was made at brigade level that resulted in high casualties. Savage may have been accusing Donelson of this blunder when it was in fact Savage that should have been responsible for the deployment. Regardless, Savage would still be left blameless if he was never informed of that responsibility.]

Savage assumes that this fatal order of Cheatham's and Donelson's resulted from one of three causes:

First. From undue excitement by the presence of the batteries and main line of the Yankee army, dethroning their reason and banishing their common sense.

Second. From drinking liquor to stimulate their courage to meet the dangers in the impending battle.

Third. To cause the death of the disrespectful, disobedient and insubordinate Colonel Savage, who was constantly declaring that the army should be reorganized, Davis removed and a dictator appointed, or the conquest of the South by the abolitionists was a certainty. This made all office-holders the bitter enemy of Savage.

[If there is any foundation to the first accusation, it is that there was a sense of urgency to seize the lone battery, and clearly, this urgency superseded the deployment of the entire division. Although Savage was brash as well as sometimes disrespectful, disobedient and insubordinate, the belief that he was targeted for death by his superiors is likely just sheer paranoia that he suffered from. But as Savage and Lord Byron point out, sometimes fact is stranger than fiction.]

Captain J. J. Womack's diary detailed the events of the day. He commanded Company E of the Sixteenth Tennessee. Like the previous primary sources, historians would have to seriously cherry-pick this record of events to make Womack's testimony coincide with their version of events. Reading this record (in order and unedited) gives the full and complete testimony of what he and his comrades witnessed. It can hardly be taken out of context. Due to Womack's position on the field and in the regimental line, his experiences were not inclusive of the Hafley cabins and are thus not mentioned in his account of the fight.

DIARY ENTRY OF CAPTAIN J. J. WOMACK[175]

Oct. 8. Wednesday—Clear & hot. The enemy began cannonading at sunrise and continued slowly till about nine o'clock in the morning, occasionally answered by our skirmishers and some pretty brisk firing was heard along our front lines. Our division (Cheatham's) changed position from where we were first formed in rear of Perryville to our extreme right and took a position in the front line about this time. Here our division remained till about noon, all of which time considerable cannonading was going on along most of the line. About twelve o'clock the batteries of our division were put in position and brought to bear on one of the enemy's now opened just in our front. The duel between these two lasted about two hours, and was said to be the briskest of the day. Here one of our Brigadiers, whose name I do not now remember, was wounded in the head by one of the enemy's shells. About this time the battery of our brigade (General Donelson's) commanded by Capt. Carnes, moved from its present position farther to the right, immediately after which, the whole division moved in double quick, forward, near one mile across some fields, and again halted and formed.

[At this halt, the division had reached the hillside near the Walker House on the southwestern slopes of Walker's Bend. At this division assembly area, the regiments were instructed to drop their extra gear and prepare to advance to their attack position.]

Here we remained but a short time, stopping only long enough to pile away all the extra weight about us, such as blankets, knapsacks etc. Again we moved forward across a small creek, and quietly formed in line of battle behind the top of the hill, lying, till the whole line would have time to cross over and form.

[As noted above, Womack stated that they crossed Chaplin River and "formed in line of battle behind the top of the hill." Realizing that the remaining regiments of the brigade and Stewart's brigade had to ascend the steep embankment and form, common sense explains that the regiment did not form within one-hundred yards of the bank. The regiment clearly had to advance due west for several hundred yards to create space for the trailing units to ascend the bank and form. This would suggest that the regiment advanced over three-hundred yards to a point north of the entrance of the park. The position would also help explain distances related by Womack in the next few lines—as well as Savage's testimony regarding the distance of the guns in the regiment's front.]

We now occupied ground about three hundred yards from where the enemy lay concealed in an enclosed wood, about one quarter of a mile in length north and south. At each extremity of this wood they had placed a battery. The one at the northern extremity, of 7 guns, that at the southern about the same.

[This mention of two batteries of artillery suggests that from their position—north of the modern-day park entrance—they may have observed Stone's battery nearly 700 yards away to their left-front and Parsons' battery unlimbering about 350 yards to their right front on Open Knob. Womack failed to mention the change of direction by the regiment after it started the advance, but he does note that the regiment was directly in front of the "seven-gun battery."]

"Victory" for our motto was shouted all along our line, and fearlessly and gallantly we charged them. The Regt. to which I belonged (Col. Savage's) was on the extreme right of Gen. Bragg's army, and was directly in front of the seven-gun battery before spoken of.

[In the foregoing, it is clear that the regiment had already conducted the change of direction and began their charge. They were then ascending the south-eastern slopes of Open Knob and approaching the fence and cabins. In the following, Womack tries to explain why the Sixteenth suffered so severely at the "onset."]

---

[175] J. J. Womack, *The Civil War Diary of Capt. J. J. Womack* (McMinnville, TN: Womack Printing Company, 1961) p. 62-4.

Donelson's brigade either executed orders too promptly, or else other commands not hastily enough, in consequence of which this brigade, and the 16th regiment especially, was exposed to a most terrific fire from both the above batteries and at the same time an opening line of infantry. Here at the onset we suffered very much both in officers and men.

[Womack made it clear that the regiment was struck by the fire of at least two batteries and the line of infantry at the fence as soon as they came under fire.]

The men from drought and fatigue were almost exhausted at the opening, but they made the charge & received the fire of the enemy, although the first battle in which most of them had ever engaged, in a manner worthy the cause in which they were engaged.

[As will be noted in this account and several others of the regiment, the Sixteenth single-handedly made no less than three charges on the enemy line at this point in the first thirty minutes of the battle. In the following, Womack describes his regiment falling back to the edge of the woods after breaking the enemy line at the fence in the face of heavy enemy fire.]

With two batteries and the whole line of infantry occupying a chosen position, pouring a destructive fire upon us, (one brigade) we were compelled, after the most stubborn resistance possibly to be made, to fall back, not without however, having first dislodged the enemy from his stronghold and chosen ground.

[Womack has made it clear that the enemy at the fence was "dislodged" in the first assault. Womack now relates that they then attempted another charge within only minutes of their first. It was likely this second charge that the regiment gained the fence on their right and the cover of the Hafley cabins as earlier explained by Colonel Savage.]

With our numbers now much weakened we rallied and charged them a second time, with about the same success as the first.

[Below, Womack describes that at least a portion of the regiment fell back to the fence and woods and the regiment prepared to charge for a third time. Historians have often taken the term "fall back" too far. In both Noe's and Hafendorfer's books, the regiment and brigade are supposed to have fallen back several hundred yards to near their starting point. Womack's and others' testimony clarify that this all took place in thirty minutes or so, and the regiment only fell back to the nearest cover to rally for another attempt. Next, Womack makes it clear that the third charge was successful driving the enemy from Parsons' battery, but he doubted that it would have been if Maney's brigade had not arrived on their right when they did.]

Again we were compelled to fall back, and again formed and charged them a third time, but our forces were so diminished by this time that I am not at all sure we would have been able to drive them from their guns had it not been for the timely arrival of re-enforcements on our right.

[Womack now explains that the appearance of Maney's brigade "struck terror to the already retreating enemy." His mention that they (Maney's men) "scarcely fired a gun themselves" illustrates the difference in time that the Sixteenth was under the fire of these guns versus Maney's brigade. He also mentions the enemy falling back to a lane three-hundred yards to their rear. This was clearly the retreat of Terrill's brigade to Benton Road at the foot of Starkweather's Heights. Other historians suggest that this is in reference to Dixville Crossroads in rear of Harris' battery; however, Womack continues that they didn't resist the Rebel advance as much at that second point. It is also common knowledge that no Confederate attacks took place at Dixville Crossroads. The Twenty-first Wisconsin was quickly routed from their position at the cornfield and Benton Road, and the remnants of that unit and Terrill's men retreated atop Starkweather's Heights.]

Fortunately however they appeared in time to gain the day, although they scarcely fired a gun themselves. But their appearance on the field stuck terror to the already retreating enemy, who fell back about three hundred yards, on their second line, but the resistance they made was very slight compared with that of their first.

[In yet another reference of Parsons' battery, Womack makes it clear that the Federals left a battery of seven guns in their possession at the point where the Sixteenth attacked. The only battery containing more than six guns at Perryville comprised Parsons' battery. He also mentions the death of General Jackson who was known by both sides to be killed at this battery. Still, historians have tried to morph this testimony to fit an attack on Harris' battery near dusk.]

They had now not only left their splendid battery of seven cross pieces in our hands, which they had been commanded never to desert, together with many a one of their fellows slain and wounded, but also their general, the gallant Jackson, who fell exhorting his men never to abandon the field.

[While historians have tried to imply that Donelson's brigade was pulled from the fight at this point, Womack makes it clear that they continued in the attack until about 5 p.m. He doesn't mention—as Cheatham did—that the brigade reformed in the ravine, but as Donelson described, the brigade was recommitted after reforming. Donelson later mentioned that the division conducted a "general falling back" when the battle slackened in their front. This was probably about 5 p.m. They then resupplied their ammunition and retrieved the Eighth and Fifty-first regiments. Both Donelson and Cheatham refer to the last attack that took place about 5:30 to 5:45 p.m.]

Soon after this, about five o'clock in the evening, the regiments of the first Tennessee brigade were withdrawn and held in reserve for half an hour, when about sunset they were marched in again; but night coming on and the enemy still retreating they were ordered to pursue no further.

[Womack has made mention of the brigade being marched back to the fight, but oddly, he included no mention of a fight near Widow Gibson's or any cabins that resulted in the capture of Harris' battery—or any other—at this time. In fact, no member of the regiment mentioned an attack that resulted in the capture of a battery at this hour. This is in complete contrast to what historians of the battle have concluded—i.e.—that the Sixteenth took part in the capture of Harris' battery near dusk. When Donelson's brigade did participate in the capture of Harris' guns, it would have been accomplished by Wood's brigade and the left of Donelson's brigade.

Farther down the line to our left, just at sunset the carnage was terrible indeed.

Thus closed the ever memorable eighth of October, 1862, on which the fierce and bloody battle of Perryville was bravely fought and nobly won.

Our loss on this occasion was heavy, but not near so heavy as that of the enemy. The 16th regiment went into the action with about 400 men, just fifty percent of whom were killed and wounded, the Col. among the latter.

Just fifty percent of my company (E) was wounded, but not a man killed upon the field; five or six had, notwithstanding, received mortal wounds.[176]

We occupied the field all night, taking care of the wounded; the enemy as well as our own comrades.

When the broad face moon began to shed her silvery beams on the faces of the dead and dying, the field presented a most horrible spectacle indeed; and the shrieks and groans of the wounded constantly pointed to where another brave and gallant fellow had sacrificed his all on the alter of liberty.

---

[176] According to the regimental casualty report, his company suffered twenty-five casualties; thus, the company probably went into action with about fifty effectives.

One of the most reliable of all the sources of the Sixteenth Tennessee is that of **Thomas R. Hooper**. He recorded the events in his 1862 diary. A copy from Stones River National Battlefield was obtained and copied verbatim from his handwriting in the original diary. This testimony helps to cement the facts and explain in detail the experiences and chronology of the battle for Donelson's brigade and the Sixteenth Tennessee. Hooper served in Company A and would have been on the extreme right of the regiment.

T. R. HOOPER'S DIARY ENTRY FOR OCTOBER 8, 1862.[177]

Wednesday October the 8th 1862 We remained in line of battle until about 11 oc A.M. When General Bragg came up and taken command in person then General Cheatham Donelson and Col. Savage all come back to their respective commands though previous to this there had been fighting going on most all day with cavlry We now had our positions on the left wing. But when Gen. Bragg taken command, our Division taken its proper place on the right as ours is the first division.

[As noted above, Bragg's presence on the field was noted and commanders returned to their original commands. However, it is still interesting to note that Bragg never actually claimed to command the forces at the battle, and he congratulated Polk in his report for his handling of the troops during the fight.]

We taken our position on the right and remained in position I guess something like 1 hour; but all this time very heavy cannonading was going on on both sides of our position for I guess something near ¾ of a mile from the enemie's line of battle. Up to this time their batteries had done but little damage to our lines. At this hour I guess about 2oc P.M. we were ordered to advance on the enemy, our brigade was in advance of the remainder of the Division.

[The brigade crossed the river in advance of the other brigades and moved to within three or four-hundred yards of the enemy. This may be where the change of direction took place. Cheatham and Polk must have been visible and within hearing distance of the extreme right flank of the regiment. This is clear evidence that the two generals were in proximity of the regiment when Cheatham told them to "Give 'em hell boy's!" and Polk declared "Go on! Do as General Cheatham says!"]

Continuing to advance the line got in 3 or 4 hundred yards of the enemy, when General Cheatham give command to charge – General Polk also told us to let the Yanks know what Tennessee steel was made for; we raised the yell and charged with few obstacles;

[After they had changed their direction to the right—as Savage, Biles and Donelson noted—they rushed up the hill attacking the 123rd Illinois behind the rail fence.]

got in 1 ½ or 200 yards where we turned loose on them, but we were now carried in advance of the other Regiments but we advanced on driving the Enemy before us; for some distance til we were about to be cut off at this critical time we got help by or from General Maney's Brigade

[Hooper failed to detail the three attacks at the fence and Hafley cabins, but clearly noted that it was the sudden arrival of Maney's brigade at the "critical time" that enabled them to capture Parsons' battery. This too is in complete contrast to historians' conclusions of the fight. If Hooper and the Sixteenth Tennessee didn't participate in the capture of a battery early in the fight, why would Hooper make this up? This is another example of "cherry picking" by historians to pick and choose what to use from a source—and when to use it.]

We were at this time and had been for some time in about fifty to one hundred yards of a battery of 8 or 9 pieces on our right and our left wing with another firing down our center, all heavily supported by infantry.

[The mention of more than one battery probably indicates Stone's battery on their left-front as suggested by Womack's testimony. The battery firing on their center may be indicative of Bush's battery. Regardless—in the following, Hooper

---

177 Thomas R. Hooper, *1862 Diary of Thomas R. Hooper*, (Photocopy on hand at Stones River National Battlefield, Murfreesboro, TN) p. 74-9.

clearly points out that "we"—the Sixteenth Tennessee—took the battery on their right with "our assistance." Hooper also makes it clear that in the supposed thirty minutes that the regiment was engaged alone, they had already "killed nearly all their horses, and a great many of their men." This too coincides with Federal accounts.]

We with our assistance now taken the battery on our right but before this I think we had killed nearly all their horses, and a great many of their men and to be regretted we had lost many of our brave fellows out of the old 16ᵗʰ. And I for one got knocked down by a grapeshot scalping me in the side of the head, but in a few minutes I was giving my lead away again

[Although Hooper received a wound in the initial attacks on Parsons' guns, he continued in the fight after the battery fell to his regiment and Maney's brigade. In the following, Hooper indicates that the regiment was relieved briefly. He—unaware of the relief—continued in the attack with the relief as he was wrapped up in the action in his front like so many other members of the regiment.]

In a short time after this our Regiment was relieved for a short time but I was a head of the rest of the company and Regiment and did not know that we were relieved til the Regiment came upon me I therefore staid a head with the relief for some time til we had driven the Yanks for near a half mile, when I got wounded again by a buckshot striking me in the left jaw knocking me down for the sixth time. I thought now that I was ruined for a few moments, for I bled liken to a hog that had been stuck where the shot entered about the mouth and impaired for a short time.

[It's amazing that Hooper was knocked down six times. Hooper was probably put out of action during one of the attacks against Starkweathers' Heights and Stone's battery alongside Stewart's relief.]

But in a few minutes I found that I was able to walk, but now very weak from the loss of so much blood. I think the shot lodged in my jaw breaking the bone I think. I was now so weak that I could not keep up. I therefore went to the rear, taken a pair of shoes off a dead Yank on my way but I would not have did it for any a account if I had not been in great need of them. I also picked up a cup and canteen could have got pistoles and a great many other things if I could have packed them. I went back through our Regiment found several wounded but did not see any one of our company killed. As I was not able to fight any longer and our surgeons had not time to dress wounds of those that were more serious than mine. I therefore started with some others of our Regiment that were able to walk to go to our Division Hospital. Walked about 1 mile then got ride 2 – 3 miles but did not find our Hospital.

First Lieutenant Jesse Walling was in Company E of the Sixteenth Tennessee. He explained his participation in the battle in a letter to Colonel Savage.[178]

"COLONEL JOHN H. SAVAGE:

DEAR SIR: In reply to your inquiry as to what I remember about the part your regiment took in the battle of Perryville, Ky., I would state that we were encamped near a creek when orders were given to break camp and move forward.

[The following lines reveal that they ascended the bank, formed line and moved "southward" a half mile. This suggestion that they moved "southward" has been taken too literally by historians as well. First, that distance south from Dug Road would have placed the regiment south of Doctor's Creek and within 230 yards of the Chatham House. It also would have placed the regiment within 700 yards northeast of Squire Bottom's and about 430 yards south-southeast of Widow Bottom's residence. To rectify this, historians have decreased that distance to only about 250 yards. However, it's likely that if his distance was that far off, his direction was probably off as well. Contemporary maps of that time have directions off by as much as 90°.]

We ascended a very steep embankment, formed line and moved southward, probably one-half mile, when General Donelson appeared, and after talking with you for about a minute or so we were ordered to charge the enemy. The first sight that we had of the enemy was a battery of beautiful cannon. We charged in right oblique course and were met by the grape and canister shot from these guns, which killed many of our men.

[Walling failed to mention the halt and redirection of the regiment, but stated that the regiment charged in "right oblique" toward the enemy guns. This was likely in reference to their change of direction. In the following, he mentions three distinct charges that the regiment made. The initial engagement is supposed to be against the 123rd Illinois. Although that enemy regiment was twice the size of the Sixteenth, the violence of action broke their regiment and allowed the campaign hardened Rebels to seize the fence. Each charge accomplished a little more—finally seizing the guns with the assistance of Maney's brigade. He then added that they continued pressing the enemy—"killing them as they ran." This is further evidence that the regiment—as a whole—didn't stop at the guns, but continued on with the left of Maney's brigade in their assault through the cornfield.]

All at once the enemy raised up from behind a rail fence, pouring a deadly fire into us and killing great numbers of our men. We fell back a short distance, rallied and charged again, meeting the same deadly fire which drove us back for the second time. The third time we went over the fence, driving the enemy before us, capturing the cannon. We continued running them, killing them as they ran. Their dead and wounded lay thick behind the fence and over the field.

[Below, Walling notes that the regiment was unsupported for "at least thirty minutes" before Maney appeared on their right.]

I was in the center of the regiment (Sixteenth Tennessee), and noticed that we were not supported either to the right or to the left. My company went into the fight numbering eighty-four men and next morning we only had sixteen men able for service. You will see that our loss was terrible, but the most surprising thing to me is that every man in your regiment was not killed, as we fought the enemy to the front, left and right flanks unsupported.

The Sixteenth was engaged with the enemy for at least thirty minutes when General Maney's men appeared to our right as we were running the enemy across the field.

[While Walling suggests that they were already running "the enemy across the field," it appears it was—in fact—the combined efforts of Maney's men and the Sixteenth in their final charge that broke Parsons' support and allowed the capture of the guns.]

---

[178] John H. Savage, *Life of John H. Savage*, Nashville, TN, 1903, p. 126-28.

I could not begin to name over all the dead and wounded as most all our company were in this list, and to name some of our brave and good and leave out others equally as honorable, I could not do.

Why our regiment was ordered to fight this battle alone and on a field where our position was decidedly against us I shall never be able to understand. To look at the great numbers of the enemy in comparison to our little regiment it seemed that we were brought up to be slaughtered.

[In the foregoing, it is clear the men in the ranks were bewildered at the lack of assistance they initially received. Their thirty minutes under fire probably seemed like an eternity.]

One of the bravest men I have ever seen was one of the enemy, who stood upon his fine brass gun, waving his hat over his head after all his comrades had fled. But he too fell in this brave act. I could not hear distinctly his words as he stood there waving his hat.

You will please pardon me for speaking of this brave fellow, but he is always before me when I think of this terrible battle. Yours very truly,

JESSE WALLING, *First Lieutenant.*"

Private Carroll Henderson Clark served in Company I of the Sixteenth Tennessee. His following account also differs in many respects to the conclusions made by historians.[179]

> We were formed into line & awaited the order to march forward. The enemy was about one half mile from us & the crack of the pickets rifle & the occasional roar of a cannon made us feel sad. The day (Oct. 8, 1862) was clear and beautiful. It was afternoon when we were ordered to move forward. We crossed a creek or brook and went out on top of the hill & ordered to halt and reform. We were in sight of the enemy & it looked to me like the whole face of the earth was covered with Yankeys *[sic]*.

[In the foregoing, Clark related crossing Chaplin River and moving to the "top of the hill." This is indicative of their movement up the western bluff of the River and onto the long finger of terrain that gradually sloped off to the south. This would probably have placed the regiment slightly north of the battlefield park's modern-day entrance. This was the ridgeline that had just been cleared of Federal skirmishers by Wharton's cavalry.]

> Shot & shell from their batterys *[sic]* made me wish that I was at home but oh my! We were ordered forward again. The whole line of battle was expected to keep in line on the forward movement, but some of the boys seemingly anxious to close in on the enemy raised the yell & rushed forward which caused our Regiment to get far in advance of our main line, & it is yet a wonder to me that any man in our Regiment escaped death.

[Perhaps, as Clark stated above, it was just sheer enthusiasm that caused the regiment to career ahead of its two sister regiments.]

> Three batteries of cannon & a Brigade of the enemy were directed at our Regiment & the boys were falling dead & wounded all around me, & I thought all would be killed. Some of my school & playmates, neighbors, and friends lost their lives there. 12 Van Buren County boys were killed & mortally wounded on Perryville's bloody field.

[Clark stated specifically that three batteries were playing on the regiment. There is no other location on the battlefield – other than Open Knob – where three batteries could have directed their fire on the regiment. These were the batteries of Parsons atop the knob and Stone and Bush atop Starkweather's Height west of Benton Road.]

> If you wish to know how a soldier feels in such a battle as that, you must ask some one else. I cannot explain, but I had no hope of getting out alive. Such trials as that has a tendency to temporarily derange the minds of some, at least it was the case with me. If you ask me if I was scared, I answer, I don't know, but I do know that I was scared before we got in the thickest of the fight. We were in 40 yards of the enemy & they were falling fast. I hurriedly glanced to the right & left to see if the main line was engaged. Genl. Maney's Brigade came to our rescue on our right, & saved the remainder of our regiment from being killed & captured.

[Although Clark doesn't indicate how long the regiment was engaged, he does relate that they were forty yards from the enemy and Maney's brigade came to their assistance on their right. This has been corroborated by both Savage and Maney as taking place within the first thirty to forty minutes of the battle.]

> Many times when thinking of that bloody battle, the tears roll down my cheeks, & I cannot force them back now while writing this article. Some sheep and rabbits were between the two lines, scared and demoralized, but I paid no attention to them. Some claimed that they never dreaded a battle & some claimed to have a gizzard full of sand…

> The enemy finally retreated & we followed on. They loaded as they fell back but would whirl & shoot back. As we passed the little cabin on the hill I was seriously wounded through my right side above my hip. We then had them on the run.

---

[179] Carrol Henderson Clark, *My Grandfather's Diary of the Civil War/Carrol H. Clark, Co. I Sixteenth Regiment Tennessee Volunteers, C.S.A.,* McMinnVille, TN: C. W. Clark Jr., Articles 14-15.

[Once again, a member of the regiment refers to a cabin in the foregoing. This could not have been Widow Gibson's as it was so far behind Federal lines in the initial combat, additionally, Maney's brigade never crossed over that portion of the field. This is more evidence of the Hafley cabins on Open Knob. Note the three batteries that could have engaged the Sixteenth Tennessee. Parsons' battery is atop the knob at the position of the 105th Ohio, with Stone and Bush approximately three to four hundred yards west-south-west.]

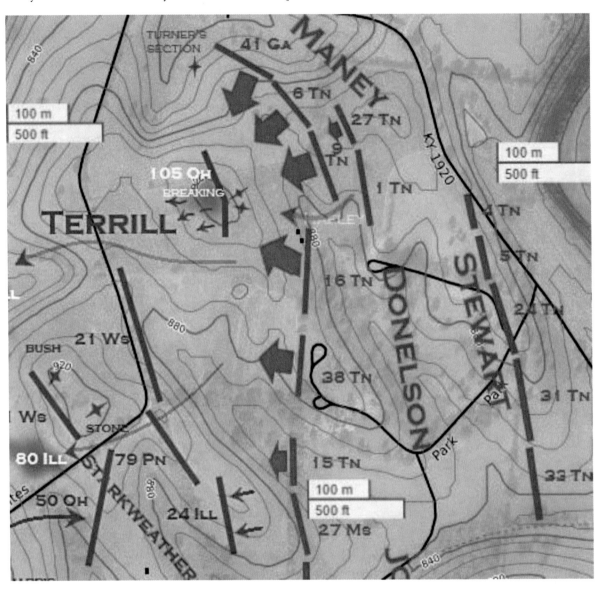

Private James R. Thompson was in Company A of the Sixteenth Tennessee. His account also makes reference to the Hafley cabins and the battery that was in such close proximity to the regiment's right flank.[180]

The weather was dry and water was scarce. There was a long hole of water in the bed of Chapman Creek and a spring near it. Buell pressed his attack to our left and in the direction of the spring and pool of water. Our Cavalry there advanced and checked it and Hardee's Corps was sent to their relief. The enemy was posted in line of battle a few hundred yards from Chapman *[sic]* Creek. We were ordered to attack him and we had to climb a hill which was difficult to ascend. We went up an old road, and the 15th Tennessee reached the top about the time we did.

[Thompson has made reference to the bluff on the west bank of Chaplin River and the Dug Road.]

We were given a few minutes rest. We were then ordered forward, which was obeyed with a loud "Hurrah!" We were perhaps two hundred yards from the enemy when we were ordered to open fire, which we did with effect on the enemy, judging from the piles of dead which were before us after firing a few rounds.

Colonel Savage who was in front of our line rode around to our site and his horse got wounded. I ran forward to a little stump six or eight inches through and about two feet high and rested my gun on the top and took deliberate aim. Before I could fire, some of our men shot a ball into the stump, which barely missed me. I stormed out at them that if any of the shot me, I would come back there and kill him. About this time we were ordered to charge, and we went forward with a rush. The enemy fell back and we crossed the fence they were behind, amid hundreds of their slain.

[Thompson made mention of the regiment's first and second charges. The first had forced the 123rd Illinois back, and the second charge had gained the Hafley Cabins and fence where Colonel Savage was wounded.]

Just at this time Colonel Savage got wounded. I was right by him, and he said to me, "I am wounded. Where is Colonel Donelson? He will have to take charge of the Regiment." Colonel Donelson appeared on the right where I was and a flanking party had started around us on our right with their guns at a right shoulder shift. Our men had failed to get up the hill as fast as we did.

[At this point, the regiment had seized the Hafley cabins and the 123rd Illinois had been routed, but a wing of the 105th Ohio was bearing down on the right flank of the regiment.]

Just at this critical moment, Maney's Brigade appeared upon the scene. With a yell they charged and drove back the flanking party. We had been in the fight 30 minutes according to Colonel Savage's statement, with no help except the 15th Tennessee. They were on our left. We would have been captured in ten or fifteen minutes longer. There was a battery just to our right side. When the flanking party was driven back, I thought it should be silenced or captured. There were two little log cabins just behind the enemy line that we had captured and a fence running about north and south.

[Maney has come to the immediate right of the regiment. Thompson has noted Parsons' battery that was a short distance to the regiment's right flank and the two cabins comprising the Hafley Cabins. He and others participate in the third and final attempt to seize the guns with Maney's brigade.]

I jumped over this little fence and started toward the battery. I came to a small shade tree and rested my gun against it. I commenced firing at the cannoneers. A ball from down the fence tore through my hat and hair. About this time Alvin Simpson, one of my company, came and rested his gun against the six or seven inch tree and fired. A ball from the same direction that had clipped so close to me, split his hat on the side about four inches. When the flanking party was driven back, it opened the way for our artillery,

---

[180] James R. Thompson, *Hear the Wax Fry*, McMinnville, TN, 1966, Ed. Nellie Boyd, p. 9-10.

which was put in use with vigor. And the enemy finally yielded this line and fell back a few hundred yards to a lane.

[In the foregoing, Thompson mentions the assistance of Turner's battery opening fire and the retreat of the Federals to a lane "a few hundred yards." This lane would have been Benton Road which is almost exactly three-hundred yards west of Open Knob. There is no other location on the field where a lane is that distance in rear of a battery that was captured in the first thirty to forty minutes of the battle with Maney's brigade. Other histories suggest the lane is the Dixville Crossroads in rear of Harris' battery, but that battery was not captured until nearly six p.m. as was seen in the reports of the Federal commanders.]

They reformed their lines and arranged their artillery. The battle now raged with terror and the slaughter was terrible. About sundown the enemy withdrew from this line and fell back to a woods about three miles. So the battle was over for the day and we had won a complete victory.

Private Thomas A. Head served in Company I of the Sixteenth Tennessee Infantry regiment. He was the first historian of the regiment and had promised his comrades he would write a history of the regiment while still serving in the ranks. Since Head was present on the field at the battle, it was assumed that his knowledge of the battle would be impeccable. However, Head may very well have been a member of the infirmary corps during the battle. Whether or not he was serving in the battle lines that day, he was detailed to remain behind to nurse the wounded following the battle. It is uncertain how accurate his minute description of the battle is. If he served with the infirmary corps, he spent his time helping wounded off the field rather than being a participant in the actions of the regiment that day. On the other hand, much of what he wrote may be eyewitness testimony, or that of comrades that described the battle to him in some detail. Either way, Head—like Marcus Toney—would reveal more than one version of the battle. But, unlike Toney—his versions of the battle differed in some substance, as he apparently learned more about the actions there in the years following the war. These accounts are provided in the same chronological order as Marcus Toney's following accounts. This first account is from a newspaper article that he had published only one year prior to the unit history's publication in 1884.

The enemy's advance having been checked by the Texas cavalry, formed line of battle in double columns about eight hundred yards from the west bank of Chaplin on the east side of a hill. Polk's corps appeared before the bluff. At the top of the bluff the men were given a moment to rest and the word "forward" was given. The men obeyed with a yell. For six hundred yards the ground was irregular, with stone fences running in different directions. At this distance from the bluff and two hundred yards from the enemy, there was slight trough shaped depression in the ground, running parallel with the enemies lines. As the 16th approached the lowest point of this depression the enemy opened a murderous fire upon them with musketry and artillery from right, left and front. The ranks of the 16th were mowed down at a fearful rate. The 8th Tennessee regiment also suffered severely. The ranks closed up and the brigade pressed onward in the charge. Col. Savage was in the lead of his regiment and directed its movements as calmly as if it had been a regimental drill. As the 8th and 16th moved up the hill the fight grew more and more desperate. Heavy charges of grape and canister were hurled into the ranks from the front and on the flanks. Stewart's brigade now came up and formed on the left of Donelson's, by which support the 8th was partially relieved of the severe cross fire upon their left wing.

[Head was wrong in his belief that the Eighth Tennessee supported his regiment on the left. This was the Fifteenth and Thirty-eighth Tennessee regiments. The Eighth Tennessee was still detached with Carnes' battery. Head was also wrong in the idea that Stewart's brigade joined to the left of his brigade. As seen in Cheatham's report, this was not done until Parsons' battery fell and then Stewart marched *through* Donelson's brigade rather than to the left.]

Buell was still bearing to his left, and a heavy force was now massed in front and on the right of the 16th Tennessee regiment. The enemy now bent his lines around the right flank of the 16th Tennessee, near an old log hut, and poured into its ranks an enfilading fire of artillery and musketry.

[The flanking force that Head mentions—was more than likely—a wing of the 105th Ohio that had just advanced from the west out of a ravine and was threatening the Sixteenth's right flank near the Hafley cabins.]

The regiment held its ground for half an hour, when Maney's brigade formed on its right and attacked the flanking party of the enemy. Gen. Maney succeeded in turning the enemy's line on the right of the 16th. This opened the way for artillery, which was hurried to the scene and planted at the point of the angle. The battle on the Confederate right now raged with fury and the slaughter was terrible.

[Cheatham had placed two 12 lb. howitzers of Turner's battery near the angle and was able to enfilade the extreme flank of Terrill's brigade.]

The enemy finally yielded this line and fell back to a lane at the top of the hill, about three hundred yards distant. In this line the enemy reformed his lines and planted his batteries. The Confederates were prompt to appropriate every inch of ground they had gained in the struggle, and were soon pouring destructive volleys into his ranks. The enemy contested this ground stubbornly and the Confederates pressed the assault with vigor. The enemy, after losing several of his guns and many valuable officers, including two Brigadier Generals, yielded this line about sundown, and the battle ended for the day.

[After Parsons' battery fell, the enemy had withdrawn to Starkweather's Heights which was along Benton Road at the top of the hill where Bush and Stone's batteries were placed.]

The enemy retired to a timbered region about three miles from his original lines of the evening. The Confederates held the field at night, and had gained a decided victory. The losses on both sides had been heavy, and the battle, for the number of men and the length of time engaged, was the severest of the war. The 16th Tennessee regiment lost over two hundred men. The 8th suffered severely, as did also the 15th Tennessee, of Donelson's, and the 1st of Maney's brigade.

[The Eighth Tennessee suffered only thirty-three casualties of nearly 440 men engaged. The Fifteenth Tennessee suffered thirty-four of less than 200 men engaged, while the Sixteenth suffered nearly sixty-percent losses. In the following, Head presents the idea that the Sixteenth Tennessee engaged the Thirty-third Ohio and the Seventh Ohio whom he attributes Colonel Moore to commanding.]

The 16th engaged the 33d Ohio in the first of the battle and subsequently the 7th Ohio, commanded by Colonel Oscar F. Moore. Col. Savage received two wounds in this battle and had his horse shot under him, but he remained on the field till the issue was decided. Late in the evening he became exhausted from the loss of blood. Bishop Quintard dressed his wounds, and Dr. Cross, Chaplain of Donelson's brigade, procured comfortable quarters for him at a farm house near the field and remained with him during the night.

[The following suggests that General James Jackson was brought into Rebel lines by the Sixteenth Tennessee. Jackson was in fact killed dead on the field and left there after being stripped of belongings. His body was found the next day by Federals on Open Knob.]

The Federal General, Jackson, was brought in by Savage's men a prisoner and mortally wounded. A Federal Colonel was also brought in a prisoner and severely wounded. This man proved to be Col. Oscar F. Moore, of the 7th Ohio, and was personally acquainted with Col. Savage in the U.S. Congress. He told Col. Savage his regiment had suffered severely, and lost over half its number. Col. Savage told him the same of his regiment. The two regiments had engaged each other during the day, and the commander of each was wounded and one commander was a prisoner. Col. Savage assured Col. Moore that he should have the best attention that was in his power to bestow, and ordered his surgeons and attendants to bestow upon Col. Moore the same attention that would be given to one of their own men. Gen. Jackson and Col. Savage recognized each other at once, having been old acquaintances in public life. The General died within a few hours.

[Savage never stated that he spoke with Colonel Moore after his capture, and he certainly didn't recognize the dead General Jackson whose body was still on the field.]

The wounded were cared for as well as the circumstances would allow. All who could travel were sent to Harrodsburg. Those not able to bear transportation were taken to the farm houses of the neighborhood where hospitals were established.[181]

The second telling of the story of the regiment came from Head's book *Campaigns and Battles of the Sixteenth Regiment, Tennessee Volunteers* that was published in 1885. By this time, he had made some corrections to his narrative, but still stated that his regiment engaged the Thirty-third Ohio. This was his belief, as the regiment had captured its commanding officer.

Some Texas cavalry charged the advance-guard of two regiments about the time of their arrival at the spring and drove them back. Polk's corps was hurried to the right. Hastening down the Chaplin at double-quick, it was formed in line of battle near the spring before mentioned. The enemy's advance

---

[181] *Southern Standard* (McMinnville, Tennessee) Aug. 2, 1884, p. 2

having been checked by the Texas cavalry, formed a line of battle in double column about eight hundred yards from the top of the bluff, on the west bank of the Chaplin and on the east side of a hill. Polk's corps appeared before the bluff. Ascending the bluff in line of battle, by brigades, the top was gained with difficulty. Donelson's brigade was the first to gain the top of the heights. The enemy was posted in their front, in double columns, eight hundred yards distant.

[In the foregoing, Head stated the distance from the bluff to the enemy lines at 800 yards. That is nearly the precise distance to Open Knob. Below he notes a "trough-like" depression in the ground two hundred yards shy of the enemy lines. This is the hollow that Savage relates that ran parallel to the Federal lines.]

The men were given a moment to rest at the top of the bluff, and the word "Forward" was given. The men obeyed with a yell. For six hundred yards the ground was irregular, and having stone fences running in different directions, the men scaled them without difficulty. At this point there was a slight trough-like depression in the ground, running parallel with the enemy's lines. As the Sixteenth Tennessee approached the lowest point of this depression the enemy opened a murderous fire upon them with musketry and artillery from right, left, and front. The ranks of the Sixteenth Regiment were mowed down at a fearful rate, and the Fifteenth Regiment also suffered severely. The ranks closed up and the brigade pressed onward in the charge. Colonel Savage was with his men directing their movements as calmly as if it had been a regimental drill.

As the Fifteenth and Sixteenth Tennessee Regiments moved up the hill and came nearer to the enemy, the fight grew more and more desperate. Heavy charges of grape and canister were hurled into their ranks from the front and on the flanks. Stewart's brigade now came up and formed on the left of Donelson's brigade, by which support the Fifteenth Tennessee was partially relieved of the severe cross-fire upon its left wing. Buell was still bearing to his left, and a heavy force was now massed in front, and on the right of the Sixteenth Tennessee Regiment. The enemy bending his line around the right flank of the Sixteenth Tennessee Regiment near an old log cabin, an enfilading fire of musketry and artillery was poured into its ranks; yet the regiment held its ground for half an hour, when Maney's brigade came up and formed on its right. General Maney charged this flanking party of the enemy, and swung it around on its main line, forming an angle in the shape of the letter V.

[Head incorrectly relates the arrival of Stewart's brigade which may have been the Thirty-eighth Tennessee arriving on the regiment's left. He does note the Hafley cabin as "an old log cabin" as well as the time-frame the regiment held their ground the initial combat. Just as Maney and Savage stated, the regiment was engaged for "half an hour" before Maney's brigade "came up and formed on its right." In the following he relates the arrival of Turner's howitzers that engage Terrill's brigade from the extreme northern flank—only two hundred yards away according to Cheatham's testimony. Note that he then adds the enemy "fell back to a lane at the top of the hill, about three hundred yards distant. This was Benton Road and Starkweather's heights.]

This opened the way for artillery, which was hurried to the scene and planted at the point of the angle. The battle on the right now raged with fury, and the slaughter was terrible. The enemy finally yielded this line and fell back to a lane at the top of the hill, about three hundred yards distant. In this lane he reformed his lines and planted his batteries. The Confederates were prompt to appropriate every inch of ground which they gained from the enemy, and were quickly pouring destructive volleys into his ranks along the lane. The enemy contested this ground stubbornly. The Confederates pressed the assault with vigor. The enemy, after losing several of his guns and many valuable officers, including two brigadier generals, yielded this line about sundown, and the battle ended for the day. The enemy retired to a timbered region about three miles from their first line of the evening. The Confederates held the field at night, and had gained a decided victory.

The losses on both sides had been heavy, and the battle, for the number of men and the length of time engaged, was the severest of the war. The Sixteenth Tennessee lost over two hundred men. The Eighth

Tennessee suffered severely, as did also the Fifteenth Tennessee, of Donelson's, and the First Tennessee, of Maney's brigades. The Sixteenth Tennessee engaged the Thirty-third Ohio, and subsequently the Seventh Ohio, which was commanded by Colonel Oscar F. Moore.

[It appears Head had read two accounts written by Savage in newspapers and somehow confused Perryville with Murfreesboro. The Eighth Tennessee was fortunate to sustain only thirty-three casualties.]

Colonel Savage received two wounds early in the fight, and had his horse shot under him, but he remained on the field till the issue was decided. Late in the evening he became exhausted from loss of blood. Dr. Charles K. Mauzy, Surgeon of the Sixteenth Tennessee Regiment, dressed his wound, and Dr. Cross, the brigade chaplain, procured quarters for him in a farm-house, and attended him through the night. The Federal general, Jackson, was killed by Savage's men. A Federal colonel was brought in a prisoner, and severely wounded. This man proved to be Colonel Oscar F. Moore, said to be of the Seventh Ohio, and was personally acquainted with Colonel Savage in the United States Congress. He told Colonel Savage that his regiment had suffered severely, and had lost near half its number. Colonel Savage told the Federal officer the same of his own regiment. The two regiments had engaged each other through the day. Both had engaged each other through the day. Both had suffered greatly, and the commander of each regiment was wounded, and one a prisoner. Colonel Savage assured Colonel Moore that he should have the best attention that it was in his power to bestow, and ordered the surgeons and attendants to bestow upon Colonel Moore the same attention they would bestow upon one of their own men. General Jackson and Colonel Savage had known each other in public life.

[Head also attributes the death of Jackson to the Sixteenth Tennessee in addition to Savage, Womack and others in the regiment.]

The wounded were cared for as well as the circumstances would allow. All who could travel were sent to Harrodsburg. Those not able to bear transportation were taken to the farm-houses of the neighborhood, where hospitals were established.[182]

Head's third telling was in a newspaper article published in 1907 that relates the story with a few more changes.

The Federals had chosen a strong position near a thousand yards from the top of the bluffs of the Chaplain. These bluffs had to be scaled by the troops in line of battle. There was a distillery at the foot of the hill and a part of the line went through the premises of the distillery. While the men halted a minute to adjust the lines before the ascent was commenced, the owners and operatives of the distillery came along the lines hurriedly each bearing a bucket of whisky with a dipper or cup, and handed the whisky out to the men by the dipperfull. It was all done in a few minutes time and only a few men got the whisky. The ascent was made and the top of the hill was gained. As the sides of the bluffs were almost perpendicular except in a gap merely wide enough for two regiments to ascend in line of battle, the Sixteenth Tennessee and the Fifteenth Tennessee were the two first regiments to ascend the hill. These were of Donelson's Brigade under Colonel Savage, and two other regiments of the brigade were sent under Colonel Wharton of the Texas Rangers along with Carnes' Battery to strike the enemy in the rear of his left flank. The remaining regiment of the foot of the bluff following with Stewart's brigade. *[sic] [The remaining regiment of the brigade was still at the foot of the bluff following with Stewart's brigade.]*

[Interestingly, Head relates in this 1907 version of the battle that Savage was in command of Donelson's brigade "under Savage."]

---

[182] Head, Thomas A. *Campaigns and Battles of the Sixteenth Regiment Tennessee Volunteers* (Cumberland Presbyterian Printing House: Nashville, TN, 1885) p. 95-98.

The enemy was posted from eight hundred yards distant in an open field. Here came a matter that has figured in history like the battle of Gettysburg. There was some confusion in commands, and Col. Savage, who was in command of the brigade, thought best to await the arrival of the other regiments of the brigade before advancing any further. General Donelson came up about this time, and, thinking the other troops were up the hill, ordered Col. Savage to advance with his column of two regiments. Col. Savage told him to give the command himself, and he (Savage) would execute it. General Donelson ordered: "First Brigade, forward, march!" Col. Savage repeated the command, and the 16th and 15th Tennessee Regiments went to the attack in which they were mowed down by a heavy fire of grape and canister and musketry in front, and a heavy cross-fire from right and left. The 38th Tennessee finally formed on the left of the 15th Tennessee, and Stewart's Brigade on the left of the 38th. Maney's Brigade came up on the right of the 16th, and until this support came up, the 15th and 16th Tennessee Regiments, for a half an hour at least, fought the whole left wing of Buell's army. The expedition under Col. Wharton on the enemy's left was a success, and Buckner's command came up meanwhile, and turned the enemy's left flank, and the day was won.

The losses on each side was fearful. The 16th Tennessee Regiment lost two hundred men before the support arrived. The 15th Tennessee was nearly destroyed. It was a mere handful of men when it went into the fight. Gen. Bragg came upon the scene from Frankfort, while the battle was going on.[183]

---

[183] "The Battle of Perryville." *Nashville Banner* (Nashville, Tennessee) Feb. 27, 1907, p. 10.

In addition to the foregoing members of the Sixteenth Tennessee—whose testimony supports historical revision—the following members of the First Tennessee *greatly supplements* the evidence provided by the rank and file of the regiment.

Private T. J. Wade was a member of **Company I—The Rutherford Rifles—First Tennessee Infantry** regiment of Maney's brigade. He wrote an article that was published in a Murfreesboro newspaper in 1880 about his experiences at the Battle of Perryville. In it he clearly states that his brigade came to Donelson's assistance *before* the attack on Bush's battery—where the First Tennessee sustained such frightful losses. He notes the attack of the Ninth Tennessee on Parsons' battery in the regiment's front and then the advance toward Bush's battery.

The storms of shell are slackened, and the arms of Donelson's men roar incessantly. We are ordered to march to his support and over rock fences, hills and every other obstacle, we double quick, and soon we form in Donelson's rear. Now the 9th of our Brigade and perhaps others enter the action, 1st regiment in reserve, and here fell the pure and spotless Sam Ransom. We are ordered to charge and passing through a cornfield, Len Smith fell. Further on we reach a fence and here we jumped Rosseau's line of battle, and as it retreated up the hill, it melted like "butter in the sun." On the top of this hill we met his reserves and here we sustained our heaviest loss, loosing six of the flower of the company, perhaps in as many minutes.[184]

Private Marcus B. Toney was a member of **Company B—Rock City Guards—First Tennessee Infantry** regiment of Maney's brigade. Toney left *four records* of what he witnessed at the Battle of Perryville. His company was on the extreme left of the First Tennessee and was nearly *adjacent* to the Sixteenth Tennessee in their simultaneous attack to seize Parsons' battery. Each of his accounts corroborate one another and each also adds a touch more detail to the experiences of his regiment. The first of his accounts was written in 1893 during an interview with a reporter—although not directly attributed to Toney—that mirrors Toney's later accounts of the fight. If it wasn't Toney, it only helps to shore up his other accounts—as it would give yet *another member* of the First Tennessee sustaining Toney's account of the battle.

It was just such a day as this, Cheatham's matchless division bore the brunt of the fight, and struggled with grim determination for victory against three army corps, and at the close of the day lay down to sleep, or rather rest, on a field literally covered with dead and wounded. I was a member of Company B, Rock City Guards, and we went into that fight thirty-three strong, and when it closed fourteen were killed and thirteen wounded. Our regiment, with Savage's, was ordered to take the enemies' artillery, and in the effort were almost destroyed. In that fight the gallant First began a record which became more glorious as the war progressed. We took Parsons' splendid battery and charged Bush's, but when we reached the second battery there were not enough men left to claim the prize, although nearly every artilleryman was either killed or wounded.[185]

[In the above, he clearly stated that his regiment "with Savage's, was ordered to take the enemies' artillery." He continued that they "took Parsons' splendid battery." He then briefly related the assault on Bush's battery which resulted in their repulse. The **second account** is directly attributed to Toney as the author of the article. It was published in June, 1904 and includes more detail.]

About 3 o'clock the artillery from the enemy began to boom, followed by musketry. The First Tennessee moved in line of battle across Chaplin River and up the bluff. When we reached the summit we came upon Gen. *[sic]* Savage's regiment and he was hotly engaged with the enemy. Gen. Polk rode up and asked what regiment. The answer from Col. Fields, the First Tennessee.

---

[184] "Rutherford Rifles." *Free Press* (Murfreesboro, TN) Apr. 23, 1880, p. 2.

[185] "Anniversary of Perryville." *The Tennessean* (Nashville, TN) Oct. 9, 1893, p. 3.

The next command was, "Move your regiment by the right flank." As soon as we uncovered from Col. Savage's right we moved against the enemy, which in our immediate front was Gen. Jackson's brigade of Ohio troops, although they were all Germans.

When we charged they fled precipitately, and in attempting to rally them Gen. Jackson was killed. We captured Parsons' eight-gun battery in Col. Savage's onslaught. He had lost heavily, and when we made another charge to capture Bush's Indiana battery, which appeared to be supported by a double line of troops, we exposed our left flank to an enfilade fire, which mowed our men like grass before the sickle. Ten men were shot down with the colors, all of whom were killed or died.

Subsequently, all of Company B except six men were place hors de combat. The regimental loss was about 250. Col. Savage lost about 199, and in the space of two hours the battle was over.

I did not wonder that Col. Jno. H. Savage of the Sixteenth Tennessee, and Col. George Maney of the First Tennessee, wept bitterly, for the flower of their regiments were dead or bleeding.[186]

[Toney's personal experiences are plain to be understood when he stated, "we came upon Gen. *[sic]* Savage's regiment and he was hotly engaged with the enemy." He continues, "As soon as we uncovered from Col. Savage's right we moved against the enemy, which in our immediate front was Gen. Jackson's brigade of Ohio troops." He then stated that General Jackson was killed and "*We captured Parsons' eight-gun battery in Col. Savage's onslaught.*" This experience is in concert with the accounts of the men in the Sixteenth Tennessee and is not arguable. To add more weight to his recollection, he states the casualties of the Sixteenth Tennessee and the fact that "Col. Jno. H. Savage of the Sixteenth Tennessee, and Col. George Maney of the First Tennessee, wept bitterly, for the flower of their regiments were dead or bleeding."

Toney's **third account** of the battle was from his autobiography that was published in 1907. This account closely resembles the above account with less detail as it wasn't an article specifically about the battle, but an autobiography that covered his experiences throughout the war.]

There had been some skirmishing before our arrival, and about three o'clock the musketry and cannonading became quite brisk, the shells falling around us as we climbed the fence in battle line. We crossed Chaplin River, ascended a high bluff, and when we reached the height Colonel Savage's Sixteenth Regiment was hotly engaged with the enemy. To uncover from Colonel Savage we had to move by the right flank, and while executing this move some of our men were wounded. When we uncovered, we again moved by the left flank. General Leonidas Polk rode up and asked: "What regiment is this?" The answer was: "The First Tennessee." He then said: "Capture that battery."

It was Parsons's *[sic]* eight-gun battery, supported by an Ohio brigade (Germans) in command of General Jackson, of Hopkinsville, Ky. They would not stand the charge, but ran in great disorder, leaving the battery in our possession. In attempting to rally them General Jackson was killed, and his body fell in our line of march.[187]

[In support of the above articles, Toney related his proximity to the Sixteenth Tennessee and that the battery that the two regiments were confronting was that of Parsons' atop Open Knob. The **final account** was written in 1912 and adds even more detail to the above accounts.]

The firing of the pickets and the booming of the enemy's cannon told the battle would soon begin. From our position in the valley we could not effectively use artillery. Near the bluff General Buell had seven pieces of a Parrott battery. Our regiment, after crossing the stream, nearly dry, climbed the steep bluff and came up in rear of the Sixteenth Tennessee commanded by Colonel John H. Savage, which he called "the Panthers." The Sixteenth was engaged in a hot contest to capture the Parrott guns which were supported by a brigade of Illinois soldiers and Ohio soldiers commanded by General Jackson, from Hopkinsville,

---

[186] "Invasion of Kentucky by Gen. Braxton Bragg." Marcus B. Toney. *Nashville Banner* (Nashville, TN) June 14, 1904, p. 40.

[187] Marcus B. Toney, *Privations of a Private* (Publishing House of M. E. Church, Nashville, TN, 1907) 42-3.

Kentucky. As we were moving by the right flank in the rear of Colonel Savage and endeavoring to uncover from his right, several of our men were shot before we got into action.

While laying down awaiting orders, General Leonidas Polk rode up and asked: "What Regiment?" The reply: "First Tennessee." He ordered Colonel Fields as soon as he uncovered from Colonel Savage to move by the left flank and assist Colonel Savage to capture that battery.

When we got into line of battle, the firing was furious, but as soon as we fired the Ohio troops fled and we captured the Parrott guns. In the meantime, Bush's Indiana Battery, supported by the First and Twenty-first Wisconsin, were reinforced by an entire brigade. The First Tennessee rushed forward under a storm of shot and shell which seemed to mow down our boys as grain by the sickle, but our thin ranks would close up and charge again only to meet with death. We had advanced so far in front of our line that we were without support, and the enemy, having no foes in their immediate front, turned their fire upon us and many of our boys were killed and wounded by this enfilade fire. Nowhere on the firing line was it so furious as where the First Tennessee was engaged, and some of our men fell in ten feet of Bush's Battery but we could not take it. Every man and horse of the battery was either killed or wounded. *When we charged the Ohio brigade with Colonel Savage of the Sixteenth Tennessee and Colonel George C. Porter of the 6th Tennessee,* General Jackson, with sword drawn, attempted to rally his men but he was killed and his body fell in the line of company F, Captain Jack Butler (which was known as the Nashville and Chattanooga Railway boys). Tip Greenhalge of the company captured General Jackson's watch.[188]

[Four separate—but corresponding—accounts confirm the validity of Toney's statements. These accounts verify the fact that Maney's brigade came to the assistance of the Sixteenth Tennessee before the fall of Parsons' battery, and that the charge of Maney's brigade was *made in conjunction* with the charge of the Sixteenth Tennessee. It is supported by Hooper's, Walling's, Head's, Womack's, Savage's, Thompson's and Clark's testimony which all state that *they took the eight-gun battery with the assistance of Maney's brigade.* This was on an open hill in the first thirty to forty minutes of the fight.]

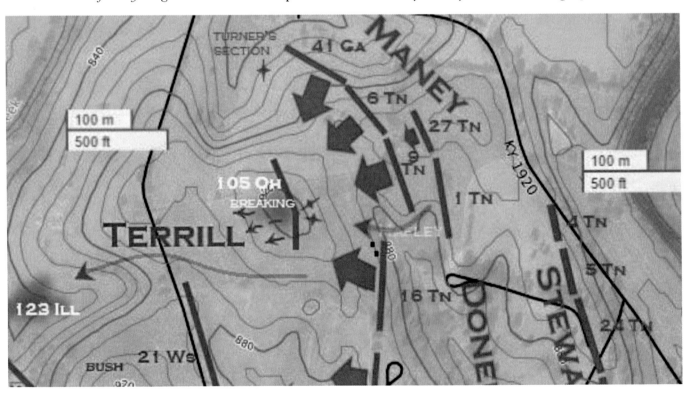

[188] "Fifty Year Ago Tuesday The Battle Of Perryville Was Fought." Marcus B. Toney. *Nashville Banner* (Nashville TN) October 12, 1912. *(Emphasis added.)*

Colonel Robert C. Tyler was the commanding officer of the Fifteenth Tennessee Infantry regiment of Donelson's brigade at the Battle of Perryville. He was also acting Provost Marshal for the army. He observed the fight but it is supposed that due to his role that he did not personally participate. He may have followed—in rear of the front-line fighting—with the headquarters and escort. His recollection of the fight can be interpreted in more than one way, *unless* one considers the corroborating evidence by the numerous other sources that help substantiate the fight. The most important piece of information that Tyler reveals is the location of Rebel forces in relation to the Federal positions at Perryville. Also, how the Rebel forces closed on the enemy. This recollection was recorded in a Knoxville newspaper about a week or so after the fight and was reprinted in a Georgia newspaper. The article is copied verbatim.

COLONEL R. C. TYLER'S ACCOUNT OF THE BATTLE.[189]

Col. R. C. Tyler, of the 15th Tennessee regiment, reached this city on yesterday directly from the scene of conflict in Kentucky. He advises us that the skirmishing commenced on the 6th between the cavalry, and occasionally there was an artillery duel. On the 7th Buell occupied Perryville, making it the centre of his line of battle. On the night of the 7th Hardee moved up his division fronting Buell's army. On the evening of the 7th, a portion of the right wing of the army of the Mississippi (Cheatham's Division, composed of Donelson's Stuart's and Maney's Brigades.) moved from Harrodsburg to Perryville, where they rested on their arms in line of battle till daylight. The pickets skirmished all night. On the morning of the eighth, at daylight, at the centre of the lines, there were cavalry fights and many were wounded on both sides. About half past nine cannonading commenced.

At half past ten we discovered that the enemy were massing troops on their left to turn our right wing. At this juncture, Cheatham's division, above mentioned, was moved from the left to the right of our lines, about one and a half miles. During this time a brisk fire of artillery was kept up. Carnes' battery was immediately brought into action, which, admirably served, did great execution. (This was Jackson's battery at Columbus, KY.)

Cheatham's Division was now about three fourths of a mile from the enemy and in line of battle, Donelson's Brigade being in advance.

[Notice that in the foregoing, Tyler stated that the brigade had moved to a distance of about three-fourths of a mile from the enemy positions. That would place Cheatham's lead brigade (Donelson's) in the vicinity of the Walker House or at least within two-hundred and fifty yards of that location inside Walker's Bend.]

The ground between us and the enemy was broken but without timber. It was found necessary to approach nearer the enemy for this reason and because of the superiority of their guns. Carnes was ordered to advance, and it was in this movement supported by Donelson's Brigade. We advanced about a fourth of a mile, and the enemy finding their position untenable, retired to another.

[After placing the division in Walker's Bend—three-fourths of a mile from the enemy lines—Tyler has just related that they then advanced a quarter mile. This placed the division near the foot of the abrupt ascent and in defilade on the east side of Chaplin River. The division would now have been located only one-half mile from the enemy lines.]

We again advanced a quarter of a mile, to the summit of a precipitous bluff, which the battery of Carnes could not ascend.

[Tyler then noted the advance up the steep western bank of Chaplin River that brought Donelson's brigade to the highest elevation—now only a quarter mile from the enemy line. This movement would have placed the brigade north of the park's visitor entrance and modern playground. This placed the brigade only 350 to 450 yards from the Federal line.]

Our lines were here reformed, and orders were received to advance upon the enemy at a double quick across open fields unobstructed, except by stone and rail fences. With terrific yells and unbroken front we advanced upon the enemy, two batteries playing upon Cheatham's Division, advancing under this fire and

[189] "Details of the Recent Battle in Kentucky." *Daily Morning News* (Savannah, GA) October 22, 1862, col. 2.

enfiladed by the batteries of the enemy. When within one hundred and fifty yards of the enemy they opened on us with grape and canister. When within eighty yards they opened on us with musketry, and now the fight became general.

[The range at which they became engaged with the enemy coincides with statements by men in the Sixteenth Tennessee.]

About this time Maney's Brigade with Donelson's were sent round to the enemy's extreme left to capture a battery that had been so destructive to us. The battery taken, and here the Yankee General Jackson fell. This was half an hour after the fight became general.

[Tyler's mention of Maney *and Donelson's* being sent around the *extreme left* makes it clear that both Donelson's and Maney's brigades were attacking Parsons' battery. Tyler—like Savage and many others in the Sixteenth Tennessee—clearly indicated that the battery was "taken," and "Jackson fell" only "*half an hour* after the fight became general." These three facts are supported by members of the Sixteenth Tennessee as well as members of Maney's brigade. The battery (Parsons') had been very "destructive" to the Sixteenth Tennessee.]

Every inch of ground was bravely contested. It became known that Jackson had fallen, and the enemy had retired, probably for this reason, but more probably because they could not withstand the impetuous valour of our troops. About this time, probably a little earlier, Stuart's *[sic]* brigade moved into action, in perfect order and with great coolness. The troops first engaged, worn and weary rushed on with Stuart's men, and the rout on the left became general.

[As was noted in Cheatham's report, Stewart was advanced just after Parsons' guns were taken. As Tyler related above, many of the troops in Donelson's brigade were too wrapped up in the fighting to stop and reorganize and "rushed on with Stuart's men."]

The enemy reformed their lines several times but were no sooner restored than they were broken.

The fighting was kept up till night put an end to the conflict. We had then driven the enemy from three to five miles along the whole line of the two armies.

We formed our lines and remained on the ground during the night. On the morning of the 9th, believing it would be hazardous with his weary troops to renew the conflict with a reinforced army of the enemy, General Bragg or Polk ordered our army back to Harrodsburg.

We captured all the artillery of the enemy except one battery, and quantities of all descriptions of small arms.

The loss of the enemy in killed and wounded was enormous. The field of battle was everywhere strewn with the killed, wounded and dying. In places they were piled up on each other.

We retired in perfect order, each regiment and brigade in proper position to Camp Dick Robinson and its vicinity, where our army was concentrated.

Our loss in killed, wounded and missing and missing will not reach 2,500. The killed in Cheatham's Division number 209 and about 1,250 wounded. This Division suffered most.

At half past 4 o'clock on Monday, 13th Instant, Colonel Tyler left General Polk, and of subsequent events, he is, of course not advised.

FEDERAL ACCOUNTS.

Captain Percival P. Oldershaw was an excellent witness of the events that transpired on the extreme Federal left until just after the death of General James Jackson. He was A.A.G. for the Tenth Division and witnessed all that transpired early on the Federal left with his own eyes. This portion of his report only applies to the Federal left and center. The account begins just after the arrival of the Tenth Division.

CAPTAIN PERCIVAL P. OLDERSHAW'S REPORT.[190]

At this time some batteries, I believe of General Rousseau's, were in action at long range on the right, and General Jackson, not then contemplating a general engagement, ordered me back to bring up the troops and to place the two brigades at rest on the right and left of the road. The Thirty-fourth Brigade, Colonel Webster, soon came up, and in my absence and delay in clearing the road of ambulances and ammunition wagons, to enable the Thirty-third Brigade to come up, the battery of Captain Harris was moved across the main road to the left and put in position on the right of a high, level ridge. It soon opened fire at long range, no enemy then being visible, and the regiments belonging to the same brigade were placed in position in the rear and left of the battery under the crest of the hill, as will be seen by the report of Lieut. E. E. Kennon, acting assistant adjutant-general, herewith submitted. Here I rejoined General Jackson. A few rounds having opened the enemy's batteries, a 12-pounder shot came within a foot of anticipating the fatal stroke our general received soon afterward.

[Note that in the above description, Oldershaw has placed Captain Harris' battery on "the right of a high, level ridge." This is not the description that members of the Sixteenth Tennessee give in relation to their attack on a battery.]

Riding toward our left and a little in advance of Harris' battery we came upon an open knob, where we found General McCook and all his staff watching some beautiful artillery practice by Stone's battery farther on our left, which was firing up a wide ravine upon the enemy's cavalry moving up a road to our front.

[Above is the first description of "Open Knob" and firing of Stone's battery at some of Wharton's cavalry near Wilson's Creek and along New Mackville Pike. Oldershaw notes that it was on this Open Knob that Parsons' battery is placed below. Contrary to the belief that only one battery was firing when the Confederate attack commenced (Simonson's according to Holman), Oldershaw witnessed Parsons' battery move into position and commence firing as they unlimber one at a time below—*before* spotting any Rebel infantry.]

Here Captain Parsons was located soon after, and by 2 p.m. opened with round shot and shell. The One hundred and twenty-third Illinois had been previously brought on the field forming our extreme left and angling toward the rear of the battery, and the Eightieth Illinois, Colonel Allen, through misdirection of the guide, came up later and formed in the valley near the edge of the woods, as will be seen by the report of Capt. William P. Anderson, assistant adjutant-general, herewith submitted.

[Note below, the battery was already firing when they realized the Rebel infantry was approaching their position.]

This battery had fired but a few shots when we heard rifle-shots below in the woods, when the enemy soon advanced and came in sight in the edge of the woods fronting our troops. No sooner was this seen by General Terrill and Lieutenant Parsons, then directing the fire of the guns, than they changed the direction of the fire, and opened at short range (about 90 yards) on the flank of the enemy with grape with deadly accuracy.

[Recall in Savage's report, he stated that "the left of the regiment was at the edge of the forest and the field, when the battery, about one hundred and fifty yards from the regiment, fired, enfilading it, sweeping the whole length of the line,

---

[190] Oldershaw, Captain Percival P., "Report of the Battle of Perryville." OR, Pt. 1, Vol. 16, p. 1059-62.

killing a captain, a lieutenant and many privates." This is descriptive of the enfilade (or flank) fire that Parsons' guns inflicted on the Rebel troops above.]

It checked the advance of the enemy, and after a few more rounds they changed front and faced the battery, which then flanked our left.

[Oldershaw stated that the advance of the enemy was checked and the enemy changed front and faced the battery. This is indicative of Savage ordering the charge to take the fence and Hafley cabins on his right flank—or Federal left—as seen in Savage's report.]

General Terrill, seeing this, ordered the advance of the One hundred and twenty-third Illinois, Colonel Monroe, and to charge bayonets. It advanced bravely, but unfortunately the enemy had not then left the woods, and there was a rail fence on its edge, which prevented their advancing promptly. The regiment fired a volley and fell back, when almost immediately afterward General Jackson, who was standing on the left of the battery, was killed, two bullets entering his right breast. At the moment I was standing on the right of the battery, watching the gallant defense then being made by the troops on our left.

[His description of the fight—above—closely resembles the fight as described by Savage and other members of the Sixteenth Tennessee. Captain J. J. Womack had made it clear that the regiment was "directly in front of the seven-gun battery"—the northern most battery as he had already related. He also mentioned a second charge by the regiment that was partially successful. Oldershaw later stated—in Buell's Court of Inquiry—that General Jackson was "killed early in the engagement, almost at the first shot."[191] This further supports Savage's earlier belief that his regiment was more than likely responsible for Jackson's death. Maney's brigade didn't appear on Savage's right until at least thirty minutes of combat had elapsed. That would hardly be considered "almost at the first shot."]

Returning to the general to report the same, I found him on his back struggling to speak, but unable to do so. He died in a few moments. His staff officers at once removed his body from the crest of the hill some 50 yards. Mr. Wing, one of the general's volunteer aides, went for an ambulance, and while I was absent, notifying General Terrill and Colonel Webster of the general's death, instructing the latter to take command of his entire brigade until he received further orders from General Terrill or myself, the battery had been taken by the enemy and the troops driven back from the open ground on the knob to the skirt of the woods, thus extending our left, and it was impossible to recover the body of our fallen general.

From this time up to 5 p.m. the battle raged with great fury and varied success on both sides. Two regiments, the Second and Ninety-fourth Ohio, belonging to General Rousseau's division, had come into our lines between the two batteries and behaved most gallantly.

[Below, it is made clear that Webster's brigade had hardly had contact up to this point—as Starkweather's right and Harris' left had shielded that brigade from heavy contact. Below, he identifies the flag of Hardee's corps—mistakenly describing it as having a white flag with a black ball. Donelson's and Wood's brigades were the ones that crashed into this position and were responsible for the seizure of four of Harris' battery after 5 p.m. as related above.]

Finding no enemy in front of Colonel Webster's brigade, which never lost a foot of ground up to this time, Colonel Webster rode off with me a little to the rear, where we found General McCook. He rode with us up to Colonel Webster's command and reported that his right was being heavily pressed and falling back. He and all of us then saw the progress of the enemy on Colonel Webster's right, as evidenced by the steady approach through the corn of a flag with a black ball in the center of a white ground, and he had hardly time to change the front of Colonel Webster's command (which was then all on exposed ground) when the enemy's infantry, arriving on the edge of the corn, opened fire upon them. The regiments moved down at a double-quick to the right face and formed in the woods, where they opened a deadly volley on the enemy, who were found in large numbers on the ground the next morning. They were killed

[191] Testimony of Capt. P. P. Oldershaw, OR, Vol. 16, Pt. 1, p. 293-96.

mostly by the rifles of the Ninety-eighth Ohio. The enemy, however, still advanced, preventing Captain Harris from getting the whole of his battery off. Heavy firing all along this changed front still continued. The line, so far as was observable from this division, was then at a right angle with the main road instead of parallel with it as before, when fresh troops from the extreme right rushed in with rapidity and gallantry, checking the farther advance of the enemy and closing the fight at dark.

Captain William P. Anderson was the A.A.G. of General Terrill's brigade. He wrote the Thirty-third Brigade's report of the battle and was eyewitness to the events that transpired on Open Knob.

CAPTAIN WILLIAM P. ANDERSON'S REPORT.[192]

The One hundred and fifth Ohio Volunteers, Eightieth and One hundred and twenty-third Illinois, a detachment of the Seventh and Thirty-second Kentucky Volunteers and Third Tennessee Volunteers, under command of Colonel [T.T.] Garrard, of the Third Kentucky Volunteers, and Parsons' eight-gun battery (made up of detachments from the regiments of the brigade), arrived upon the scene of action about 3 o'clock in the afternoon of the 8th instant. The One hundred and first Indiana Volunteers was not present, having been sent that morning as a guard to a train to Springfield.

A short time after its arrival General Terrill was ordered by General Jackson to occupy a hill upon the extreme left of the line. General Terrill immediately rode forward to survey the position, directing the brigade to follow. During the time occupied in marching from the place where the general left the brigade to the position we occupied several messages were sent me by him to push forward with it as rapidly as possible. The distance was probably three-quarters of a mile.

[This "hill" on the extreme left was Open Knob. Below, Anderson describes the deployment of the 123rd Illinois. As Oldershaw stated, they had arrived just before the guns of Parsons' battery began firing at the approaching rebels.]

The One hundred and twenty-third Illinois Volunteers, being the advance regiment, arrived upon the ground first. It was marching by the flank right in front, and the rebels at the time could be seen within 200 yards advancing to occupy the same ground. The One hundred and twenty-third was immediately brought to face the enemy. The position of the parties unluckily threw the rear rank in front, which produced much confusion, the regiment being a new one. For 100 yards in front of them the ground was clear. The rebels were advancing in and protected by the woods beyond. They commenced pouring a heavy fire into the ranks of the One hundred and twenty-third, to which they nobly responded.

[The description of the field closely resembles the description Colonel Savage gave of the battlefield. The Rebels were mostly covered by woods. Oldershaw's report also noted that when the Federal left was threatened, Terrill ordered the bayonet charge of the 123rd Illinois that was broken up by the fire of the Sixteenth Tennessee and the fence that separated the field from the woods.]

Parsons' battery immediately took position in the rear of the One hundred and twenty-third. Six of his guns were brought to bear upon the enemy and drove them back. At this instant General Jackson was shot dead. He, with General Terrill, had been standing to the left of Parsons' battery, encouraging the men to stand to their places.

[Only after the rout of the 123rd Illinois and death of General James Jackson, is the mention of a "heavy force of the enemy" mentioned. The one on—what has become—the right is the Sixteenth Tennessee that has already been engaging

---
[192] Anderson, Captain William P., "Report of the Battle of Perryville." OR, Vol. 16, Pt. 1, p. 1082-62.

the Federal force. The new force is on the newly extended left—Maney's brigade has entered the action. Approximately thirty minutes had elapsed.]

A heavy force of the enemy was now seen advancing upon both of our flanks. The One hundred and fifth Ohio Volunteers was ordered to meet them upon the left and the Eightieth Illinois Volunteers, with Colonel Garrard's detachment, upon the right. The One hundred and fifth were marching unfortunately like and thrown into line in the same form as the One hundred and twenty-third Illinois Volunteers, viz, rear rank in front. They at once opened fire upon the enemy, but did not succeed in stopping their advance.

[Anderson then describes Maney's advance with the Forty-first Georgia, Sixth and Ninth Tennessee regiments.]

They moved up to within 100 yards of our line without discharging a musket. They then opened a deadly fire. In spite of the efforts of the officers most of our men broke and fell back in great confusion. Lieutenant Parsons at the time was placing his seventh gun into position, when every man at the piece deserted him. He was then ordered by General Terrill to withdraw his battery. He succeeded in bringing away but one gun, four caissons, and two limbers, the horses in the other carriages being killed or disabled.

[As described in reports of the three Confederate regiments that made this assault from Maney's brigade, the Federals had fallen back a short distance and the fight was renewed as Rebels encompassed the abandoned guns of the battery.]

General Terrill, assisted by some of the officers, succeeded in rallying about 200 men of the One hundred and fifth Ohio Volunteers and One hundred and twenty-third Illinois Volunteers at a fence about 100 yards in the rear of our first position. Here the conduct of some of the officers, I am sorry to report, was disgraceful. The Eightieth Illinois and Colonel Garrard's detachment behaved well. When the left gave way they were obliged to fall back, which they did in good order. The general ordered the fragment of the One hundred and fifth and One hundred and twenty-third to fall back, which they did in good order. He ordered me to find General McCook and to tell him his position and to ask for re-enforcements. General McCook informed me every regiment he had was in the hottest of the fight, but that he had asked for re-enforcements from General Gilbert, and as soon as they arrived General Terrill should be supplied.

[He then noted that the force was withdrawn to the vicinity of Bush's Battery where they continued resistance.]

Had the enemy pursued his advantage at this crisis the most disastrous results must have followed his vigor. Nothing but a very small, disorganized fragment of the division remained to dispute his possession of the Mackville road, upon which lay our ammunition train, ambulances, and such supplies as had accompanied us. Trusting that re-enforcements might yet reach him, General Terrill rallied the few troops he had left near the place where Bush's battery had taken position. While thus engaged he fell mortally wounded and was carried from the field. Although the command of the division devolved upon General Terrill after the death of General Jackson he fell before he assumed the command.

The brigade was in action less than an hour. Its loss during this time was very severe, as will be seen by the report of Colonel Hall, who assumed command upon the fall of General Terrill.

[Note that Anderson specifically noted that the brigade was in action *"less than an hour."* This chronologically falls in line with the times consistent in Maney's report, Savage's account and all of the accounts of men in the Sixteenth Tennessee.]

BIBLIOGRAPHY

Works Cited

Primary Sources
Manuscripts

Alabama Department of Archives and History

    Preston, William E. *Diary of William E. Preston and History of the 33d Alabama*, SPR393.

Stones River National Battlefield

    Hooper, Thomas R. *1862 Diary*

    Quarles, John S. *Memoir of John S. Quarles*

The Huntington Library, San Marino, California

    Simon Bolivar Buckner Papers

        Buckner, Simon B. *Report of Battle* (mssSB 1-1197: Box 2)

Western Reserve Historical Society, Cleveland, Ohio

    Braxton Bragg Papers

        Cheatham, Benj. F. *Report of Battle* (William P. Palmer Collection: Box 1, Folder 6)

        Donelson, Daniel S. *Report of Battle* (William P. Palmer Collection, Box 28, Folder 9)

Books

Clark, Carroll H. *My Grandfather's Diary of the War* (C. W. Clark, Jr., Ed., TN, 1963)

Dyer, Gustavus W. & Moore, John T. *The Tennessee Civil War Veterans Questionnaires.* (Rev. Silad Emmett Lucas, Jr., Southern Historical Press, Inc., Easley, SC)

Head, Thomas A. *Campaigns and Battles of the Sixteenth Regiment Tennessee Volunteers* (Cumberland Presbyterian Printing House: Nashville, TN, 1885)

Liddell, St. John R. *Liddell's Record* (Nathaniel C. Hughes, Ed., LSU Press, Baton Rouge, LA, 1997)

Rennolds, Edwin H. *A History of the Henry County Commands.* (Sun Publishing Company, Jacksonville, FL, 1904)

Savage, John Houston. *Life of John Houston Savage*, (John Houston Savage, Nashville, TN, 1903)

Supplement to the Official Records of the Union and Confederate Armies, Pt. 3, Vol. 2 (Broadfoot Publishing Co., Wilmington, NC, 1994) Pt. 2, Vol. 3.

The War of the Rebellion: A Compilation of the Official Records of the Union and Confederate Armies (Washington, D.C.: Government Printing Office, 1896) Series I, Pt. 1, Vol. 16.

Thompson, James R. *Hear the Wax Fry* (Nellie P. Boyd, Ed., Cookeville, TN, 1966)

Toney, Marcus B. *Privations of a Private* (Publishing House of M. E. Church, Nashville, TN, 1907)

Winters, Erastus. *Serving Uncle Sam in the 50th Ohio.* (East Walnut Hills, OH: 1905)

Womack, James J. *The Civil War Diary of Captain J. J. Womack* (Womack Printing Co.: McMinnville, TN, 1961)

Newspapers and Periodicals

Cleveland Morning Leader (Cleveland, OH)

Daily Morning News (Savannah, GA)

Memphis Daily Appeal (Memphis, TN)

Perrysburg Journal (Perrysburg, OH)

Portsmouth Daily Times (Portsmouth, OH)

Southern Bivouac (Louisville, KY)

Southern Standard (McMinnville, TN)

The Louisville Daily Journal (Louisville, KY)

The Nashville Banner (Nashville, TN)
The Nashville Daily Union (Nashville, TN)
The National Tribune (Washington, D.C.)
The New York Herald (New York, NY)
The Spirit of Democracy (Woodsfield, OH)
The St. Cloud Democrat (Saint Cloud, MN)
The Tennessean (Nashville, TN)

Secondary Sources
Books
Gillum, Jamie. *The Battle of Perryville and the Sixteenth Tennessee Infantry Regiment: A Reevaluation 2nd Edition* (Jamie Gillum, Spring Hill, TN, 2015)
Noe, Kenneth. *Perryville: This Grand Havoc of Battle* (Lexington, KY: The University Press of Kentucky, 2001)
Sanders, Stuart W. *Maney's Confederate Brigade at the Battle of Perryville* (Charleston, SC: History Press. 2014)

Documents
Unknown. *Owners of the Perryville Battlefield* (Perryville Battlefield State Historic Site: Perryville, KY, 2014)

Websites - Electronic
Ancestry.com – for family information
CaliTopo – for maps
Effectiviology.com – for definition of straw-man argument
Email Correspondence – for differing views
Fold3 – for military experience
Google Earth Pro – for perspective
Library of Congress, Chronicling America – for contemporary soldier accounts
Library of Congress, Map Division – for contemporary maps
Newspapers.com – for contemporary soldier accounts
Perryvillebattlefield.org – for "Owners of the Battlefield" document
Terrystexasrangers.org – for Wharton's brigade information
Uchicago.edu – for biographical information
U. S. Army Heritage & Education Center of Carlisle Barracks, MOLLUS Collection – for contemporary photos
Wikipedia – for definitions of cherry picking, confirmation bias and attitude polarization

Confederate Unit Index

Union Unit Index

Alphabetical Index